KEIR HARDIE

CROOM HELM SOCIAL HISTORY SERIES
General Editors:
Professor J.F.C. Harrison and Stephen Yeo
University of Sussex

CLASS AND RELIGION IN THE LATE VICTORIAN CITY
Hugh McLeod

THE INDUSTRIAL MUSE
Martha Vicinus

CHRISTIAN SOCIALISM AND CO-OPERATION IN VICTORIAN ENGLAND
Philip N. Backstrom

CONQUEST OF MIND
David de Giustino

THE ORIGINS OF BRITISH INDUSTRIAL RELATIONS
Keith Burgess

THE VOLUNTEER FORCE
Hugh Cunningham

RELIGION AND VOLUNTARY ORGANISATIONS IN CRISIS
Stephen Yeo

CHOLERA 1832
R.J. Morris

WORKING-CLASS RADICALISM
IN MID-VICTORIAN ENGLAND
Trygve Tholfsen

THE COLLIERS' RANT
Robert Colls

THE ORIGINS OF BRITISH BOLSHEVISM
Raymond Challinor

THE MERTHYR RISING
Gwyn A. Williams

KEIR HARDIE

THE MAKING OF A SOCIALIST

FRED REID

CROOM HELM · LONDON

Croom Helm Ltd, 2-10 St John's Road, London SW11

British Library Cataloguing in Publication Data

Reid, Fred
    James Keir Hardie.
    1. Hardie, Keir 2. Statesmen – Great
    Britain – Biography
    941.081'092'4   HD8393.H3
    ISBN 0-85664-624-5

Printed in Great Britain by offset lithography by
Billing & Sons Ltd, Guildford, London and Worcester

CONTENTS

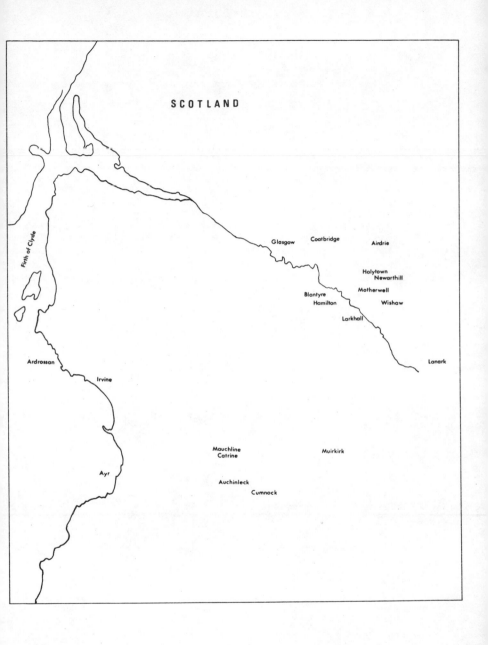

SCOTLAND

Firth of Clyde

Glasgow   Coatbridge   Airdrie

Holytown
Newarthill
Motherwell
Blantyre
Hamilton   Wishaw

Larkhall

Lanark

Ardrossan

Irvine

Mauchline
Catrine   Muirkirk

Ayr

Auchinleck
Cumnock

PREFACE

This book began as an Oxford D.Phil. thesis. After many revisions and developments, it still bears, I hope, an evolutionary resemblance to its ancestor. At one time, I intended it to form the first part of a full-length biography of Keir Hardie. Many of the complex investigations of popular history which such a study would entail remain unfinished, however, and the pressures of many commitments seem to postpone their completion indefinitely.

Meanwhile, two useful contributions to our knowledge of Hardie's career have appeared from the pens of K.O. Morgan and Iain McLean. A full-length treatment therefore seems less urgent and, since my conclusions differ from theirs on a number of central questions concerning Hardie's personal and political development, it has seemed better to publish this account now, ending in 1895, without waiting the outcome of further research which would need to be excessively prolonged.

I owe debts of gratitude to far more people who have helped me than I can possibly acknowledge here by name. I hope anyone who feels left out will accept my apologies at once.

Mention must first be made of my parents, whose years of service to the labour movement laid the foundation of my interest in it. I owe much, also, to Mr W.H. Marwick, formerly of the University of Edinburgh, whose teaching and writing helped to shape my interest in Scottish labour history. Mr Henry Pelling, as a Fellow of Queen's College, Oxford, made available to me his invaluable private copies of manuscripts (many of which are still not readily available to scholars). His encouragement extended far beyond the formal duties of supervision. In recent years, I have benefited much from the friendship and stimulation of colleagues at the Centre for Social History in the University of Warwick. Students and staff alike have helped with their insights and enthusiasm.

A number of fellow research-workers provided valuable pieces of information. Mr Gordon Wilson of Hamilton Technical College allowed me to use his index of Lanarkshire miners' wages from 1860 to 1873. His intimate topographical knowledge of the Hamilton area was also of great value. Dr J. Strawhorn of Cumnock supplied valuable extracts from local records. Miss Wilhelmina S|hreuder and Dr C. Tsuzuki helped me to obtain copies of manuscripts from collections in the

9

International Institute for Social History, Amsterdam. Dr J.G. Kellas kindly allowed me to read his then unpublished paper on Highland immigrants in Glasgow, from which I obtained information concerning William Small. Mr Paul Watmough of the Centre for Social History in the University of Warwick allowed me to read his valuable unpublished paper on the South West Ham election of 1892 and Mr John Battie from the same Centre gave me invaluable research assistance at various times. Mr E.P. Thompson shared with me his close understanding of the socialist movement in the 1890s and allowed me to borrow items from his private collection of rare books and sources for its study. His own writings have been an inspiration.

Dr A.B. Campbell read and commented on a draft of chapters 1 and 2. Professor Royden Harrison and Dr Tony Mason of the Centre for Social History at Warwick read the final draft and offered many valuable suggestions. None of these is, of course, responsible for the final text in any way. That responsibility is solely my own.

I received unstinted help from the library staffs of the British Museum, London School of Economics, the Scottish National Library and the public libraries of Bradford and Hamilton. Mr John Pemberton and Mr William Pine-Coffin at the Library of the University of Warwick were never-failing sources of patient and expert guidance.

I am also indebted to the University of Warwick for its enlightened sabbatical leave policy and its generous financial assistance, which gave me freedom and means to continue post-doctoral research. I acknowledge with thanks the grant from the Twenty-Seven Foundation which also helped the work forward.

My warm thanks are due to Mrs Vera Collett and Mrs Valda Reid for coping so cheerfully with my difficult manuscript.

Last, but by no means least, I will always be grateful to my dear wife for her support during the years when this book demanded so much of my time and hers.

INTRODUCTION

This book is an essay in labour biography. Labour leaders of the nineteenth century are often enigmatic personalities, and James Keir Hardie is no exception. Recent scholarly investigation[1] has failed to portray a convincing human personality. It has concentrated on dismantling the legend created by hagiographers of the Independent Labour party, but has put in its place either a puzzling series of apparent contradictions or the two-dimensional stereotype of the party politician. One comes away from all this work feeling that one does not know Hardie as a man.

What these studies lack is any convincing account of the process by which Hardie came to be a socialist. To K.O. Morgan, for example, Hardie is on the face of it a contradiction, 'Radical and Socialist'. Hardie socialism is apparently the product of personal psychological deprivations, giving a *fin de siècle* colouring to a broad progressivism gradually picked up in his early career. Iain McLean has denied that socialism had any relevance whatever to Hardie's life-work of building a Labour party. He sees Hardie as a protagonist of labourism and an old-fashioned land radical, who adopted socialism gradually into his rhetoric in order to widen the electoral appeal of the Labour party he was trying to build.

These approaches are of value in focusing attention on the ambiguities of Hardie's political outlook, but they remain unsatisfactory. Morgan underestimates the strength and consistency of Hardie's commitment to the idea of an independent Labour party from 1887 and therefore sees no need to explain this sudden and dramatic change in his political outlook. McLean pays no attention to Hardie's demand for the nationalisation of mines in 1887 or his continuing concern for it throughout his career. Yet the early appearance of this demand is surely fatal to his view that Hardie's socialism in 1887 was only a version of old-style land radicalism and had nothing to do with the modern idea of the nationalisation of the means of production.

This study, however, is not a tedious wrangle over the significance of this or that missing fact. Its main purpose is to penetrate to the heart of the enigma. Why does Keir Hardie remain so puzzling? Are we condemned either to explain him away or to reduce him to an extended entry in the *Dictionary of National Biography*? Must we debunk the myth of the cloth cap only to substitute for it the misleading image of the *déraciné* Bohemian?

It should not be necessary to do so if we can only penetrate to an understanding of the complex process by which Hardie's personality (both private and political) was formed. To do this, we need to explore far more deeply into his early childhood — his illegitimacy and his upbringing — than has so far been done. We need also to explore the class-relationships of the troubled mining communities in which he learned to perceive his status as a worker. We need to place this investigation in a wider setting than the narrowest questions of trade unionism and to see how Hardie was affected by two contradictory pressures. These were on the one hand, the backward-looking pressures of tradition — what I have called the myth of the independent collier — and on the other hand the forward-looking pressures of the proletarianised miner. Hardie embodied in his own personality the ambiguous outlook of the Scots miner of the 1870s and 1880s, and his class-consciousness, decisively shaped by the events of these years, was shaped in an ambiguous form.

Curiously enough, the materials for which such a reconstruction of Hardie's personality can be attempted have been substantially ignored by historians and biographers. Morgan hurries breathlessly through them, on his way to the 'fruitful years' of progressivism after 1895. For Hardie's personality he falls back on a few rather misleading hints and guesses and sometimes misconstrues the manuscript material. Early hagiographers shrouded the origins of the legendary hero and martyr in a suitable veil of myth and obscurity. This, therefore, must be the present writer's excuse for demanding so much of the reader's time for a period in the life of his subject which the biographer usually consigns to one or two pithily written chapters.

Notes

1. Henry Pelling, *The Origins of the Labour Party* (2nd edn., Oxford, 1965), pp.62 ff; F. Bealey and H. Pelling, *Labour and Politics, 1900-1906* (1958), pp.186 ff; K.O. Morgan, *Keir Hardie, Radical and Socialist* (1975); I. McLean, *Keir Hardie* (1974); F. Reid, 'Keir Hardie's Conversion to Socialism', A. Briggs and J. Saville (eds.), *Essays in Labour History* (1970), pp.17-46.

1   INFANT SENSIBILITIES

I

James Keir Hardie was born in the tiny hamlet of Legbrannock, in Lanarkshire, Scotland, on 15 August 1856. He was the illegitimate son of a Scottish farm servant, Mary Keir, and a miner, William Aitken. Thus were united, in the circumstances of his birth, the two spheres of mining and agriculture which were to influence so much of his political outlook in later life. He continued to live at Legbrannock until his mother married David Hardie, in 1859. His grandmother looked after him while his mother earned their livelihood by working long hours on the local farms.

Legbrannock lay, in 1856 and for some years to come, on the margin of heavy industry. It was situated at one corner of a triangle formed by the towns of Coatbridge, Airdrie and Holytown. Although the sides of this triangle were only three miles long, it contained within its area no fewer than sixty-six coal-mines, many of them owned by iron-smelting companies, of which the largest was that of the Bairds, whose Gartsherrie works at Coatbridge were the second largest iron works in the world. Within this triangle, known as 'The Monklands', lay the heartland of Scottish heavy industry, whose growth, since 1830, had been relentless. Within a generation, its rural character had been obliterated. Coatbridge had mushroomed from a tiny village into a great company town. Immigrants, many of them from Ireland, had poured in to work in the new coal-mines and smelting furnaces. Black smoke by day and the lurid glow of the furnaces by night hung over the whole district, giving it a hellish appearance which visitors often commented on.[1]

To the east of Holytown and Legbrannock, however, the scene gradually changed. Coal-mines became smaller and more scattered, standing isolated among the fields and farmhouses of the rich, mixed farming countryside of the upper Clyde. Across the river stood the fashionable burgh of Hamilton, seat of an ancient line of dukes. In the 1850s and 1860s, it had not yet acquired the ring of large collieries that were to destroy its character as a ducal seat. Further up river stood New Lanark, where Robert Owen had dreamed of reuniting agricultural and industrial life in his famous model village.

It is important to bear constantly in mind that Keir Hardie's child-

13

hood was thus spent in intimate contact with Scottish rural life as well as with heavy industry. The land question was to come to have a powerful fascination for him and he would dream, like Owen, of a socialist Utopia in which the hell of modern industry would have given way to pastoral peace and innocence. Too often, biographers have dwelt only on his later memories of urban life, which were usually unpleasant, and have failed to pay sufficient attention to his recollections of Arcadia. Yet his village experiences may have played an important part in shaping his character and outlook by providing a nostalgic escape world to set against his urban and industrial memories in later life.

On 22 April 1859, Mary Keir married David Hardie, a thirty-four-year-old ship's carpenter from Carron in Stirlingshire. They left Legbrannock and settled first in the nearby village of Eastfield, where Mary Hardie bore him a son in 1860.[2] At some time between 1860 and 1862, David Hardie decided to seek employment in the shipbuilding yards of Govan, in Renfrewshire, where Mary Hardie's third child, a daughter, was born in the latter year. Time-served craftsmen like David Hardie often formed an aristocracy of labour in Victorian Britain. They could hope to earn higher wages than unskilled labourers and had the chance of achieving some respectability. Such good fortune, however, eluded the Hardies. Three more pregnancies followed in quick succession by 1866 and, at the very time when David Hardie's services as breadwinner were most needed, he struck a period of very bad luck. A serious accident kept him off work for months. Mary Hardie was forced to sell the furniture to make ends meet and eventually they had to move across the river to the poorer district of Partick, where they lodged in a back room in a mean street. Then, shortly after David Hardie had recovered his health and returned to work, the shipyards were stopped by a prolonged strike in 1866. During these long periods of enforced idleness, David Hardie became moody and frustrated. He took to drink, and there were frequently violent quarrels between him and Mary, in which he reproached her with 'the bastard'.[3]

Mary Hardie, who was a hard-working, striving countrywoman,[4] had hoped for better things than this for her son James from the marriage. She had sent him to school, but that had lasted only a few months, as there was soon no money to pay the fees. She continued to encourage him to develop the skill he acquired in reading. His natural intelligence enabled him to do so by studying the captions of eye-catching advertisements in the window of Thomas Lipton's grocery shops. Later, he was able to study sheets of newsprint picked up in the streets. His mother had also tried to get him apprenticed to a trade, by means of which he could have some hope of a decent start in life. He began work in a brass finishing shop, but had to leave almost immediately when it was discovered that he would have to serve the first year of his apprenticeship without wages. By this time, the family's deepening poverty required him, at the age of eight, to contribute to its breadwinning. He drifted through a series of casual jobs. The first was in the shipyards, working as a rivet-heater for the skilled platers, high up on the hulls of the iron ships. The boy next to him fell to his death and Mary Hardie took James away.

During the shipyard strike of 1866, he worked as delivery boy for a baker. His mother was then in an advanced stage of pregnancy and a younger brother was down with fever. David Hardie rose very early each day to wander the city in search of work and young James had to help his mother nurse the sick child and prepare breakfast before setting out for his work at the shop, where his attendance was required by six a.m. Not surprisingly, he was often late and his irritated employer finally warned him that another offence would mean dismissal. Next morning he arrived fifteen minutes late, breakfastless and drenched with rain. The shop assistant told him the master wanted to see him. Upstairs, he was kept waiting outside the master's dining-room until prayers were finished, then ushered into a room in which the breakfast table was laden with dainties. Hardie often recalled the scene in later life with bitter reproaches on those who professed Christianity while intensifying the sufferings of the poor:

> My master looked at me over his glasses and said in quite a pleasant tone of voice: 'Boy, this is the second morning you have been late, and my customers leave me if they are kept waiting for their hot breakfast rolls. I therefore dismiss you, and, to make you more careful in future, I have decided to fine you a week's wages'.[5]

Biographers have retailed faithfully these bitter memories of Hardie's city childhood. There can be no doubt about the scars they left on his later life, yet they have perhaps been given an undue prominence. Hardie also set down pleasant recollections of his childhood. Significantly, such early memories are always connected with rural life, the escape from city and mine. The earliest of these is, perhaps, a children's story which Hardie wrote for publication in his paper, the *Miner,* in 1887. The story is a conventional melodrama, such as might be found in many popular papers of a Christian moral tone at that time, but there can be no doubt of the autobiographical character of some of its contents. The hero is abducted and then abandoned by a wicked uncle in order to prevent him inheriting his father's estate. This infant has the name James. He is found and fostered by a country couple. The foster-mother is loving and loyal, but the foster-father, a miner, is given to drink and comes to a horrible end in a pit accident. Misfortune is heaped upon misfortune. The child suffers a second abduction, this time to California. At last, after discovering his true identity, he returns to claim his fortune and just in time to comfort his loyal foster-mother on her death-bed. The most lively part of the tale is Hardie's description of the childhood of the hero in the village of his foster parents, where he becomes known by the nickname, 'Wee Jamie Keekie'. The origins of this alliteration on his own childhood name, Jamie Keir, are explained in the following nostalgic manner:

> Wee Jamie Keekie was everybody's wean [child]. There were few houses Righa' that Jamie had not made his way into, and not into the houses only, but somehow he managed to get into the hearts of the people as well. Whenever a 'tap, tapping' was heard at the door of a house, the following colloloquy was always sure to follow: —
> 'Wha's that?'
> 'Wee Jamie Keekie wantin' in, for his feet's caul' an' his shin's din' [feet are cold and his shoes are worn out].
> And then the door would be opened and the little fellow admitted. Though the door stood wide open, and the day was the hottest in summer, the formula had to be gone through. Little wonder he was a favourite. When he turned up his round laughing face, and looked with his clear blue eyes that seemed, young as he was, to be wells of liquid light, and said in his own simple, childish way — 'Wee Jamie Keekie, let me in, my feet's caul' an' my shin's din'.[6]

It is impossible to doubt the autobiographical quality of this recollection of an idyllic childhood and it may refer to the short period which the Hardies spent at Eastfield after their marriage and before moving to Govan. We shall have to note presently the bearing of the tale on the question of Hardie's view of his own illegitimacy, but for the moment what needs to be stressed is that Hardie could recall village life as a kind of innocence of early childhood, before the fall into the Glasgow years of the drinking step-father and the master who treated him with cold indifference. Hardie did not experience village life as, say, Joseph Arch knew it, an exploited child-worker, drudging to augment the family income. For Hardie, the countryside was always to be an escape from the city of dreadful night. The contrast in his own childhood helps to explain his penchant in adult life for rural Utopias such as farm colonies for the unemployed and for the strong 'Back to the Land' strain in his socialism. It was with a veiled autobiographical reference that he could write in 1893:

> The divorce of the worker from the forces of Nature is to me a most lamentable thing. Imagine the hapless lot of the poor child, born and reared in the working-class quarters of a city, surrounded by hard, cold and unsympathetic stone walls, no green fields, no summer birds or music of brooks, no communication with the silent, yet all powerful force of Nature. How can healthy life, physical or moral, be expected under such conditions?[7]

II

The contrast between the life of heavy industry and that of agriculture continued to run, like dark and bright threads, through the texture of Hardie's experience in his teens. In 1867, his parents left Glasgow and returned to the district of James's birth on the edge of the Monklands. David Hardie had decided to resume his old occupation at sea, no doubt for him the quickest way of restoring the family's fortunes. Mary Hardie was perhaps reassured to be back beside her mother in familiar surroundings while her husband's absence imposed on her the burdens of a single-parent family. They made their new home in the village of Newarthill. James was now ten, the age at which a boy could legally be employed to work in a mine, so he was sent to eke out the family income by working as a trapper in the Moss pit of The Monkland Iron Company.[8]

Mary Hardie hated having to send her first-born child, for whom she had evidently hoped so much, to work in the dark and dangerous pit. As she bustled about getting breakfast on that cold, winter morning when she sent her husband back to the sea and her eldest child to the mines, her silence was hard and resentful. To cheer her up, David Hardie joked grimly: 'Ye hae this consolation at least, that sailors and colliers are the twa classes that meenisters pray maist for, if that does ony guid.'[9] Silently, she turned away and pretended to be making up the fire.

James hated the work in the mine. He began at the very bottom of the hierarchy as a trapper, a boy who sat at a door or 'trap', which had to be closed to regulate the flow of fresh air through the mine, and

opened whenever a train of coal tubs had to pass through on its way
from the face to the shaft bottom. Hardie wrote later:

> Try to imagine my position in this place day after day, sitting alone,
> only seeing a human face as the driver passed and re-passed with his
> rake [train], no sound except the dripping of water into the
> [horse's] trough . . . or the tip-tapping sound occasioned by contin-
> uous drippings from the roof, or the occasional scamper of a mouse,
> frightened in the midst of a meal which he would be making in the
> horse's stable.[10]

He was all the more frightened when he heard from his workmates that
the trapper before him had been killed in an accident. He found his one
consolation in the friendship of dumb animals, who seemed victims,
like himself. He shared his tea and 'piece' with the pit ponies, whose
stable he had to muck out, and he even got friendly with the rats.

Gradually he learned not to be so frightened and the restless
temperament he had inherited from his mother began to find
distractions to while away the lonely hours. He blackened a whitish
stone with the smoke of his pit lamp and taught himself to write by
scratching characters on it with a steel pin. He developed his reading
too, mostly with tales of adventure, but also with *The Pilgrim's Progress*.
After two years as a trapper, he began to move up through the hierarchy
of underground jobs. For a time he worked as a pony driver and afterwards, as his strength increased, he went to the coal face to work with
the hewers. Often, he discovered, boys like him did the hardest work,
for which they received only a fraction of the man's wage. Thus he
recalled the work of cutting through solid rock to make a tunnel
connecting one mine with another:

> The man for whom I worked blasted out the rock, a kind of half-
> clayey shale, and my work was breaking up the rock into small
> pieces and taking it to the mouth of the mine in a box mounted on a
> pair of skidders, the same shape as the rockers of a cradle . . . The
> air was so bad, especially after a blast, that breathing was a big job,
> and the lamps at times would not burn. When things got so bad as
> this, I had to take my jacket and 'waft oot the reek', that is, drive
> out the smoke and foul gas by waving my jacket in all directions. My
> wage was one shilling and threepence, fifteen pence for a shift of ten
> hours [11]

What made such experiences more bitter was the fact that the workman often joined in the exploitation of boy labour:

> I have had to work at the face for three or four hours in the morning, helping to make ready a shot, and then, when a day's darg [output] had been blasted down, have had to begin to draw them [haul away the coal] while the man went home to enjoy himself.[12]

He also had early experience of the dangers which miners seemed to take for granted. He worked as pony driver on a nightshift in an old, wet mine. Suddenly, the cry went up that the walls of the shaft were closing in. Everyone rushed to the bottom, only to find that their means of exit had been closed off. Much later, Hardie recalled the scene:

> The men gathered in groups, each with his little lamp on his bonnet, their black and serious faces discussing what should be done. The roaring and cracking, as if of artillery, went on overhead and gloom began to settle on every countenance. Some of the more susceptible were crying, and I remember two by themselves who were praying and crossing themselves. There was nothing that could be done unless and until the shaft was reopened.

The boy grew weary and went to lie down on the straw in his pony's stable, where he fell asleep. While he slept, men were lowered into the shaft and succeeded in clearing the obstruction. A rope was lowered and the entombed miners were raised to the surface. Everyone was so relieved that they almost forgot about the pony driver: 'Perhaps in the excitement of the moment no one would have missed him had there not been a mother there, waiting for him'. Rab, the foreman, was sent back into the workings with two other miners to look for him. Finding James asleep on the straw, they roused him with curses and punches. The excitement at the surface when the last boy emerged safely from what had nearly been a disaster was so intense that James broke down and cried.[13]

In later life, Hardie would recall these searing experiences again and again in order to justify his outspoken denunciations of the rich, the churches and the politicians of the Establishment, who, as he saw it, callously neglected the toilers in industry who produced the world's wealth. Biographers have often repeated them in a way that adds to the picture of Hardie's early years as a period of unrelieved darkness and misery. Yet it may be at least as important, if we are to understand the complex labour politician, to pay more attention to his recollections of sunnier and happier moments. Once again, these are associated with rural life and agricultural surroundings.

The village of Newarthill, where the Hardies lived in the late 1860s, had lost little of its old agricultural character as a result of the rise of heavy industry. Set a little apart from the Monklands, it lay on the edge of a large, unenclosed moor, known locally as 'the Moss'. The village was practically one long street of thatched cottages, straggling along the road from a cross, where stood a kirk and three public houses. Mary Hardie occupied one of the cottages and Grannie Keir the one next door. They had small gardens in which they grew kitchen produce. During the long winter evenings, the neighbours would gather in Mary Hardie's house, round a coal fire whose dancing flames gave the only light in the room, casting weird shadows on the black earth floor, the open thatch above and the earthenware sitting on the wooden dresser. On such occasions, young James would hear his grandmother telling one of her old ghost stories in her soft-voiced, broad-vowelled, Lanark-shire dialect.[14] These stories transported the boy back into a much older Scotland, older than heavy industry, the peasant world of Robert Burns. Gradually, the Scottish past began to fascinate him. He read tales of border warfare in *Wilson's Tales of the Borders* and he became aware of the legendary deeds of the Covenanters, whose 'martyrs'' graves and monuments lay all around him, and who had preached at lonely conventicles on the Moss against the wicked godlessness of the rich and powerful of their day. Neither the Border chieftains nor the Covenanting prophets were, perhaps, as glamorous as they seemed to Hardie, but to him they represented a time when men did great deeds against the seemingly overwhelming odds of nature, magic and social coercion. The Moss, across which young James walked three miles to work every day, came to seem a spot haunted by more than his Grannie's bogles.

In winter, the Moss was dark and desolate and when James was on a day shift he never saw the sunlight. But in summer, at hay-making and harvest time, the local farmers needed every hand they could get, and James was able to leave off mining work and earn a few shillings at agricultural labour. Once again, we have to note that Hardie's recollections of these times are not presented in terms of rural realism − no *Jude the Obscure*, lonely and bored at crow-scaring under a tyrannical farmer. The employer whom Hardie recalled was known to him as 'Uncle Willie' and took on, in memory at least, the aspect of a god-fearing, patriarchal peasant reminiscent of Burns's ideal:

> 'Uncle Willie' [was] a veritable patriarch, in whom all that was best in the old Covenanters still lived. Fond of a joke, practical in everything, he managed his farm and all thereon with a degree of conscientious scruple all too rare. Sitting at the head of the table, round which were ranged his kinsfolk and hired servants, male and female, he made all feel at home. It was in the evenings, however, that he impressed himself most upon my mind, when conducting family worship. There was a dignity, a sincerity, a grandeur about the old man and his words as he knelt by his old armchair and poured out his supplications.[15]

III

Sunny intervals of harvest time and hay-making apart, however, Hardie's lot was mainly cast in the hell of mining in the west of Scotland. As he grew older, the reality of miners' conditions was impressed upon him, and this fostered in him deep class resentments against the tyranny of large-scale iron companies. His direct experience of the powerful ironmasters of Lanarkshire was increased when, in 1871, David and Mary Hardie again moved home. This time they shifted from Newarthill to Quarter, a large, squalid mining village outside Hamilton. It had a population of nearly seven hundred, most of them recent immigrants, crowded into rows of drab company houses around the works of the ironmaster, Colin Dunlop.[16] The move enabled David Hardie to give up his work at sea and settle down in a job which proved permanent as a joiner in the company's mines. James was also taken on by the company, as, in time, were his two younger brothers.

Joiners like David Hardie were usually employed as 'on cost' men, that is, permanent employees of the company, receiving a regular, fixed weekly wage, instead of the day wage paid to the mass of miners, whose earnings therefore fluctuated from week to week, according to the number of days they were given work. The years 1871 to 1873 saw a sharp rise in miners' wages and, in these conditions, the Hardie family began at last to enjoy some of the prosperity which had so long eluded them. But for James, now entering his late teens, this improving fortune was accompanied by a gradually increasing awareness of the low esteem in which miners were held by other classes in the community and of the resentment which many of his fellow colliers felt at the tyranny exercised over them by companies such as the Clyde.

The expansion of the iron industry had led to the mushrooming of villages like Quarter during the second and third quarters of the nine-teenth century. Inadequate services were provided in these towns for a rapidly expanding population. Housing became scarce and over-crowded, and piped water-supply was almost unknown. Since the towns were often distant from older settlements with established shops, miners' wives were often wholly dependent on stores provided by the companies, stores in which all the old evils of truck survived. Miners in these communities came to be regarded as a rough, undisciplined mass of black heathens who had to be civilised in the same way that David Livingstone of Blantyre was then civilising the natives of darkest Africa. Referring to the inhabitants of Quarter in 1850, the land agent of the Duchess of Hamilton had commented:

> The male collier population is made up of the old collier race, the Irish immigrants and worst Scotch of other counties. It has till of late, to a considerable extent, been rude, vulgar, ignorant and savage in the extreme. Low as the state of education and morals was among the aboriginal collier population during the slavery, it has since sunk still lower, owing to the vast influx of Irish of the lowest grade from Connaught.[17]

Such attitudes were widespread among the better-off sections of the mining communities and James became aware of them as he grew to manhood. 'I can remember', he wrote, after the great Scots coal strike of 1894, 'shop labels which read, "Good pit butter, one shilling per pound". Anything in the food line is deemed good enough for our collier laddies.'[18]

The heavy hand of the iron companies was also experienced in the Quarter days. Mary Hardie, hard-working and independent as ever, scraped enough savings together in these prosperous years to open a little shop in the village. It sold sweets and other provisions and came directly into competition with the company store, which had hitherto enjoyed a monopoly. The works manager ordered David Hardie to see that the shop was closed, under threat of dismissal. David Hardie refused to comply and once again found himself out of work. Mary's trade prospered, however, and they decided to sit it out. Writing of the incident some ten years later, Hardie recalled that his father:

> cared nae mair for th' shop than he did for th'man in th'mune,
> But there was a principle at stake, an' he left the wark. It wisna lang,
> hooiver, tae th'storeman failed an' th'manager got th'sack, an' then

oor yin wis sent for again, an' noo I believe ma mither wid get keepin' jumbo th'elephant if she liked.

Th'store still exists, but there is mair liberty than formerly.[19]

It is interesting that Hardie's step-father should emerge from this anecdote as a stubborn figure of resistance. No doubt the characteristic independence of the craftsman had something to do with his reponse to the company, but there may have been more to it than that. The harsh experiences of the Glasgow years had turned him towards secularism and the republican movement with which it was closely associated. The anti-clerical propaganda of Charles Bradlaugh's National Secular Society had spread into Scotland and David Hardie had become a reader of his paper, the *National Reformer*. A copy of Tom Paine's *The Age of Reason* is said to have stood on the bookshelf in his house, alongside the Bible and *The Pilgrim's Progress.*[20] Bradlaugh's secularism was interlocked with republicanism, because the power of the Church was thought to rest on the political and social privileges of the Court, the aristocracy and the House of Lords. David Hardie's interest in the movement rubbed off on James, whose earliest political memory was the stir created by the Republican Clubs which spread in the North of England and Scotland in 1871.[21] David Hardie was in the habit of expressing in his son's hearing his contempt for petit-bourgeois toadies in Hamilton, who fawned on the Duke. He said the Duke of Hamilton got fourteen thousand pounds a year in royalties from the coal-mines on his estate, while the miners like themselves were lucky to get twenty-five shillings a week.[22] Republicanism carried even more far-reaching implications. There were those in the Land and Labour League who wanted to nationalise land and to create work on it for the unemployed in 'home colonies', financed by state credit.

But republicanism was of less immediate relevance to a young miner than trade unionism. The veteran Scottish miners' leader, Alexander McDonald, was making renewed efforts to organise a Scottish miners' union. In 1871, he helped set up the Miners' Association in Fife, a county whose brisk export trade with the Baltic set it somewhat apart from the industry in the west of Scotland. Organisation grew more slowly in the west, but there was an inchoate Ayrshire Miners' Union in 1872. Lanarkshire possessed no county-wide organisation. There, the great iron companies, such as Bairds, were strong and had not scrupled to make full use of migrant agricultural labour from Ireland and the rural areas of Scotland to break the resistance of miners' unions. Only in those districts where iron companies were less predominant did trade unionism flourish among coal-miners. The best organised was Larkhall, which included the Hamilton miners in the early 1870s. In 1872, McDonald decided that the moment had come to try to weld these scattered forces into a federal structure to be called the Scottish Miners' Association.[23]

McDonald stood at the peak of his reputation. Wages had risen since 1869, from three shillings and sixpence a day to ten shillings, in the best paid districts in 1872.[24] Wages had never before reached this astonishing level and the size of the increase brought about something like a revolution of expectations among the Lanarkshire miners. The press began to carry tendentious reports of miners' new expectations. It was said that they rode to the butcher's in carriages to bring home roast beef. Speakers at miners' meetings did not deny at least the beef, but asked who could be more entitled to it than a hard-working miner.[25] What the boom years of 1870-2 really changed, however, was not this or that item of diet, but the miners' belief that wages must fluctuate with trade between subsistence and comfort levels. It seemed at last possible that a 'fair' wage could be established as a permanent feature of their industry. Wages had now risen so high that, it seemed, they could never again slide back as low as three and sixpence a day.

Alexander McDonald cultivated this new hope with an ambiguous rhetoric that was more persuasive because of his almost legendary standing in the Scots coalfields. Everyone knew the stories and rumours that hung about him. He had begun work as an ordinary collier. By undertaking the toughest and dirtiest jobs in the pits, he had saved enough money to attend classes in Latin and Greek at Glasgow University. He had been in his time a mine manager, a school-teacher and a strike leader. Somehow, he had amassed a small fortune (by investment, some said, in contraband shipping during the American Civil War) and he had become a partner in a small coal company in Hamilton, where he lived in an imposing country house and kept a groom and stables. His wealth had enabled him to conduct a series of campaigns for improvement of the law regulating the safety and working conditions of miners and he had just played a large part in framing the Coal Mines Regulation Act of 1872. By this time he was nursing the English mining constituency of Stafford, which returned him to Parliament in 1874 as one of the first two working-class representatives to sit in the House of Commons.[26]

James Hardie's imagination was touched by the legend of this self-improving working man who had risen from humble beginnings without deserting his class. He first heard him address a Lanarkshire miners' meeting in 1870, in an open-air amphitheatre at Powburn Toll, near Uddingston. Hardie had to get up at six o'clock and walk some eight miles to attend the meeting. He was too tired and hungry to pay close attention to the speaker, and spent most of the time hunting the hedgerows for edible herbs, but the occasion stuck in his memory because he had to defy a company prohibition in order to attend the meeting.[27]

The iron companies of Lanarkshire looked with concern on the growth of trade unionism among coal-miners in these years. Their great mid-Victorian heyday was in decline. They had neglected the Bessemer steel-making process and were now faced with sharp competition from English and Continental steel-makers. The unprecedented demand for coal which followed the Franco-Prussian War in 1871-3 further eroded their profits by pushing up the wages of coal-miners. By 1872, therefore, the Lanarkshire ironmasters had a strong motivation, not only to check the rise in miners' wages, but to depress their own miners' wages below the rate earned by men employed by the coal or 'sale' masters, and at a meeting in Glasgow they resolved to pursue this policy by collective action.[28]

The new Scottish Miners' Association met the ironmasters' demands with optimism. The 'coal famine' which had pushed wages up so high seemed to have placed them for the first time in a position to resist the dictates of the 'iron ring'. McDonald told them that by the power of their organisation they could prevent wages ever again falling below a level that was 'fair' alike to miner, masters and consumers of coal. By restriction of output, the union could balance the supply of coal to the demand and so prevent prices from falling below a level that would guarantee miners a 'fair' wage. Should the ironmasters persist in their determination to pay their miners less than men in the sale pits, the Scottish Miners' Association would respond by 'putting on a block', that is, by bringing out on strike the miners in the offending iron companies and providing for the strikers by levies on those who remained at work in the sale pits. Sale masters, miners and the coal-consuming public would thus be banded together in a coalition to break the power of the 'iron ring'. The ironmasters would be forced to abandon their old strike-breaking tactics and submit to the practices of civilisation. Harmony and class-collaboration would be restored.[29]

McDonald's strategy fascinated many of the delegates who attended the monthly conferences of the Scottish Miners' Association. Yet it rested on three erroneous assumptions. The first assumption, whose error was already quite apparent, was that all sale masters were ready to collaborate with the miners' unions. It is true that small coalmasters, often little removed socially from their men and less burdened than larger companies with heavy capital costs, sometimes looked favourably on restriction of output as a means of keeping up coal prices. But the 'coal famine' had encouraged the formation of large coal companies to exploit the deeper seams around Hamilton and these tended to side with the ironmasters in opposing restriction of output. The second assumption (whose erroneous character was also already apparent) was that sale masters would refrain from supplying coal to iron companies whose miners were on strike. The union hoped to constrain them to do so by restricting output, but this tactic was seen to be hopeless when the error underlying the third assumption began to make itself clear. This was the assumption that coal and iron prices would not fall very much. At the end of 1873 they began to collapse all over the world and their fall lasted until 1887. The 'Great Depression', as contemporaries called it, drove Lanarkshire miners' wages inexorably downward from about eight shillings a day in 1873 to about four in 1874 and three in 1878. The depression broke the fragile solidarity of the Scottish miners. Men would not practise restriction of output when they needed to produce more coal in order to compensate for lower piecework rates. Union districts not involved in strikes refused to pay heavy levies out of falling wages in order to support strikers in Lanarkshire iron companies who, if successful, would have been better paid than the men who had supported them.

These weaknesses of McDonald's policy led to revolts against his leadership in those districts of Lanarkshire where miners' unions had to confront ironmasters or large coal companies. Hamilton miners were involved in a long and bitter strike with the men of Larkhall, Motherwell and Holytown in 1872, resisting the efforts of ironmasters and large coalmasters to lower their wages. In 1874 they again found themselves at the storm centre, when ironmasters decided to reduce their miners' wages by four shillings a day, to meet the drastic fall in pig-iron prices occasioned by the 'Great Depression'.[30] During these disputes, local strike leaders pointed out the weaknesses of McDonald's strategy and demanded that the Scottish Miners' Association call a 'universal strike' throughout Scotland to resist the demands of the ironmasters. As we have seen, there was no hope of commanding support for such tactics. Yet it was equally clear that, as far as the maintenance of a fair wage for miners was concerned, McDonald's strategy was also in ruins. McDonald himself made the fact painfully obvious to the strikers when he announced in 1874 that he had negotiated privately with the

director of a large iron company to establish a sliding scale for the
adjustment of miners' wages. According to its terms, miners would get
three and sixpence a day when pig-iron sold at fifty shillings a ton.[31]
This 'standard rate' provoked sharp reaction among rank-and-file
miners. Though in theory only a basis for arithmetical calculation, the
'standard' was regarded by miners as the 'minimum' rate to which the
masters expected prices and wages to fall in the worst market conditions. Miners' meetings denounced McDonald's scale and demanded
that the 'minimum' should be higher.[32] McDonald's leadership and that
of the conference delegates were repudiated and a series of mass
meetings instituted at Powburn Toll, where Hardie had first heard
Alexander McDonald in 1870. This time he heard McDonald vilified by
a veteran miner, claiming fifty-one years' experience of pitwork:

> Their leader was now said to be a capitalist [the speaker said] and
> how could he be expected to work in the interests of labour? . . .
> He characterised the miners as slaves in a Scotch Siberia under an
> Emperor Alexander and he called upon them to free themselves
> from his rule.[33]

A makeshift Lanarkshire Miners' Association was formed under an
elected 'County Board'. Old followers of McDonald were repudiated and
new, untried men pushed forward. One of them was a reticent,
reluctant lad of less than eighteen, James Hardie.[34]
    To these developments McDonald responded with negative vitupera-
tion. Characterising the new leaders as 'silly fools and blind bats', he
stated, in an open letter to the strikers, 'I will leave your present
advisors to complete their work of ruin and confusion and, what is
more, I will allow them to extract themselves and you from the mire
they have dragged you into.'[35]
    He did not have long to wait for his satisfaction. Strikers were
evicted from company houses. Blacklegs were employed in their places.
Union funds built up during the years of the 'coal famine' were
exhausted by strike pay. After sixteen weeks the strike was called off in
ignominious defeat. In Hamilton, miners blamed the Larkhall leaders
for the disaster and broke away to form their own district union.[36]
The rout of the Scottish Miners' Association was complete.
    Apologists for Alexander McDonald[37] have sometimes under-
estimated the force of the criticisms made against him during the
turmoil of 1872-4 and the constructive stimulus given by rank-and-file
militancy to trade union policy. There is no need to deny McDonald's

great achievements. He had done much to lay the foundation principles of miners' trade unionism. He had demonstrated the power of the state to control mining operations. He had pointed to national federation as the goal of miners' organisations. His rhetoric had upheld the belief that miners should be guaranteed a 'fair' wage by masters and the community at large in return for supplying a vital commodity to the nation. But in 1874 he counselled retreat and negative despair in a situation of world depression, which called for new thinking on the means of pursuing these highly desirable ends. He was, of course, perfectly correct in his view that a 'universal strike' of Scottish miners was out of the question, but his vituperative attacks on those who led resistance to the ironmasters' demands helped to confuse the issues and check the development of new strategies. Strike agitation was the only means by which such new strategies could be stimulated and publicised among miners. At one of the mass meetings at Powburn Toll in 1874, the first glimmering of a new view emerged. The Larkhall miners' agent felt moved to exclaim:

> He wanted the miners to call upon the Legislators of Great Britain to take up the question in dispute. Some cried out that it would bring starvation. If it did bring starvation to families were they not the subjects of Queen Victoria? Were they not the upholders of Great Britain?[38]

In this confused outburst of a reluctant strike leader, hitherto a devoted follower of Alexander McDonald, we can discern the first stirring of a new departure, which was soon to direct itself much more consciously at bringing the state further into the operations of coal-mining than McDonald had been prepared to allow. What the 'Legislators of Great Britain' might be asked to do was, in 1874, left unexplained, but the question was to preoccupy the taciturn youth who found himself caught up in the turmoil.

Hardie had been shocked to find that the iron companies could, in sixteen short weeks, reduce the wages of their miners by nearly half. There had been no question of negotiation, no chance for the union leaders to put the men's case, simply a tyrannical exercise of power by the companies over the miners' livelihoods. Hardie, already irked by the condescension of social superiors towards miners and aware of his father's republican views on mining royalties, felt 'resentful and vengeful'.[39] The episode seemed to sum up the low esteem in which people like him were held. He had become an ardent reader of Robert

Burns and some lines from 'Man was Made to Mourn' seemed to sum up his feelings:

> If I'm designed yon lordling's slave,
> By Nature's law designed,
> Why was an independent wish
> E'er planted in my mind?[40]

Hardie was developing into an agitator, but his feelings about the strikers were as confused as his feelings against the ironmasters were resentful. New influences were at work in his life, drawing him apart, alike from the class-consciousness of the militant rank-and-file and from the sectarian isolation of his father's secularism. These were the influences of middle-class evangelicalism, towards which he was pushed by his mother's deeply-engrained temperance views. Evangelicalism encouraged him to see the rank-and-file miners as in some measure victims of their own weaknesses of character. Trade unionism could never be respected until all miners learned to live and work like Alexander McDonald. This view was powerfully reinforced by the myth of their own history which Scots miners commonly cherished. They believed that their forefathers had ranked as an elite of skilled, independent workmen, whose prosperity had been undermined by ignorant and worthless immigrants from Ireland and elsewhere. These miners aspired to restore their occupation to the honourable dignity of a skilled trade whose members would rank among the aristocracy of labour and they looked to the state, in common with middle-class evangelicals, to coerce and discipline those 'interlopers' who had degraded and dishonoured the dangerous and demanding trade of collier. It is the ambiguity of Hardie's developing relationship to the militancy of the rank-and-file on the one hand, and the sense of superior independence fostered by evangelicalism on the other, which forms the characteristic polarity within his political outlook.

Notes

1. A. Miller, *The Rise and Progress of Coatbridge* (Glasgow, 1874); F.H. Groome, *Ordnance Gazeteer of Scotland* (1885); D. Pollock, *Dictionary of the Clyde* (Edinburgh, 1891); R. Hunt, *Mineral Statistics of the United Kingdom,* annual (see esp. 1855); Gordon M. Wilson, 'The Industrialisation of Hamilton', in *Hamilton, 1475-1975* (Hamilton, 1975).
2. The General Index of Births for Scotland, Register House, Edinburgh, shows a child David, born at Eastfield, Parish of Bothwell, to David Hardie, ship's carpenter. Ms. Report of the Scots Ancestry Research Society, commissioned

by the present writer, from which this and other genealogical data have been taken.

3. D. Lowe, *From Pit to Parliament* (1923), pp.10-16; Stewart, *Hardie* (1921), p.1ff; E. Hughes, *Keir Hardie* (1956), p.14.
4. Hardie recalled that 'Her idea o' Heeven seemed tae be that it wis a great big fairm whaur ye could get workin' on frae year's end tae year's end withoot stoppin'.' *Ardrossan and Saltcoats Herald*, 3 June 1882.
5. Hardie in *Merthyr Pioneer*, 26 December 1914.
6. *Miner*, December 1887. See Appendix I.
7. *Labour Leader*, February 1893.
8. Hardie, 'Christmas Ghost', *Labour Leader*, 23 December 1904.
9. H. Fyfe, *Keir Hardie* (1935), p.17.
10. *Ardrossan and Saltcoats Herald*, 3 June 1882.
11. *Labour Leader*, 23 December 1904.
12. *Ardrossan and Saltcoats Herald*, 1 July 1887.
13. *Labour Leader*, 26 March 1893.
14. Ibid., 23 December 1904; 24 August 1906.
15. Ibid., 24 August 1906.
16. Census records give them as living in Darngaber Row, Quarter, in 1871.
17. Quoted in J. Handley, *The Irish in Modern Scotland* (Cork, 1947), p.135.
18. Hardie, 'Our Collier Laddies', *Labour Leader*, 10 March 1896.
19. *Ardrossan and Saltcoats Herald*, 3 June 1882.
20. Stewart, *Hardie*, p.6; Lowe, *Pit to Parliament*, p.19.
21. *Labour Leader*, 3 July 1908. There is a good account of the republican movement in Britain in R. Harrison, *Before the Socialists* (1965), pp.109ff.
22. Hardie in *Labour Leader*, 29 May 1905.
23. See *Hamilton Advertiser*, 31 August 1872, for a full report of the conference. This newspaper is hereafter cited as *Hamilton Adv.*
24. I am indebted to Dr Gordon Wilson of Hamilton Technical College for permission to use his unpublished index of Lanarkshire miners' wages.
25. *Hamilton Adv.*, 28 December 1872.
26. The other was Thomas Burt, the Northumberland miners' leader. See J. Saville and J. Bellamy (eds.), *Dictionary of Labour Biography*, I (1972), p.212.
27. *Ardrossan and Saltcoats Herald*, 2 April 1882.
28. *Hamilton Adv.*, 23 and 30 November 1872.
29. Ibid., 31 August 1872.
30. Ibid., 14 December 1872-22 February 1873 and 7 March–15 August 1874.
31. Ibid., 28 March 1874.
32. Ibid., 23 March and 4 April 1874.
33. Ibid., 11 April 1874.
34. Hardie, 'Reverie and Reminiscence', *Labour Leader*, 6 January 1905.
35. *Hamilton Adv.*, 9 May 1874.
36. Ibid., 8 August 1874.
37. H.A. Clegg, A. Fox and A.F. Thompson, *History of British Trade Unionism since 1889*, I (Oxford, 1964), p.18.
38. *Hamilton Adv.*, 16 May 1874.
39. Hardie, 'Reverie and Reminiscence', *Labour Leader*, 6 January 1905.
40. Ibid.

2 THE INDEPENDENT COLLIER

I

Historians who have focused their attention on the national organisation of British miners have long followed G.D.H. Cole in regarding the Miners' National Association of Great Britain and Ireland as a union different in kind from the mid-Victorian trade unions of skilled craftsmen.[1] According to this account, skilled craftsmen such as the engineers founded their trade union strategy on an attempt to exclude from their jobs labourers who had not served a regular apprenticeship. By contrast, miners' trade unionism developed differently, since miners, unlike engineers, were not surrounded at their place of work by a large mass of unskilled labour capable of taking over their jobs in times of industrial dispute.

When we examine miners' trade unionism at the level of the district unions which constituted the Association, however, we see that this is a wholly misleading view. The district unions of Lanarkshire whose rules have survived were just as concerned to keep unqualified men out of their trade as any Victorian aristocrats of labour. The only respect in which they differed from the craftsmen is that the latter were more often successful in operating this exclusive trade unionism to their own advantage.[2]

Lanarkshire miners tried to impose what amounted to apprenticeship by laying down a course of training for a boy entering the mines. He would begin work under the supervision of an adult hewer, who, it was assumed, would usually be his father. For the first two years he would be treated as a 'quarter-ben', that is, he would only receive one-quarter of the tubs normally allocated to a hewer, restricting him, in effect, to one-quarter of a man's pay. During this time, his work would consist of the most menial tasks of coal-getting, breaking up the coal into lumps, loading it into tubs, hauling the tubs from the work place to the nearest railhead underground, and otherwise acting as fetcher and carrier for the hewer. During the following two years, as a 'half-ben', he would begin to take a hand in the less difficult tasks of cutting the coal. His hewer would do the most difficult part, known as 'holing' or 'bottoming', by which the lower part of the coal seam would be cut out to a height of some eighteen inches and a depth of several feet. This would leave the upper part of the seam hanging, and the boy would be shown how to 'rip down' this hanging coal by means of wedges and pick, so as to get it out in large lumps with as little dross as possible, for the collier was not paid for dross and tiny lumps. During these years, the boy would also be taught how to recognise dangers and difficulties at the work place, such as the presence of noxious gases or the sounds which heralded an imminent roof-fall. After four years, the boy would graduate to the status of 'three-quarter ben', undertaking for himself the work of holing, and would be initiated into the dangerous work of shot-firing when explosives were necessary to get at the coal. Not until the end of these six years did the boy become entitled to be regarded and paid as a 'full ben'.

Lanarkshire miners tried, by trade unionism, to exclude from their work all who had not undergone this training. 'Strangers' coming into a district were expected to bring 'clearance lines' from the district they had left, showing that they were qualified men, and those who did not bring such lines were to be charged 'entry money', in some cases fixed as high as five pounds. In the days of James Hardie's boyhood, district unions in Lanarkshire were still trying to operate this apprenticeship system.

It had long proved hopeless. The coming of the iron companies had led to the exploitation on a large scale of the thickest seams, at which wholly inexperienced agricultural workers and general labourers could be employed. The systematic use of this unskilled labour outraged Scots miners, who looked upon their trade as a kind of hereditary calling, stretching back to and beyond the days of serfdom which had been ended by Act of Parliament in 1799. These men did not regard themselves as proletarian hands, but as independent contractors who controlled their own pace, rhythms and methods of work in return for an agreed price or 'cutting rate' from the owner or lessee of the coal seam. They were proud of their agility in thin and difficult work places, their knowledge of geology, which enabled them to anticipate faults in seams by knocking or boring into them, and their skill in handling explosives in dark, unlit mines where dangerous gases lurked to wreak havoc and destruction if they should miscalculate. As one of them put it in the 1880s, 'To hew coal skilfully is at least as hard as to hew stone'.[3] They resented immigrant and untrained workmen, who not only lowered wages, but endangered everyone in the pit by their ignorance of the signs of danger.

In the 1860s there was prevalent, among the skilled Scots colliers of the Larkhall and Hamilton district, a myth that their forefathers had been free and independent peasants, working the land and the mines as independent tradesmen.[4] According to this myth, Scots miners had reaped the reward of their struggle for emancipation from serfdom by becoming free workmen at a time in the first decade of the nineteenth century, when coal was in great demand and their skill was needed to work the narrow seams. In those days, ran the myth, pits were small and shallow, the working miner could enter and leave at will by means of ropes, ladders and stairs. As men of small capital, masters were not socially distanced from their men. Rather, they were often local tenant farmers who enjoyed a smoke and a good dram with their workmen during frequent breaks from labour in the pit. Markets were local and the rhythm of their demand from summer to winter well known and understood. Miners could offset the slack times of summer by moving to agricultural work. Often, they had a little land themselves, or at least large gardens on which to keep animals and grow vegetables. They did not need to depend wholly on pit work for their subsistence. Finally, the demand being well understood and masters and men knowing and trusting each other, they would cooperate to regulate output to the exact quantity needed by the consumers, so that the wages of miners fluctuated little and the industry provided a good return. Like all myths, this one had its basis in fact. Wages had been high in the Napoleonic wars and even the brothers Baird had begun their mining enterprise as tenants working a pit on their land with a horse gin.[5]

In the folk memory of Larkhall and Hamilton colliers, the transformation of the brothers Baird into the lords of the iron ring had been the harbinger of disaster to their way of life. The great iron companies were built on large capital investment. They sank a great many pits to work the thick 'ell' seam of coal and introduced unskilled labour. Their mode of operation imposed restrictions which the independent collier regarded as tyranny. Instead of being treated as an independent contractor, the working miner was a company hand under their regime. He could not enter and leave the pit as he pleased, for the mechanised winding gear of the new operations imposed a daily routine of raising coal and men at fixed times. The iron companies had no interest in regulating output, since increased output was necessary to get the maximum return on capital and, as their output of coal expanded beyond the consumptive capacity of their smelting furnaces, they entered into competition with the small sale masters for a share of the domestic and exporting markets. When the Scots miners tried to impose restriction of output by getting every trade unionist to reduce his daily 'darg' or output of coal, the iron companies responded by evicting the men from the company houses and bringing in blacklegs, often Irish, protected by troops and police. Company houses had no gardens or, if they had, the keeping of pigs and cows was prohibited.[6] Thus the miner saw himself as having been transformed from an independent collier into a degraded wage-slave.

Yet for two generations after the coming of the iron companies in Lanarkshire, the characteristic response of the Scots miners was to try to restore the old Arcadia. Those who looked back nostalgically to the post-emancipation decade continued to urge the iron companies to behave like the traditional small sale masters. They urged them to cooperate with the unions in restricting output. They stressed the common interest of master and man in good iron prices. They sought to regulate entry into their trade in order to enhance their power of restriction and they looked to the empty lands of the New World to provide the alternative in agricultural work for miners hard pressed by falling markets for coal. In their yearning for independence, they turned to cooperative production, banking the funds of their unions with a view to one day leasing coal land on which to sink a pit and employ themselves.

The lingering of this nostalgia in a coalfield long polarised into a class society of company masters and proletarians is to be attributed to the survival of many vestiges of pre-iron-company mining operations and to the rewards which mining could still offer the exceptional individual. Many of the coalmasters were still, in the 1860s and 1870s, small sale masters owning one or two pits and employing twenty or thirty workmen in each. Even in the great iron companies, large outputs were usually obtained from the proliferation of relatively small pits rather than the development of a few very large ones. Moreover, the development of large-scale company mining with hierarchical work forces went hand in hand with the maintenance of an archaic production system in which the muscle, sweat and sometimes still the skill of the collier was the basic productive energy. Opportunities therefore existed for individual miners to make better money than the mass of workmen and to rise into supervisory grades as certificated oversmen and even mining engineers. Social mobility in the Scots coalfield of the mid-nineteenth century was not entirely mythical, though beyond the power of the great majority to command, and there were even stories of miners who became ministers of religion and doctors.[7]

The continuous thread of trade union organisation in districts of Lanarkshire such as Larkhall throughout the 1850s and 1860s is to be attributed to the persistence of Scots miners who looked on themselves as the aristocrats of the work force and who wanted to turn the clock back to the good old times of the early nineteenth century when the collier had been independent and, as his dialect-borrowing from the French had it, 'bien'. Leadership from this stratum, however, would only have a mass appeal in an industry like mining so long as wages were rising. Entry restrictions could hold no attraction for most of the working miners, who had had to break them in order to get in. Sliding scales in the international world of pig-iron production meant only poverty and intermittent plenty. The mass of working miners were only interested in policies which offered hope of bettering this basic fact of their working lives. They would be attracted by the concept of the minimum wage rather than the sliding scale. They would pursue restriction only if it was directed at pushing up wages, not as a means of adjusting supply to demand in order to prevent them from falling.

After his temporary disorientation in 1874, McDonald pursued his customary ambiguous strategy of building the trade unionism of the independent collier while appealing rhetorically to the solidarity of all miners. He urged the Lanarkshire unions to restrict their output as the best way of defending themselves against the falling market. At the same time they should work to rebuild the Scottish Miners' Association so that one day the universal strike of Scottish miners, so dear to the hearts of the rank-and-file, would be possible. He was even prepared to threaten the ironmasters with a sympathetic strike of miners, seamen and engineers.[8] Throughout the years 1874 until his death in 1881, however, he persistently ignored the new directions indicated by the agitations of the best organised Lanarkshire districts. The mass of the miners grew increasingly disillusioned with his policies, though he could still command the support of closed conferences of delegates. The miner knew the hollowness of restriction of output in an industry where conditions varied so much from district to district and even from seam to seam in the same pit. He knew too the solidarity of the 'iron ring' in the face of low pig-iron prices and he had no belief in the policy of picking them off one by one by the tactic of selective strikes. What he wanted was a policy that answered to his own militant will to resist.

II

In the 1870s and 1880s, James Hardie came to occupy an ambivalent position towards the militancy of the rank-and-file of miners in the Hamilton district. He was drawn powerfully towards the myths and traditions of the independent collier, and towards the trade unionism of sliding scales, output regulation and class collaboration. He came to share the miners' nostalgia for a lost Arcadia and their resentment of depraved interlopers as well as high-handed iron companies. The acquiring of this labour aristocratic outlook was a dialectical process between certain middle-class religious elements in his community and his own inner sense of alienation.

Hamilton was the latest district of Lanarkshire to be transformed from the small-scale operations of sale masters to the operations of large-scale mining. The process had begun in the mid-1850s, when Colin Dunlop had leased land at Quarter, between Hamilton and Larkhall, for the development of his iron works. Elsewhere in the district, the great depths at which the coal seams lay had delayed the application of investment to their exploitation. The very high coal prices of 1870-3, however, stimulated investment and, by the end of the 1870s, the town of Hamilton stood in the centre of a wide arc of large-scale pits. The population, which had been nine and a half thousand in 1931, was nearly three times that figure in 1881. The transformation of what had until recently been an elegant ducal seat, fit for the entertainment of Napoleon III, into a centre of modern heavy industry elicited a steady stream of nostalgic reminiscences of the district before the pollution of mines and miners had overtaken it.

They were assiduously cultivated by Thomas Naismith, editor of the *Hamilton Advertiser,* who encouraged Scots colliers with literary aspirations to publish in his columns. They filled many of them with dialect accounts of the district in their boyhood and offered their homely wisdom on the issue of how best to restore the comfort and harmony of the old days. In these reminiscences, mining at Quarter on the Duke's estate and under his agent was recalled in an idyllic glow. The mines had served the local market for house coal. Miners had been kept busy with pit work in winter. In summer they turned their attention to 'country wark . . . in stone quarries and lime kilns and for the farmers at hay-time and harvest.' Memory recalled well-stocked vegetable gardens around the cottages of the 'bien colliers'. A number of them 'kept a cow for the use of their families and all of them a pig.'[9] The Larkhall miner-poet, Thomas Stewart, remembered how his father had worked a pit on his smallholding in the early nineteenth century. It had been so shallow that his wife could converse with him from the top of the shaft. His son had learned to look on him as a hero and to yearn for the day when he too would venture down into the dark and dangerous mine. In Stewart's Larkhall, the distance between master and workman seemed non-existent. All knocked off for a game of football when work was slack or sat round a dram in the farm kitchen, chaffing the Irish harvester who was casually employed there.[10]

The burden of such nostalgia was that latter-day miners had lost the heroic virtues of their forefathers. Knowing nothing of the trade, they gave themselves to drink and refused to make necessary sacrifices for the improvement of their lot. They must learn to drink less, smoke less, live simply and frugally, and so they would be able to accept the lower wages which restriction of output required in return for a regulated output and a steady market. In such vein, more than one 'Auld Collier' took up his pen to write to the *Hamilton Advertiser* in good broad Scots, and more in sorrow than in anger deploring the sight of working miners lounging of a Saturday night about the Cross:

> no' passin' time, but killin' it . . . smokin' tobacco, talkin' gie coarse language whiles . . . sair gie'en tae drink . . . oot et elbucks [elbows], oot o' meal an' money, the feck o' them oot o' credit. Poverty's nae sin, but plenty o' them brin on their ain poverty, an' that's whaur the sin lies.[11]

Hardie found himself drawn powerfully towards this view of the case. He had his own psychological reasons for being attracted by rural nostalgia. The Quarter he knew in the early seventies could hardly have contrasted more sharply with Naismith's recollection or with the isolated village of Newarthill. The mass of its near eight hundred inhabitants, overcrowded into company 'rows', seemed to the Hardies to be sunk in drunkenness and animal vices. A regular visitor at their home was a woman who had worked in the mines until excluded with women generally by Act of Parliament. Writing of her in 1882, Hardie stated that she could

> drink, smoke, swear and fight like a man . . . I remember her coming to the house of my parents one evening and, being a little tipsy, she showed us how she used to fackin the stuff doon that way, and showed a stump, all that was left of a little finger and told how a stone had one day fallen on her while she was whackin' ower the lag, lad, as she put it, and had almost cut her finger clean through. And even yet I can almost shudder at what follows. Instead of going home to have the injured finger dressed, 'I juist took ma teeth an' bit it clean aff.'

'The mental and moral debility', Hardie commented, 'engendered by such a state of matters . . . is too deep-seated to be eradicated in forty years, but there can be no doubt that the next generation will show a marked improvement over the present.'[12]

This last comment betrays Hardie's characteristic ambiguity towards the mass of working people around him. His discontented, rebellious temperament was powerfully attracted by the old 'pit wife', who no doubt played up to the boy's wide-eyed curiosity, but the grown Hardie carried the evangelical's distrust and disdain for those who gloried so openly in an unconventional role. Herein lay the origin of his later penchant for ideas of racial degeneration and coercive social reforms.

Hardie's mother continued to encourage him in self-improvement. The bond between them certainly did not diminish as years passed. Her patient, steady influence drew him away from the atheistical rebellious-ness of his father towards the virtues of sobriety and self-help. She became a symbol to Hardie of everything that was best in working-class family life and motherhood generally. 'The face of the eident [busy], thrifty, hard-working mother and housewife', he wrote years later 'who toils early and late for those she loves, acquires a sweet dignity which, betimes, I could almost worship.'[13] She fostered in him the horror of drunkenness engendered by his father's unemployed years, and encouraged him to join a temperance organisation in Quarter called the Independent Order of Good Templars. He threw himself into it with a will and became secretary of the Quarter Lodge by 1877.[14] The Good Templar movement had been an importation to Britain from the United States in the 1860s. It was encouraged by middle-class Christians, who hoped to recruit working men as total abstainers from drink to help in the campaign for an Act of Parliament which would permit local authorities to close all the public houses in their areas. This was known as the 'local veto' or 'local option' principle and was an aspect of the long-run movement for prohibition of the drink trade both in Britain and in America. Like some of the religious sects rooted in working-class life, the Good Templars offered men like Hardie opportunities for democratic organisation and for the achievement of a measure of social approval by rising through the hierarchy of its offices. It was rich in distinctions, with quasi-Masonic insignia and rituals and grandiloquent titles such as 'District Deputy' and 'Worthy Chief Templar'. It would not be many years before Mr J.K. Hardie would be affixing the letters 'DD' after his name. The order also insisted on purity of morals and encouraged women to take an active part in its organisation, because women were thought to have the primary role in rearing the new generation in temperance and purity. Hardie's lifelong concern to attract women of refinement to the labour movement and his interest in socialist Sunday schools began here.

In Hamilton, the Good Templars were under the patronage of

Thomas Naismith, editor of the *Hamilton Advertiser,* and of a prosperous tailor with a shop in the High Street, Mr Gavin Cross. Both were
members of a Hamilton Church known as the Evangelical Union. The
Union, established in the 1840s, entertained a sense of its special
mission to the mining community and rejected all Calvinist doctrines of
predestination for the belief that the atonement of Jesus Christ was
universal. Hardie now fell under the influence of its Hamilton pastor,
Rev. Dan Craig. Craig was himself a model of working-class self-
improvement. The son of an Ayrshire weaver, he had begun life as a
joiner. After some years as a lay preacher in the Evangelical Union, he
had been sent to its theological college in Glasgow and had become the
ordained pastor of the Hamilton congregation in 1871. His eloquent
preaching filled the church and the grateful congregation raised his
salary in the first six months from eighty pounds to one hundred and
sixty pounds.[15] His sudden accidental death in 1874 was a shock for
James Hardie, who recalled: 'He took a great interest in me and
completely changed the course of my religious thought, which, up till
then, about my nineteenth year, had been of a very negative
character.'[16]

In fact, Hardie did not become 'converted' to Christianity until
1878, four years after Craig's death,[17] but there is no reason to doubt
that Craig set him on the road. Perhaps the shock of Craig's sudden
death in 1874 precipitated a spiritual crisis in the impressionable young
man, and perhaps, too, his public acknowledgement of conversion had
to be delayed because of uncertainty as to David Hardie's reaction.
Hardie's friend and biographer, David Lowe, stated that father and son
talked the issue out one day while walking home and agreed to differ.[18]
There was certainly no bitterness in the parting of the ways. Hardie
admired the stubborn independence of his father in the face of ungodly
might and came to believe that the prophet of God's truth required the
same dauntless courage. 'My father', he was to tell an American
audience of ministers of religion, 'was a very militant atheist, yet he
ever exhibited more genuine Christianity, charity, tolerance, brotherly
love and morality than nine-tenths of those who sail under Gospel
colours.'[19] If his mother's influence was pushing him towards respectability, his father's helped him to retain a pride of class which made
him prickly towards cant and condescension. In the early 1890s, when
socialism had become popular, he would even use his father's name to
claim descent from the Scottish revolutionary, Hardie, executed after
the Bonniemuir uprising in 1820.[20]

Many early influences, however, now drew Hardie towards the

Evangelical Union. His mother and grandmother had both been members of the Church of Scotland and Mary Keir had been both baptised and married in the Auld Kirk.[21] Grannie Keir had been a strange mixture of rural paganism and evangelical piety. Her connection with her daugher's family had always been close and in the evenings she would gather the children round her knee to pray that Jesus would take them after death to 'the land abune'.[22] On the other hand, his mother's harsh experience of Christian charity in the Glasgow years had turned the family away from established religion. Peasant paganism, childhood piety and parental opposition turned Hardie away from coldly rational theology such as Calvinism towards a mystical view of Grace which emphasised the Fatherhood of God and the Brotherhood of Man. By the same token, however, he would have found dry and uninspiring the secularist radicalism of Charles Bradlaugh.

But perhaps the influence which prepared him most for the Evangelical Union was the sense of stigmatisation which rankled in him. He was made to feel degraded as a miner, and the knowledge that he was illegitimate in Calvinist Scotland did nothing to enhance his sense of social worth. There is some evidence that the stigma of illegitimacy was a very sore point with him. In the years following his death, one of his political opponents in the socialist movement was to find in Lanarkshire a boyhood friend of Hardie's who recalled that Hardie believed his real father to have been a doctor from Airdrie, who bribed the miner, William Aitken, to leave the district so that his name could be used in an action of paternity which Mary Keir brought in the Sheriff Court. Hardie, this witness declared, was 'a damm sight prouder to think himself the son o' a doctor than the dacent man wha gae him and his mother a name and brocht him up'.[23] Clearly, the source from which this testimony emanates is suspect as politically inspired, but Hardie's own story of Wee Jamie Keekie, with its harping on the theme of the abandoned child and the lost inheritance, strongly suggests that such fantasies really existed in Hardie's mind.

What the Evangelical Union offered Hardie, therefore, was reassurance. It gave him a socially acceptable role as a lay preacher and temperance organiser, and the esteem of ministers, newspaper editors, shopkeepers and others who welcomed him, though a humble miner, into their congregation. Like black people in the United States, British miners in the nineteenth century often found in evangelical religion the assurance of dignity in the sight of God which compensated for the low esteem in which their secular calling was held. We are given more than a hint that this was the attraction for Hardie in a sermon which he quoted verbatim and with personal endorsement for his fellow miners in 1885:

> Only a miner! Say that and believe that and you will become only a miner, and lose all your self-respect. What I wish you to feel now and always is that you are men. In fact, you are not miners at all . . . you are God's children. Your work is mining, but the blackest work to which a man may put his hand can never disguise or blot out the image of him in whose likeness he was made.[24]

Hardie was thus drawn towards a a section of middle-class life in Hamilton at a time when its leaders were concerned to recruit energetic miners as coadjutors in their mission to raise and uplift the degraded heathens of the mining villages. The old self-help virtues of the independent collier were to be re-established and universalised among the turbulent, hard-drinking miners of the district. Temperance, thrift, industry and piety were to be the virtues which would restore the fallen to the dignity and self-respect that had reigned in the garden of their early-nineteenth-century existence. There was nothing new in all this. It had been the creed of the paternalistic ironmasters like the Bairds, who had built churches and schools and organised soirées and lectures for their workmen. What was new was the desire to encourage working-class self-activity in alliance with middle-class philanthropy. So far as Lanarkshire was concerned, it was novel to find respectable people who took an interest in organisations composed of and run by working people. The Good Templars were needed in a more democratic age when working men would be called upon (it was fervently hoped) to vote for the closure of their own public houses.

But the socialisation of a complex man like Hardie could never be so straightforward. He was not merely a temperance organiser and preacher, he was a trade unionist. The Evangelical Union wanted nothing to do with strikes and class conflict. They regarded these as evidence of ignorance and barbarity on the part of the men. Yet they were not altogether hostile to trade unionism, as Naismith's wide coverage of it in the columns of the *Hamilton Advertiser* amply demonstrates. They had their own reasons for resenting the ironmasters, who were usually Conservatives in league with the brewing interest. They gave general support to the class-conciliation side of Alexander McDonald's ambiguous rhetoric. They wanted trade unionism to be founded on the principles of reason and justice to master as well as man. They favoured sliding scales and were unhappy about the ironmasters' efforts to drive down coal-miners' wages to the lowest point needed by the iron market. They exhorted ironmasters and miners alike to practise regulation of output in harmonious recognition of their common interest. They looked to leaders like Mr J.K. Hardie to continue the work of Alexander McDonald in teaching the men the value of such trade unionism and its justification in the teaching of political economy.

Hardie's reading fostered his ambivalent view of his relationships to the mass of miners as missionary and class leader. At the age of sixteen, a friend (probably Rev. Dan Craig) gave him a copy of *Sartor Resartus* by Thomas Carlyle. He struggled with it, reading it three times, until 'the spirit of it somewhat entered into me'.[25] What could he, an under-educated youth, have made of Carlyle's complex prose and cloudy, rhetorical argument? To answer this question, we must recall what Carlyle was preaching in the 1830s. He was trying to communicate to his countrymen the lessons he had drawn from German idealist philosophy. He believed that industrialising England was moving towards a revolution which would outdo the French Revolution in the anarchy which it would unleash. Starvation stalked in the land. Agricultural workers were crowding, herd-like, into the factory towns. Cynical, aristocratic politicans looked on indifferently, heedless of the misery. Soulless millocrats dehumanised their workers into 'hands' bound to them only by the cash nexus. Masses of these same hands were recruited from the ranks of the starving into the army to fight wars in which they had no conceivable interest or understanding.

Hardie could certainly identify the Lanarkshire coalfield in much of Carlyle's picture of England under the impact of the industrial revolution. Hamilton, indeed, was simply going through another stage of that process rather later than the rest of the west of Scotland. The poverty and alienation of the miners was as Carlyle described. The Duke of Hamilton with his gambling debts and declining fortune was the cynical, indifferent aristocrat. In place of hard and unfeeling millocrats were hard and unfeeling ironmasters, concerned, as Hardie felt, only with self and place. All these parallels Hardie noted. But there was another side of Carlyle which also influenced him. The Sage of Chelsea had had no belief in democracy or in popular radicalism as a solution to the turbulent disorders of reform demonstrations and Chartist assemblies. He equated democracy with anarchy, the blind upheaval of the instinct to destroy, which broke through in every age when social relationships were dehumanised by selfishness on the part of the elite. The abandoned millions were 'mostly fools', who would rise in blind fury, like the Bastille mob, and impose a reign of terror and destruction on their rulers. History revealed many such ages, of which the French Revolution had been but the latest. Society, however, was like the phoenix, it perished in flames, only to rise again. Out of the fires of social conflict had always arisen a new elite of heroes, to reimpose the laws of God on a Mammon-worshipping age: charity for the poor on the rich; obedience to the great on the poor. The hero was he who intuitively understood these divine laws and who could 'body-forth' their meaning to ignorant and irrational men. He needed no election and he owed his authority to no process of law or appeal to custom. He was known by his deeds. If, at first, the people rejected his teaching, they would, like the Hebrews of old, learn in suffering and misery to follow his course. Equally, if the hero were a sham, he could have no possibility of permanently holding sway. His misguided courses would only deepen the chaos and hasten his own destruction. The cult of the hero, which Carlyle did so much to popularise, was a starting point for the interest of twentieth-century sociologists in the role of the charismatic leader.[26]

The importance of the hero in Carlyle's thought was that he would be, as far as possible, a substitute for brute force in governing the passions of common men. The hero would gain obedience through the manifestly divine origin of his teaching. Carlyle, who sprang from the same Scottish traditions of the Covenant as Hardie, appealed ambiguously to generalised ethical values which he never analysed: to discipline, justice and charity. He never conceived the rebellious poor as historical agents of these values, but as dumb, suffering creatures whose grievances had to be pacified before they drove them to outrage. What appealed strongly to Hardie was that his heroes were as likely to spring from among the lower classes as from the upper. They were the best teachers of the common people because they knew the life of the common people. They identified with their sufferings, but not with their ignorance and their blind, destructive passion.

Here was a role that appealed strongly to this romantic, alienated young miner in Hamilton. He felt himself called to the lonely and heroic struggle against Mammon-worship in all classes. It justified his resentments and feelings of alienation against both the great and powerful masters and the ignorant and drunken men. It gave him a conviction that, though humbly born, he could still be numbered with the mighty dead. Why should not he, the step-son of a carpenter, rise from among the despised and rejected to teach the rich their duty to the poor and the poor their duty to themselves? Throughout his life, he would see himself as the Moses, even the Jesus, of the poor and oppressed, the fearless champion of their sufferings, and the moderate constitutionalist who compromised their demands in the interests of discipline and social harmony. He would encourage agitation as a stimulus to social righteousness, but he would never identify himself with the revolutionary actions of the dispossessed. This deep cultural ambivalence gave him an ambivalent role in working-class agitations for the rest of his life, an ambivalence which appeared as soon as the militancy of the Hamilton miners swept him into trade union agitations in 1879 and 1880.

Notes

1. G.D.H. Cole, 'Some Notes on British Trade Unionism in the Third Quarter of the Nineteenth Century', *Int. Rev. Soc. Hist.*, II, 1936, 1-27.
2. The following argument was first presented in F. Reid, 'The Independent Collier', *New Edinburgh Review*, 1975, pp.30-3. For an extended version see F. Reid and A.B. Campbell, 'The Independent Collier', unpublished paper. For the engineers, see J.B. Jefferys, *Story of the Engineers, 1800-1945* (1945). pp.51ff. On the labour aristocracy, see E.J. Hobsbawm, *Labouring Men* (1964), pp.272ff. Then cf. H.M. Pelling, *Popular Politics and Society in Late Victorian Britain* (1968), pp.147ff.
3. R. Haddow, 'The Miners of Scotland', *Nineteenth Century*, September 1888, p.362. Miller, *Rise and Progress of Coatbridge*, p.126.
4. T. Stewart, *Among the Miners of Larkhall* (1893), pp.4ff.
5. T.C. Smout, *History of the Scottish People, 1560-1830* (1969), p.434. A. MacGeorge, *The Bairds of Gartsherrie* (Glasgow, 1875), p.46.
6. *Ardrossan and Saltcoats Herald*, 3 June 1882.
7. Haddow, op.cit.
8. *Hamilton Adv.*, 14 November 1874.
9. *Hamilton Directory* (1879), p.22.
10. Stewart, *Among the Miners of Larkhall*, p.4ff.
11. *Hamilton Adv.*, 12 September 1874.
12. *Ardrossan and Saltcoats Herald*, 2 November 1883.
13. Hardie, 'The Banner of Labour, *Labour Leader*, 29 April 1910, p.263.
14. See advertisement for District Lodge, No.36 (Lanark, Middle Ward South-Western), Independent Order of Good Templars, *Hamilton Directory*, 1878-9.
15. J. McBryde, *Park Road E.U. Congregational Church, Hamilton: Centenary Brochure* (1954).
16. Quoted by Hughes, *Hardie*, pp.23ff.
17. Hardie, ms. diary fragment, 1884.
18. Lowe, *Pit to Parliament*, p.19.
19. *Chicago Chronicle*, 10 November 1895.
20. Hardie, *The I.L.P.: A Historical Sketch of the Movement* (1894), p.1.
21. Her birth and baptism are recorded in the Parochial Register of Airdrie, 27 September 1830 and 9 June 1831.
22. Hardie, 'Evening Prayer', *Labour Leader*, 12 May 1894.
23. A.A. Durward, 'The Truth about James Kear alias James Keir Hardie', undated manuscript, about 1948. See Appendix 1. Hardie's birth was registered under his mother's name, Kerr, then pronounced in Lanarkshire as

Kear or Keir.
24. *Ardrossan and Saltcoats Herald,* 6 March 1885.
25. Hardie in *Review of Reviews,* June 1906, pp.57ff.
26. H.H. Gerth and C. Wright Mills, *From Max Weber* (1948), p.53.

3 'BLACK DIAMONDS'

I

The Hamilton district remained very disorganised for some years after the débâcle of 1874. Nearby Larkhall continued to maintain its local trade union and tried to stem wage cuts by the old policy of restricting the size of the 'darg' or output of each miner. Wages, however, continued to fall below the level of five shillings reached in 1874 and the severe fall in pig-iron prices depressed them to around four and sixpence by the end of 1878. There was also the perennial problem of short-time working in the pits. A report in the *Hamilton Advertiser* put the average wage for miners in Scotland at four shillings a day, the lowest rates being paid in iron works, and declared that the average weekly earnings of miners could not exceed a pound a week.[1]

In 1877, however, a terrible accident occurred at the Holm Farm colliery near Hamilton. Mines had been opened up hastily in the boom years of 1870 to 1873. Insufficient attention had been given to safety considerations, and over one hundred men lost their lives at Holm Farm when water from an old working burst in upon the new large-scale development. The accident brought Alexander McDonald to the district to represent the miners' interests in the legal inquiry which followed. It also stimulated local leaders who had given up trade union activity and returned to pit work. In the worst depths of depression, therefore, a Hamilton district union was formed to pursue a moderate policy of restriction of output, and to work for the re-establishment of a Lanarkshire County Union.[2]

In 1878, Hardie became secretary to the new Hamilton union. He had attracted the approving attention of Alexander McDonald, who was on the lookout for teetotallers to staff the official positions in the new Lanarkshire organisation which he hoped to rebuild. He wrote personally to Hardie, urging on him the efficacy of restriction of output and the need to avoid strikes. 'It will bring freedom and fair wages', he stated, adding that it was important to organise the miners of Ayrshire, since they competed in the same markets as Lanarkshire.[3] Hardie appears to have had some success with this policy among the coalmasters of the Hamilton district. Coal prices steadied and began to edge upwards, while pig-iron prices remained depressed. By the autumn of 1878, the Hamilton union had pushed wages in sale pits up to five shillings a day. Hamilton once again became the premier district of trade union agitation in Lanarkshire and it was to Hamilton that Alexander McDonald came to inaugurate a new Lanarkshire county union in August 1879. Hardie moved a fulsomely worded resolution of congratulation to McDonald, but his speech on that subject was received with loud barracking. He later attributed this to the resentment of Irish Catholics in the audience when he compared McDonald to Martin Luther, but there was, no doubt, something of the old mistrust hanging over from 1874.[4]

The new Lanarkshire union now appointed Hardie as a paid agent for the Hamilton district. It was a timely opportunity, for he had been dismissed from the Dunlop Iron Company for his trade union activities shortly before.[5] The ironmasters were concerned that rising wages in the sale works would attract their own miners away and the Dunlop manager had marked Hardie as a dangerous agitator. His summary dismissal left Hardie dependent for his income on a union which was a byword for instability, and this at a time when he had just taken on the responsibilities of marriage to a Hamilton girl, of whom more later. Hardie was soon to find himself torn between his admiration for McDonald and his loyalty to the union rank-and-file in Hamilton.

At the beginning of November 1879, the ironmasters decided that the time had come to force miners' wages back to a level commensurate with the needs of iron-smelting. They formed a Lanarkshire Coal Masters' Association, in which some of the larger sale masters joined them, and announced an immediate reduction of wages in the mines of the Associated Masters by sixpence a day, to be followed by a further reduction of sixpence a day on 29 November. Their aim would thus appear to have been the closing of the gap of about one shilling which had opened up between wages in sale and iron works. Recalling the strikes of 1874, they declared further that any attempt to resist on the part of the new Lanarkshire union would be met with immediate retaliation. Wages would be reduced by a third sixpence and the Associated Masters would support financially any company whose works were stopped by selective strike action.[6]

As in 1874, Alexander McDonald's response to this situation was outwardly ambiguous. He met with the Board of the Lanarkshire Miners' Union and advised them to submit to the masters' first sixpence and, meantime, to send fourteen agents into Fife, Clackmannan and Ayrshire to organise movements for wage increases there which would bring miners' wages up to the same level as in Lanarkshire. This seemed to indicate a policy based on national solidarity and a common wages strategy, but McDonald was really only playing for time. As he admitted shortly afterwards, he expected the iron market to improve and hoped that the second reduction of sixpence would prove unnecessary. His real aim in counselling submission to the first sixpence was revealed by his further advice that the union should offer the masters a sliding scale.[7]

The Board of the Hamilton district met shortly after the county meeting. At this meeting, the agent for the Larkhall district arrived late and caused a sensation by declaring that his men had decided to come out on strike in defiance of the County Board's instructions. The Hamilton men were immediately swept into the movement and called for a national strike of Scottish miners. A week later, the County Board was again convened, this time in Hamilton, to consider what it should do about these unofficial stoppages. There were fifteen hundred men on strike in Hamilton alone, with support in the Larkhall and Motherwell districts. But in the big iron company districts of Coatbridge, Wishaw and the environs of Glasgow, the strike movement had no appeal. As the Board met and debated the situation, a noisy meeting of strikers outside clamoured for the support of the county union. Inside, Hardie, as the Hamilton representative, appears to have urged that the county union could not simply surrender to the masters' terms. At least some show of resistance ought to be put up, even if it were impossible to get the whole county to support all the men now on strike. In the end, it was agreed to recommend that all the men on strike should return to work, except one sale works in Larkhall, which would stay out, supported by the rest of the county until the reduction was withdrawn. A Hamilton works would then be struck, then a Glasgow one, and so on until all the reduction notices were withdrawn.

As we have already seen, this policy of selective strikes had a long history. It was known locally as 'putting on the block'. It could be of no avail in the existing conditions, in which the large-scale companies, iron and coal, were solidly united. It was a survival of the independent collier's dream that big business could be brought to heel by the collaboration of trade unions with small business. Most of the delegates to the County Board were men drawn from the self-improving strata of the Lanarkshire coalfield to whom such fantasies were plausible descriptions of the real world. To the massed rank-and-file outside, they were not. When Hardie put the plan to them as their district secretary, he was greeted with jeers and derision. In vain he pleaded that only one week of strike action had cost the district union four hundred and fifty pounds in strike pay. The men shouted back their defiance. They would stay out till the grass grew on the pit winding gear. In the end the meeting voted to carry on the strike at all the works then stopped and to pay no more financial contributions to the Lanarkshire Miners' Union. Reluctantly, Hardie agreed, warning them that each man at work would have to pay one shilling and sixpence a day for the support of those on strike. He could only hope, he said, that they would stick to their pledge.[8]

As a result of the Hamilton decision, the Lanarkshire Miners' Union split into two. The Hamilton, Larkhall and Motherwell districts, where sale masters predominated, formed a breakaway Lanarkshire Miners' Union, while the iron company districts of Coatbridge, Wishaw and Glasgow formed a Lanarkshire Miners' Association under McDonald's direction and resolved to exclude from office any official of the Hamilton union. The Lanarkshire Coal Masters' Assocation took advantage of the situation by imposing the threatened punitive reduction of sixpence, as well as the two reductions announced at the beginning of November. At the beginning of December, they announced a third (actually, therefore, fourth) reduction, of sixpence, which would bring wages to three shillings a day. The response was a total stoppage of work throughout the Hamilton district. In the iron districts, McDonald went about negotiating sliding-scale agreements with any masters who were prepared to accept them. He also singled out for sharp recrimination the agent of the Larkhall district who had begun the militant action and soon widened his abusive comments to include the strike leaders in general.[9]

Hardie now found himself in a difficult position. He was dependent on the Lanarkshire organisation for his salary and there would be little hope of getting work in the pits if the union movement collapsed again. On the other hand, his only claim to hold office in a Lanarkshire union would be as leader of the Hamilton district.

John Gray, the agent of Larkhall who had first broken the McDonaldite strategy, was touring the district making inflammatory speeches. Hardie knew that a strike policy could not be successful without the support of the other districts of Lanarkshire and the other counties of Scotland. But there had not been time to organise this support before the crisis had been created by the Masters' Association, while the McDonald policy of always fighting any reduction except the one actually being threatened seemed to him to be damaging to the men's will to resist. The problem seemed to him, therefore, to require that the Hamilton men get out of their present strike with whatever saving of face could be managed and the shattered unity of the Scottish

Miners' Association should be gradually pieced together. He therefore followed a policy of building bridges towards the other Lanarkshire districts while dissociating himself from the extreme militancy of Gray, who did not, in any case, enjoy the full support of the Larkhall men. His next task was to guarantee enough support for the Hamilton men to keep them out on strike until a compromise could be patched up with the masters. To this end, he arranged with local shopkeepers to provide potatoes on the credit of the union, and began to focus public attention on getting the fourth sixpence reduction withdrawn by the masters as a condition of the men's return to work. At the same time, he attended a meeting of McDonald's Lanarkshire Miners' Association and declared from its platform that he had never been a supporter of the strike policy, but appealed for support for the Hamilton men in the just cause, on which all were now agreed, of resisting the fourth reduction. Finally, he patched things up with McDonald by helping him to negotiate a sliding scale with his own former employer, the Dunlop Iron Company, and called upon Hamilton ministers of religion to arbitrate between the other masters and the union for a settlement of the strike.[10]

In spite of these efforts, the Hamilton strike dragged on into 1880 and became known ever after as 'the Tattie Strike' because of Hardie's arrangement with the shopkeepers. In the new year, iron prices rallied a little and the ironmasters decided to withdraw the reduction of the fourth sixpence. This enabled the Hamilton sale masters to make a similar concession and the men returned to work. Much bitterness and distrust remained, however, between the leaders of the Lanarkshire districts. Although the county union seems to have been formally reunited under the umbrella of the now almost moribund Scottish Miners' Association, the union repudiated the debts of the Hamilton district to the shopkeepers who had sold potatoes on credit. Hardie was branded by McDonald as an irresponsible agitator.

His response was to emphasise the need to do something practical about the strategy which McDonald himself had always advocated, that of bringing the Ayrshire miners into a common movement with the Lanarkshire men. During the summer of 1880, he toured the districts of Lanarkshire, urging the need to build up the solidarity of the Scottish Miners' Association. Towards the end of the summer, coal prices began to fall and a new round of wage reductions precipitated another wave of strikes in Lanarkshire. The county union decided, therefore, to send its firebrand, Hardie, down to Ayrshire to try to mobilise that remote county where trade unionism had long been a

weak growth, confined to the larger towns near the coast. Iron companies dominated the remoter southerly parts, but unionism had always
had a foothold in Irvine and it was agreed that Hardie should go there
as agent of the Lanarkshire Union to help form a county union.

He was warmly welcomed in Irvine by the old trade union stalwarts
and, on 18 August 1880, addressed his first open-air meeting on a hill-
side near the town, known as Craigiehill. More than three thousand
were present on a beautiful summer day. Those assembled on the hill
could see contingents of marching miners approaching from outlying
districts: 'gathering like the clans, each accompanied by bands and
carrying old Chartist symbols and other emblems on their flags'. Cheer
after cheer rose from the waiting watchers as each new contingent was
seen in the open spaces of the winding road.

Hardie was now confronted with a difficult problem. The events of
1874 had shown that Ayrshire men were not prepared to make sacrifices by striking to help Lanarkshiremen defend larger wages than their
own. If solidarity were to be built throughout Scotland, it would have
to be built on a policy that offered hope to all the counties and districts
that their standards of living would be defended. The press report of
Hardie's speech that day, which has fortunately survived in a very full
form, shows him arousing the élan of the Irvine rank-and-file by
sketching a policy of sweeping state intervention in the coal industry,
so far-reaching as to anticipate the approach of social democracy taken
up by the Hamilton miners in the mid-1880s and discussed below. With
characteristic realism, he began from the old sliding-scale policy,
familiar to his hearers. The men, he said, were willing to accept a fair
sliding scale after an initial advance in wages, but: 'There were different
kinds of sliding scale. There was the sliding scale that was always sliding
down and there was a fair one, and they did not object to the latter.'
The hallmark of a fair sliding scale, he went on to say, was that it
recognised a minimum standard of living for all miners:

No matter what the market was able to afford, the time had now
come when they must tell their employers, 'We will work no longer
for the wage you offer us, because it cannot keep us' (cheers). No
nation had the right to exist unless it could keep its workmen
comfortable. If the time had now come when this Great Britain, the
pride of the world, which ruled the waves and upon whose territory
the sun never set, was unable to keep its working men, the sooner it
disappeared the better for all concerned (loud cheers). Other nations
would have their day. In Australia, the sliding scale had been

brought into force by the Government, who had also appointed a
Minister to look after the mining community.[11]

Hardie was clearly anticipating the policy soon to be advocated in
Lanarkshire by socialist agitators, the policy of a state-imposed
minimum wage for miners coupled with nationalisation of their
industry. In doing so, he was clearly not drawing on any socialist
propaganda, of which there is no evidence in the west of Scotland
before 1884. His inspiration seems to have been the Australian colonies,
the 'laboratory of the South', then pioneering many experiments in
state intervention.[12] Hardie knew many Lanarkshire miners who
emigrated to the colonies and kept in touch with them by correspondence. Hamilton, moreover, was the kind of place where a young man
might be stirred by the expansion of 'Greater Britain'. David Livingstone, son of a weaver from nearby Blantyre, had only recently
returned from his long mission to darkest Africa, and Hamilton had
celebrated by conferring the freedom of the town on H.M. Stanley. It
was no empty jingoistic sentiment that found its way into Hardie's
rhetoric on Craigiehill, but a pride in what Scottish working-class
emigrants could achieve in lands beyond the seas.

Hardie was desperate to sweep the Ayrshire men into the
Lanarkshire strike movement and he tapped every vein of oratory
which his father's republican-radical background afforded. There were
echoes of Mazzini when he declaimed:

It had been said that if a nation desired to be free it had only to will
it. It simply wished to be free and there was no power on Earth that
could keep it from being free. Now they wanted their wages
advanced, and show him the power on Earth that would stop them.

There was an even older echo, evoked perhaps by the Chartist symbols
on the miners' flags, when he dealt with the question of how they
would support themselves during the prolonged strike about to ensue:
'They could not work and starve . . . Therefore, if they were forced to
strike, it simply came to this, that they must just take it, that is, food,
wherever they could get it. (Loud and prolonged cheers.) That was the
plain fact.'[13]

It was a rousing speech and achieved its immediate tactical aim of
obtaining support in Ayrshire for the Lanarkshire strike. Men in the
Ayrshire sale works came out and an Ayrshire Miners' Association was
formed. But the power of the ironmasters had still to be felt. At a

meeting in Glasgow, they agreed to put their furnaces out of blast in order to force down coal prices. In Ayrshire, they set their 'on cost' men to supply coal from their 'bings' or pit-head stockpiles. Hardie responded with militant measures. He organised a picket line of tough miners' wives to try to dissuade the 'on cost' from going to work at the 'bings'. The companies responded in traditional manner. Extra police were drafted into the mining villages to escort the 'on cost' to work, and some of the picketing women were arrested. After the strike, they were prosecuted for intimidation and received prison sentences.[14] Under these hammer blows, the morale of Ayrshire miners in the iron works crumbled. Most of them drifted back to work within a week and the new Association called off the strike. In Lanarkshire, also, the men were far from solid. The Glasgow district had stayed at work as in the previous year, and other districts were returning to work in disorder by the end of August. In Hamilton, the shopkeepers refused to give the strikers credit. Suffering was intense and on 7 September 1880, Hardie advised them to return to work on the masters' terms.[15]

II

The dismal failure of the Ayrshire strike seems to have further damaged Hardie's reputation in Lanarkshire. Alexander McDonald attacked him publicly, blaming him for the prosecution of the picketing women, inflaming the resentment left by the unpaid debts of the Tattie Strike.[16] Hardie evidently decided to make Ayrshire his base of operations while things cooled down in Lanarkshire. There may have been more personal reasons for this move. On 3 August 1878, he had married Lily Wilson, a Hamilton girl. Little is known about the intimate details of Hardie's life-long relationship with her. She was the daughter of a Hamilton publican, but seems to have repudiated her father's trade. Hardie met her in the Independent Order of Good Templars and she appears throughout her life to have valued self-help and respectability more highly than the ambiguous role of trade union activist into which her man was being drawn at the time of their marriage. She had little enthusiasm for the working-class movement. In the 1890s she refused to patronise the Cumnock cooperative store, a fact which caused Hardie some embarrassment with local labour activists.[17] Hardie also let slip on one occasion that she always read the *Glasgow Evening Times* in preference to his own *Labour Leader*.[18]

Hardie chose his wife at a period in his life when he had a marked evangelical tendency to exaggerate the importance of the idealised feminine virtues of chastity and dedication to the domestic arts. We get a glimpse of his ideals in a diary entry of 1884, referring to a sweetheart who had preceded Lily in his fancies:

> 4 March, 1884. Called on M. Found her married with two children and evidently not long for this world. Poor Maggie. Many a happy evening I spent in same company with her when she was young, pure and innocent as a dewdrop, but a time came when our roads divided and it is better for one of us at least that this was so.[19]

Lily Wilson, with her dark hair flowing down her back,[20] had something of the same charm. Her father's trade would have elevated the family slightly in a working-class community, while her teetotalism shielded her from any reproach it might have incurred.

If Lily married Hardie as an earnest young temperance worker, ambitious for self-advancement through involvement in good causes, she may well have been alarmed at the notoriety which began to gather around him for his trade union activities. Hardie's diary again suggests that Lily's mother was even more anxious to see her apparently wayward son-in-law settle down to a steady job:

> Mrs W. went away today. Very anxious that I should try to get a situation in Glasgow where we might be near each other. I am anxious the other way for an opposite reason. Think more of her now than ever I did but as distant fields look greenest it may be as well that we should not be too close to each other.[21]

This was written in 1884, when Hardie had been resident in Ayrshire for three years, and it no doubt provides a clue as to the more private reasons why he should have welcomed an opportunity to put nearly a hundred miles between himself and his wife's family at Hamilton.

On his move to Ayrshire in 1881, he took up residence in Old Cumnock, a town of some two thousand inhabitants remotely situated in a hollow of the hills in south-east Ayrshire. It was a good centre for anyone who hoped to extend miners' trade unionism into virgin territory. It stood on the edge of the central Ayrshire coalfield which, in contrast to that of north Ayrshire, was dominated by two great iron companies, the Eglinton (owned by the Bairds of Lanarkshire) and the Dalmellington. These two companies owned forty of the ninety-five coal mines in Ayrshire.[22] The miners, many of whom were Irish immigrants, were concentrated in company towns around Cumnock, such as Muirkirk, Auchinleck and Dalry, mushroom growths into towns of several thousands population from tiny villages of the mid-century. The companies exercised supreme authority in these single-industry communities and trade union organisation was non-existent.

There was a foothold, however, for a trade union activist in the town of New Cumnock, another mushroom growth in the next parish to Old Cumnock. The miners here were more independent than in the iron company towns, partly because the town was dominated by a prosperous sale company,[23] and partly because the proximity of a prosperous market town reduced their dependence on the company for vital services such as shops, medical attendance and the like. In 'The Cumnocks', therefore, Hardie could hope to find scope for organising work. He chose not to settle down amidst the miners in New Cumnock, but took a single-room dwelling for himself, Lily and their first child in Old Cumnock, a situation which, as we are about to see, implied a certain ambivalance about his chosen role in life.

III

Old Cumnock was not the sleepy hollow which might have been suggested by its remote, secluded situation.[24] For years, radicals and Conservatives had been fighting a sharp local battle for control of the community. On the Conservative side were the great landowners, from the Marquis of Bute downwards, and the great ironmasters, whose trade had flourished through collaboration with the aristocracy. On the Liberal side were ranged a close-knit group of prosperous tradesmen and professional people, whose social standing had grown with the prosperity of farming and mining in the region. They included Thomas and Alexander Barrowman, mining engineers, John and Adam Drummond, agricultural machine makers and ironmongers, D.L. Scott, a schoolteacher with interests in mathematics, physics and astronomy, and the ministers of the United Presbyterian and Congregational churches. These men met together regularly in the Cumnock Literary and Debating Society and contributed from time to time to the pages of the *Ardrossan and Saltcoats Herald,* whose radical editor, Arthur Guthrie, published a local edition called the *Cumnock News.* In 1866 some of them had led a successful campaign for municipal self-government for Cumnock, which had brought them into open conflict with the local 'Chartists', who saw the demand for police burgh status as a diversion from the main issue of the Parliamentary franchise just emerging into practical politics.[25]

By the early 1880s, however, the middle-class radicals were anxious to mend their bridges to working-class radicalism. The Liberal party had just been returned to power with a great majority in 1880. Scotland had contributed handsomely to the Liberal triumph and many middle-class radicals there hoped to see old scores settled. Some looked to the disestablishment of the Church of Scotland, some to bringing the drink trade under local veto. Others wanted more 'home rule' for Scotland and some wanted to attack the monopolies of the great landowners. But as Gladstone's ministry advanced, it was clear that the extension of the suffrage to the counties on the same terms as the towns would be the next great Liberal cause. In Ayrshire this meant enfranchising some-thing like thirteen thousand miners, and middle-class radicals there, as elsewhere, were wooing the miners' support.

So far as we can judge from the columns of the *Ardrossan and Saltcoats Herald,* the aim of these middle-class radicals was to contain the miners' activities within the boundaries of political economy as understood by themselves. The *Herald* regularly editorialised on the strategy which miners' unions should adopt. Their main aim should be to improve the law relating to their working conditions. Under no circumstances should they pursue an aggressive wages policy. The best they could hope to do was to defend themselves against price-cutting by coalmasters and ironmasters who drove prices below their 'natural' level by over-producing and selling surplus stocks in 'over-competition' with each other. The miners should 'regulate' their output so as to prevent this stockpiling, but the *Herald* was adamantly against 'restric-tion' of output, conceived as a means of forcing prices above their 'natural' level. This would merely drive trade away to other suppliers. Strikes would have the same effect and would damage the miners and their families even more than restriction. Thus the *Herald*'s policy provided a framework that could unite small coalmasters and tradi-tionally-minded colliers against the stockpiling, highly capitalised iron-masters whose Conservative politics made them an object of condemn-ation to middle-class radicals. It was, furthermore, a framework which held no place for Mr J.K. Hardie, whom the *Herald* denounced in round terms as a hothead who fomented strikes.[26]

The *Herald*'s opinion of Hardie was shared by other good citizens of Cumnock and he was not at first welcome in the town. One day, as he walked down the main street, he overheard an old woman remark, 'Oh, there's Hardie back again. We'll be hae'in' anither strike.' Hardie was quick to deny his reputation. He told a meeting of Cumnock miners that 'he did not take it as a compliment as he was no advocate of strikes'.[27] As secretary of the Ayrshire Miners' Association, he toured the coalfield in 1881, advising them to avoid strikes, regulate their output, support their union loyally with financial contributions and make political representations on such current issues as the Employers' Liability Bill. This was to remain his consistent approach to miners' problems until 1886. The fiery orator and strike leader of 1879-80 was transformed into a cautious moderate. He still believed in trade union organisation as the miners' first and most necessary step. He still believed in a national federation of miners' unions, but he now appeared to reject the path of agitation on which he had set foot less than eighteen months before.

Hardie's rapid transformation from strike agitator to counsellor of moderation was both chameleon-like and understandable. Pit managers were only too ready to victimise and blacklist stubborn leaders who refused to knuckle under. Many a good man had been driven from district to district in search of work until he finally came to accept it on the masters' terms. It must have been with a very wry consciousness of himself that Hardie quoted from a letter in which a friend outlined the qualities of an ideal miners' agent: 'You know the requirements of miners' agent. He must be honest, sober, possessed of neither wife nor family, have no personal feelings, be prepared to receive kicks from the Pulpit, the Press and, what is worst of all, from the body he is trying to serve.'[28]

Hardie was indeed a man with a wife, and a growing family. His sense of class injustice made it impossible for him to contemplate a quiet retreat into a life of self-advancement. On the other hand, he could not afford to run the risks of a miners' agent. He had hoped to avoid them by becoming secretary of the Ayrshire Miners' Association, but this body was never able to pay him full wages.[29] As Alexander McDonald found before Hardie, there were only two possibilities for a miners' leader. He had either to accept the wandering and impoverished life of the agitator, or find for himself a safe position in the middle class from which to act as spokesman for his own class. In Victorian Britain, however, there were few safe middle-class occupations which gave much independence. Middle-class radicals, on the lookout for working-class allies, would set limits to the toleration of it, and the working-class radical who sought independence would find himself subjected to heavy pressure to conform more or less to the middle-class outlook.

Hardie's moderate line of policy adopted in 1881 began to attract the favourable notice of the *Ardrossan and Saltcoats Herald*.[30] At the end of the year the paper's Cumnock editor and mining correspondent resigned and Hardie was offered the job. It must have seemed the safe position he needed. It gave him an office in the town, an assured salary of one pound a week and the opportunity to write for a wide audience of Ayrshire miners. He accepted the job and resigned his secretaryship of the moribund Ayrshire Miners' Association, declining at the same time a post in the Glasgow office of the equally moribund Scottish Miners' Association.[31]

With this change of occupation came a noticeable change of life-style. He began to approximate to the manners and interests of the Cumnock middle-class radicals. With his wife he joined the Congregational Church, a prosperous body long-established in the town.[32] He threw himself energetically into lay preaching and purchased a top-hat and frock-coat for services. About this time, he moved from his one-roomed dwelling to a two-roomed one on the Barrhill Road.[33] He redoubled his activities in temperance work and became a 'District Deputy' in the Good Templars. He quadrupled their membership in Cumnock by his mission work in the pit villages and was congratulated by the Grand Lodge of Scotland as their most successful District Deputy in 1882.[34] He was also busy in good works for the poor. A diary, which he kept for a brief period in 1884 to record his efforts at self-improvement, reveals him organising a benefit concert, a free breakfast and a free supper for the aged, at which suitable temperance lectures were served up with the food.[35]

Not content with merely preaching temperance, Hardie was keen to see the drink trade put down by political action. He became one of Cumnock's most zealous guardians of sobriety. He organised a petition to the magistrates to have the back entrances of public houses bricked up to prevent illegal sales off the premises and to have table games prohibited in the pubs so that young people would not be so readily enticed into them.[36] Shortly after taking up residence in the town, he wrote to the Cumnock News complaining that the Temperance party had allowed its electoral organisation to decay. Soon he was collaborating with the ironmonger, Adam Drummond, in the building of a Total Abstinence League, and in 1884 he was one of the delegates from Cumnock to a convention of temperance bodies organised in Edinburgh in support of local veto.[37] The high moment of acceptance by the town's middle-class radicals of this energetic disciple of improvement came in 1884 when he was asked to second a motion at a meeting called to establish a Junior Liberal Association.[38]

Hardie's accommodation with the middle-class radicals of Cumnock was brought about in no spirit of class-desertion. His sense that he was working for the improvement of his class at the same time as his own improvement remained strong. 'Oh that I could apply myself in some way to self-improvement', he exclaims in his diary in 1884, then adds, 'And yet perhaps after all there is no self-improvement that can be compared with the real pleasure derived from seeking the happiness of others.'[39] He continued to identify strongly with the working class with a sense of solidarity that transcended miners' trade union consciousness. Referring in his 'Mining Notes' (which he wrote under the pen-name 'Trapper') to the case of a cotton worker prosecuted for failure to pay school fees, he commented: 'Your Trapper, Mr Editor, is not one of those whose sympathies are confined to one class. True, they go out most to the class to which he belongs, but he is not conservative in this respect.'[40]

These weekly mining notes also gave him an opportunity, afforded by the political requirements of his editor, to pursue his vendetta with the ironmasters. He accused them of systematically flouting all the safety legislation governing mining, of victimising check-weighmen, of dishonest weighing and illegal deductions from pay.[41] The so-called cooperative stores run by the companies were really, he alleged, no more than truck shops with the companies nominating their foremen and cashiers to rule over the committees of management. The companies used the threat of illegally withholding dividend to discipline their employees. Noting the companies' excuse that the mining villages were isolated from town shops, he commented: 'There are places in Ayrshire at the present day (Benquhat for instance) where strong iron chains are set across the road at the end of the miners' row to prevent grocers' or butchers' vans from entering'.[42]

These early instances of Hardie's exposé-journalism should not be allowed to mask the ambiguity of his social position. It remained characteristic of him throughout his life and is the key to the ambiguities of his political outlook and actions. He wanted to be the spokesman of his class, but he was resolved not to live among the communities of his class, sharing its hardships and oppressions. He threw in his lot with those middle-class elements who showed themselves sympathetic towards the poor and concerned for their moral elevation. He relied on them for his occupation, his income and for confirmation of his position as a responsible politician who, however much he might be misrepresented by enemies, pursued the true path of moderation.

His diary fragment provides insights into the warm respect he felt for middle-class people who showed sympathy for the poor and who accepted men of humble origin like himself without trace of condescension or snobbery:

5 Jan. 1884. Went to Mauchline, Catrine and Auchinleck and then took train to Sanquhar and from there went to Kirkonnell. Fine people the Hendries of Kirkonnell. Very kind-hearted and good to poor. Jean was cooking and because I said I had a fondness for tattie scones she insisted that I should take home a dozen. Memo. This has no connection with her being good to poor. I wrote her eight or nine verses of sorry stuff in praise of those wholesome articles of diet.

Another entry reveals his exaggerated respect for the education, refine-ment and culture of middle-class people, a respect which made him feel guilty because he could not accomplish the self-imposed task of studying Latin and French for two hours every day before breakfast.

14 Feb. 1884. Our little girl was baptised tonight by Rev. A.N. Scott. Had the Elliots, Whites and Smiths together with the minister and his wife at tea. Very merry party. Mrs Scott in great spirits and declared that if she was going to be changed to a beast she would be a lion and then she would gobble all the rest of us up. Suggested some of us might get turned into whales which would tax her swallowing powers. Minister proved all five senses can be summed up in that of touch. Never had looked at it in this light but can see how it is.

To be welcome as a coadjutor in the homes of these prosperous country people, to make merry and philosophise in your own home with the minister and to be hired by a newspaper to interpret the miners' point of view to a middle-class readership — these were salves to the soul of a young man who had been born illegitimate and who had been made to feel himself among the despised of the Earth on account of his occupa-tion. The way seemed open for him to become the spokesman of the Scottish miners in succession to Alexander McDonald.

What was less obvious to Hardie, and has received little attention from his biographers, was that this ambiguous social position involved him in important concessions to stock middle-class notions about the working class. The toleration which middle-class people like Hardie's editor extended to working-class people had its necessary limitations. In return for their sympathy, they expected conformity to their own standards. They demanded respect for the so-called laws of political economy. They insisted that poverty was, at least in part, the personal responsibility of the individual. They rejected strikes as nothing but a threat to the social order and they demanded acceptance by the working class of a social elite as its natural political leaders. Hardie had to defer to such values before his role of blunt, outspoken champion of the workers was accepted. What emerges from his mining notes, published under the heading of 'Black Diamonds' between 1882 and 1886, is an ambiguous Hardie, now tribune of the people, now their 'Candid Friend'. The uneasy assortment of these roles often led him to give confused and contradictory advice to the miners, urging moderate tactics in pursuit of an *avant-garde* strategy.

Again and again Hardie urged the Ayrshire miners to organise a union, and to participate in national conferences with other Scottish miners to coordinate wages policy.[43] But the years from 1882 to 1885 passed with the Ayrshire miners paying little heed to his call. No Ayrshire delegate attended the conference of Scottish miners held in Glasgow in 1882, when delegates from Lanarkshire and Fife decided to make a simultaneous demand for a wage increase.[44] In 1883, when the miners in the sale pits around Irvine and Kilmarnock staged a county conference with Hardie as the chief speaker, the miners from iron companies failed to attend.[45] The years of bad trade in 1884 and 1885 found ironmasters lowering their men's wages without resistance.

Hardie's explanation of the weak trade unionism of the Ayrshire miners tended to conform to the views of the editor of the *Ardrossan and Saltcoats Herald*. He placed the blame equally on the terrorism practised by the ironmasters and the moral depravity of their men. In 1883 we find him writing:

> On Saturday I had the pleasure of visiting Dalry. I found that things are very much there as everywhere else where a great iron company has the control, plenty of good men, but each one afraid to say what he thinks for fear of someone carrying the news to the oversman.[46]

Hardie had come to believe that there was among the miners a class of sober, thrifty, self-reliant men who wanted to organise a union, but who were frustrated in their desire and actions by another class, which was given over to the pursuit of Mammon in the forms of drink, gambling and improvidence. Far from encouraging the sense of class solidarity among all miners in the teeth of exploitation, Hardie often resorted to the language of the independent collier, looking down his nose at the incomers who flouted his work practices and his standard of morality: 'A certain class of the men would sacrifice anything to get a big fuddle [drink]. The respectable men are rendered helpless by them.'[47]

At times Hardie attacked the unregenerate miners in tones almost as strident as those he used for the ironmasters. Writing of the bad housing in the mining villages around Cumnock in 1883, he commented:

Thousands of these men and women never enter a church door or hear the Gospel preached from one end of the year to the other. In many cases a whole family have no clothes except that which serves to cover them for the time being and which is worn Sunday and Saturday alike. The wives in many cases are slatternly and untidy, having nothing to encourage them to make their dwellings tidy, and they have never learned that cleanliness should be practised for its own sake. The men have no ambition and, beyond getting a drink occasionally, have no amusements. They are completely alienated from all refining or elevating influences. There is the store at the end of the row where all his [sic] wants can be supplied, so long at least as his money lasts.[48]

Hardie could not see the mass of miners as people who, despite an unrelenting struggle with extreme wage fluctuations, under-employment and low take-home pay, could, nevertheless, create brief intervals of warmth and human pleasure in the knowledge that middle-class virtues of saving and abstinence were futile. He was censorious about their improvidence:

Hungers and bursts are the rule. On a cash night, a load of provisions will be brought in − jellies, biscuits, ham, fancy bread etc. are all spread out and everybody has a feast. Then, for a day or two previous to the next cash day, they are in semi-starvation.[49]

To Hardie, the lower strata of the mining communities needed reclamation, not by giving them hope in their own power of learning through self-activity, but by teaching them the habits of their superiors. The remedy lay in: 'better education in youth, regular family entertainment, lessons in temperance and thrift'.[50]

This view of the rank-and-file miners was derived from evangelical notions of the residuum. It was closely akin to the belief that industrialism was breeding a degenerate class and it amounted to a serious distortion of the real situation.

These stock middle-class distinctions between the respectable and the unrespectable working class undoubtedly weakened Hardie's agitational élan between 1882 and 1886, engendering in him feelings of

caution amounting almost to despair. Effective trade unionism among
the miners was impossible, he felt, until the mass had undergone a
moral conversion. Why should men like himself, who had achieved a
modicum of security and respectability, risk their position in leading
agitations of men so unsteady of purpose? It was no doubt with himself partly in mind that he wrote in 1883, after the failure of the
Irvine miners' conference to revive the Ayrshire union:

> Hard words are being used by the men against some of those who in
> times past have acted the part of guides, but who have hitherto held
> aloof from the present movement. I thoroughly believe that these
> old warriors are still heart and soul in sympathy with their fellows
> and would be prepared to do as much as ever for the elevation of the
> class to which they belong or did belong. Many of them, however,
> fill positions which they would first require to resign before they
> could be allowed to take part in miners' affairs, and their past
> experience tells them that to do so would be suicidal to their best
> interests as the probability is that any organisation which they might
> build up would speedily be allowed to collapse through indifference
> on the part of the members and the agent or leader might then shift
> for himself as best he might.[51]

As Hardie presented the problem, such an outcome was certain, not
merely because the men lacked disciplined solidarity, but because they
were ignorant of the laws of political economy.

> If a man were possessed of the eloquence of a Demosthenes . . . and
> the intellectual power of a W.E. Gladstone, all would avail him
> nothing if he counselled submission to a reduction in wages, no
> matter how inevitable. Those who were loudest in shouting hurrah
> when wages rose would be the first to decry him on the occasion of
> a reduction, and until the united power of the Pulpit, Press and
> Platform have elevated the men from their present state of mere
> animated machines, swayed by a fitful gust, whether of enthusiasm
> or passion, and transformed them into reasoning human beings, all
> the agents that ever lived will not keep them straight in the face of a
> falling market.[52]

It is difficult to recognise in these hard words the Hardie who, only two
brief years before, had been leading stubborn resistance to wage-cutting
and propounding a new policy of state intervention in coal mining.

That programme — government control of mines, a minimum wage and an aggressive wages policy — was never mentioned in Hardie's mining notes for the *Ardrossan and Saltcoats Herald* between 1882 and 1886. Instead, Hardie advocated sliding scales, restriction of output, trade unionism based on high friendly benefits and a system of apprenticeship to keep interlopers out of the mines. It was the model of the miners' unions of Northumberland and Durham which he held up before the men for their emulation:

> Hitherto, miners' unions [in Scotland] have been formed without any clear idea among the men as to what were the uses of unionism, the principle idea being that a union should send wages up to, say, six shillings or seven shillings a day and then prevent them from coming down again, forgetting that unionism only helps the workman to make the most of the wages market, but does not affect the market itself, the immutable law of supply and demand doing that. Besides, as I have pointed out over and over again, this wages question is but a tithe of the questions affected by union, perhaps the least question of all. The securing of proper laws and the putting of these in operation, the freeing of the workmen from the petty tyranny so often exercised by small contractors and the like, making sure that when a bargain is made it is fulfilled, and the prevention of that barefaced system of robbery practised on the pithead — these are a few of the objects to which a union could and should attain, to which may be added provision for sickness and death.[53]

This was the kind of trade unionism which appealed strongly to the traditions of the independent collier, with his insistence on rewards to skill in hewing. But to the ordinary run of miners, who came into the coalfields from agriculture and other industries, there was little attraction in a view of trade unionism which offered so little hope of controlling the violent fluctuations in wages experienced since 1873. Whenever money wages were depressed too far, the miners would strike more or less spontaneously in resistance, but without a common wage policy it was difficult to maintain solidarity between high-paid and low-paid districts. A federal union with a coordinated minimum wage policy was urgently needed and the men's spontaneous strikes were the only means available for forcing such a view of policy into trade unionism and politics generally. Hardie failed to see that progress depended on the heroism of the rank-and-file: their willingness to undergo hardships, to lose wages, suffer eviction from hearth and home, mount picket lines in defiance of police and blacklegs. He turned away from the fighting colliers' wives of his 1880 picket line to play the part of the hero in politics, speaking as the superior workman, condescending to his class while believing that he championed it.

Thus, after his appointment as sub-editor on the *Cumnock News,* Hardie made a great parade of his opposition to strikes. They could only be successful if universal through the mining industry and, if the miners were as well organised as that, it would be unnecessary for them to resort to a strike. Strikes without complete organisation were bound to be defeated, bringing suffering to women and children. Even in 1882, when the miners of England held a national conference (their first for many years) at Manchester to discuss common wage policy, passing a resolution to enforce a wage demand by strike action, Hardie adopted an apologetic tone about the conference in face of criticism by his editor, although rising coal prices offered favourable conditions for an aggressive strategy. He insisted that the conference had been packed with delegates from weakly organised districts, who had clamoured for a strike and who had carried their resolution in confusion at the end of the proceedings. Taken as a whole, the conference provided 'complete refutation of the old time fallacies, still held by some, that unions are good only for promoting strikes'.

> True, the closing scene was in favour of such a course, but it can be shown that the parties who opposed the strike in favour of restriction were those representing the best organised districts or counties, while, as is always the case, the very parties who clamoured most for a cessation of work were those who have neither an organisation to carry a strike nor funds wherewith to support themselves.[54]

Hardie now insisted that restriction of output was the only means of securing an advance in miners' wages, but even here he was at odds with the editorial chair and had to modify the men's case. As we have seen, Arthur Guthrie rejected restriction as a means of forcing up coal prices and advised only regulation, as a means of preventing the masters from forcing prices down to 'unnatural' levels by over-competition. The rank-and-file miner might have seen little advantage in a policy which still permitted fluctuation and which disregarded his claim for a living wage, which the consumer must pay for as part of the price for a vitally necessary commodity.

Hardie was at his most confused when defending the policy of restriction in his mining notes. On the one hand he had to present it to the miners as a policy which had a better chance than strikes of forcing wages up. On the other, he was constantly trying to meet the objection of his editor that anything in the nature of a conspiracy against the consumer was contrary to the laws of political economy. He was keen to devise a form of restriction that would work. He knew that the 'wee darg' method sowed jealousy and dissension among the working miners and he urged the simultaneous operation of three restrictionist practices: reduction of the working day to eight hours, reduction of the number of days worked from six to five, and the fixing of a uniform wage rate above which a man would cease to hew coal. All the evidence suggests that coalmasters and ironmasters everywhere were opposed to any such serious limitation of the output. Even in Fife, where an eight-hour day had been worked since 1872, the masters had stubbornly resisted reduction of the working week and had imposed on the miners contracts which bound them to work a fixed number of days. As we shall see, Lanarkshire coalmasters and ironmasters were to unite solidly against the miners' practice there of working only eleven days a fortnight. The policy of restriction, therefore, was almost as sharp an issue as that of strikes.

Hardie's comments in his mining notes veered erratically between restriction as the independent collier had always conceived it and regulation as his editor conceived it. He seems to have wanted to believe that coalmasters would approve of the men's attempts to force up the price. Urging the employers to maintain a high price of coal in 1882, he wrote: 'It does not say much for the credit of the latter [consumers] if, after having had their coal for years at a dirt cheap price, they should attempt to resist an increase that will give better wages to the labourer and higher prices to the capitalist.'[55] Later he argued, however, that restriction of output was a misleading term. What he advocated, he said, was not a violation of the laws of political economy but 'a fore-stalling and mitigating of their effect'.[56] This was the method of 'regulation', often called by that misleading term 'restriction'. Masters objected only to the carrying of regulation to extremes, 'when it, in reality, becomes obstruction'.[57]

In 1882 he commended the Fife miners for shortening their working week to four days on the ground that reduction of the working day to eight hours would not have enough effect on the level of production, yet in the very next issue of his paper he declared, 'I am opposed to idle time', and warned the Ayrshire men against taking an idle day to hold a union meeting.[58]

The same uncertainty can be seen in his advocacy of the eight-hour day:

> I have always advocated the serving of an apprenticeship in mines as
> being the most practical remedy for over-production, but until this
> be adopted, the limitation of the output presents itself as the next
> best course. I don't mean that the men should go half-time idle, but
> that they should be content with working eight hours per day and
> producing a fair day's work.[59]

Since, however, the respectable men could not form a viable union in
Ayrshire, he accepted the demand for a legal eight-hour day proposed
at the Manchester conference of 1882: 'Miners would do well to get up
an agitation in favour of getting Parliament to pass a Bill making it
imperative that eight hours underground should constitute a day's
work.'[60] Although he argued that such a measure was for the physical,
intellectual and moral improvement of the miner, there can be little
doubt that the consideration uppermost in Hardie's mind was the
contribution which such a measure would make to the policy of restriction. Like his Covenanting forefathers, he was calling in the power of
the civil magistrate to enforce righteous conduct on the ungodly
colliers who were too given to money and drink to undergo the self-
discipline of restriction. 'Nothing', he wrote, in a scantily-veiled
comment on the Irish immigrant:

> angers the miner so much during a period of restriction as to find a
> fellow working at stoop, where the requisites are a big shovel, a
> strong back and a weak brain, said fellow having been busy a few
> weeks before in a peat bog or tattie field and who is now producing
> coal enough for a man and a half.[61]

The legal eight-hours measure would have the great advantage, he
argued, of 'compelling the stiff-necked workman to do as his neighbour
does'.[62]

In this way, Hardie made the demand for the legal eight-hour day
sound less like a new way of enforcing restriction and more like a
measure conceived by the respectable men for bending the Mammon-
worshippers to compliance with their own work practices and interests.
And as if to add final weight of confusion to the whole argument,
Hardie even came to deny that an eight-hour day would have any
restrictive effect whatever, in order to rebut the charge that the demand
was only intended as a way of getting Parliament to restrict miners'

output.[63]

Between 1882 and 1886, therefore, this rebellious and discontented young miners' leader fell into an uneasy compromise with middle-class radicalism and evangelicalism. It is not difficult to understand the social pressures which pushed him towards class collaboration. A young married man with a growing family, he shrank from the life of a miners' agitator. Yet his own experience of class injustice and the legacy of pride and independence received from his parents made it impossible for him to settle into a life-style of complacent self-advancement. He sought an occupation that offered him both security and the opportunity to play the role of hero for his class. Journalism seemed to offer the only way of combining both roles, but in reality it could not offer him the independence he sought. He became a highly ambivalent personality − and was seen as such by the working miners of Ayrshire. Some admired him for sticking to their cause while making his way in the world. During these years he helped at least two working miners to bring legal actions against their employers, and letters praising him for this appeared in the press.[64] Such praise was justified. There were, after all, working men whose dearest wish was to forget their class origins as soon as they could. But not all working miners could feel as enthusiastic about their hero as he clearly would have liked them to feel. They regarded with suspicion this black-coated evangelical who adopted a killjoy attitude to the public house, who berated their employers from the safety of the sub-editorial desk and avoided the risks and hardships of the class struggle.

One gets a sense in those weekly columns headed 'Black Diamonds' and signed 'Trapper' of Hardie conducting this other running battle, less explicit than that with the ironmasters, but nonetheless bitter, a battle with the working miners who saw no hope in the policies he offered and who refused to acknowledge him as their prophet. They suspected the bureaucratic implications of his belief in a high-subscription union with a paid secretary who would give more attention to what would nowadays be termed 'job evaluation' than to the general level of miners' wages. 'Some of them', Hardie taunted, 'are far too wise to pay a penny a week to keep a man going about with his coat on to look after their welfare'.[65] Apart from the sneer in Hardie's tone here, we need to notice the sleight-of-hand in the argument (which, doubtless was not lost on some of his critics), for Hardie himself calculated that threepence a week was the minimum subscription necessary to run an Ayrshire union for trade purposes alone. If friendly benefits were added, as he advocated, the subscription estimated rose to ninepence or one shilling.[66]

It was another source of dissension that Hardie was inclined to use for his exposures of the ironmasters evidence gathered in talks about the pits. Many working miners have felt that this was very good for Hardie's standing with his editor, but that it was they who had to face the music with the pit managers. A friend working in a Cumnock pit wrote on this point to Hardie: 'You are very much blamed here and about this pit for being the means of bringing upon us these grievances which I have now spoken about, I suppose through some paras that you have written of late.'[67] To this Hardie replied with an arrogance that became the Carlylean hero: 'this is just what has to be expected. The same thing happened—how long ago? when Moses was leading the Children of Israel forth from their bondage in the land of Egypt.'[68]

A good deal has been written rather loosely about Hardie's 'charisma'[69] without analysing that greatly overworked sociological concept in terms of the specifically historical theories of leadership on which Hardie drew. Here, as in so much else, Carlyle was his mentor. The heroic leader in politics was to be the instrument of the voice of God. He was no mere mouthpiece of the masses, who were, as Carlyle had said, mostly fools. The followers must take him or leave him for what he was, right or wrong. From this heroic concept of leadership it followed that the leader could never allow himself to become entirely the creation of the followers whom he led, never entirely dependent on their electoral will or material support. Throughout the ages, heroes had depended for subsistence on rich sympathisers who responded to their call. The heroic leader of the working class would be independent of his class in the prosecution of its struggles.

At many points in his career, this dependence on middle-class sympathisers and independence of rank-and-file struggle fudged Hardie's views on policy, causing him to present an image of ambiguity. In these years, 1882 to 1886, they limited his appeal to the miners and his effectiveness as a trade union leader. It was not from this temperance preacher and self-improving radical journalist that the Scottish miners would receive the further stimulus needed for their trade union development. His words were now confused, oracular and timid. The minimum wage, state control of mining and agitational strikes were not heard of again in Scotland after 1880 until 1887. By then new agitators had appeared, inspired by the propoganda of social democracy in its early and most revolutionary phase. It was that agitation which would once again give substance and goal to the agitation of the rank-and-file. It also forced Hardie to face up squarely to the limits which his middle-class radical allies imposed upon him, limits of which he had long been half-consciously and uneasily aware.

Notes

1. *Hamilton Adv.*, 14 April 1877.
2. Ibid., 2 June 1877. It is not clear whether the union formed in 1874 had lapsed; *sup.*, p.27.
3. *Ardrossan and Saltcoats Herald*, 10 August 1883.
4. *Glasgow Weekly Mail*, 23 August 1879; Stewart, *Hardie*, p.11.
5. Ibid.
6. *Glasgow Weekly Mail*, 6 November 1879.
7. Ibid.
8. *North British Daily Mail*, 21 November 1879.
9. *Glasgow Weekly Mail*, 20 December 1879; *Hamilton Adv.*, 20-7 December 1879.
10. Ibid., 3 January 1880, 24 December 1879; *Glasgow Weekly Mail*, 10 January 1880.
11. *Ardrossan and Saltcoats Herald*, 19 August 1880.
12. A. Briggs, 'The Welfare State in Historical Perspective', *Archives Europeénnes de Sociologie*, II, 1961, pp.221-58.
13. *Ardrossan and Saltcoats Herald*, 19 August 1880.
14. *Ardrossan and Saltcoats Herald*, 11 and 28 August 1880; *North British Daily Mail*, 5 September 1880.
15. Ibid., 8 September 1880.
16. Hardie, 'Reverie and Reminiscence', *Labour Leader*, 6 January 1905.
17. Hardie to unnamed correspondent, 4 December 1896. Murray Collection.
18. Lowe, *Pit to Parliament*, p.85.
19. Dairy Fragment, 4 March 1884.
20. Hughes, *Keir Hardie* (1956), p.27.
21. Ibid., 14 January 1884, K.O. Morgan apparently overlooks the fact that W. was the initial of the surname of Hardie's mother-in-law and thus gives this diary entry a most improbable sexual significance. Morgan, *Keir Hardie*, p.12.
22. *Report of H.M. Inspector of Mines for the Western Division of Scotland, 1882*, XXVII, 418.
23. J.L. Carvel, *The New Cumnock Coalfield* (Edinburgh 1946), pp.25ff.
24. This point is well established by J. Strawhorn, *The New History of Cumnock* (1966), pp.77ff.
25. Ibid., p.77.
26. *Ardrossan and Saltcoats Herald*, 19 September 1880; 22 October 1881.
27. Ibid., 8 January 1881.
28. Ibid., 14 October 1882.
29. Letter from 'Lugar Union Man': ibid., 4 February 1882.
30. Ibid., editorial, 26 February 1881.
31. Ibid., 15 April 1882.
32. Strawhorn, *Cumnock*, pp.153-4.
33. Ibid., p.110; the frock-coat and hat are recalled in H. Escott, *History of Scottish Congregationalism* (Glasgow, 1960), p.328, and confirmed by Hardie in a speech reported in *West Ham Herald*, 22 July 1893.
34. *Paisley Daily Express*, 25 July 1883; *Ardrossan and Saltcoats Herald*, 27 May 1882.
35. Diary Fragment, 4, 8 January 1884.

36. *Ardrossan and Saltcoats Herald,* 20 April 1883.
37. Ibid., 2 April 1881; 28 May 1882; 1 June 1883; also Diary Fragment, 2 March 1884.
38. Diary Fragment, 17 March 1884.
39. Ibid., 31 March 1884.
40. *Ardrossan and Saltcoats Herald,* 24 June 1882.
41. Ibid., 2 February 1882; 2 September 1883.
42. Ibid., 27 May 1882.
43. E.g. ibid., 29 April, 20 May 1882.
44. Ibid., 9 September 1882.
45. Ibid., 10 November 1883.
46. Ibid., 18 May 1883.
47. Ibid., 30 November 1883.
48. Ibid., 5 January 1883.
49. Ibid.
50. *Ardrossan and Saltcoats Herald,* 5 January 1883.
51. Ibid., 7 September 1883.
52. Ibid., 14 October 1882.
53. Ibid., 14 September 1883.
54. Ibid., 9 September 1882. For hostile editorial and Hardie's reply see 7 October 1882.
55. Ibid.
56. Ibid., 2 February 1883.
57. Ibid., 28 March 1884.
58. Ibid., 21, 28 October 1882.
59. Ibid., 7 October 1882.
60. Ibid., 26 January 1883.
61. Ibid., 8 September 1882.
62. Ibid., 1 June 1883.
63. *Miner,* January 1887.
64. E.g. *Ardrossan and Saltcoats Herald,* 15 July 1882.
65. Ibid., 4 November 1882.
66. Ibid., 14 September 1883.
67. Ibid., 2 April 1886.
68. Ibid.
69. Morgan, *Keir Hardie,* p.57.

4 CRISIS AND CONVERSION

I

Hardie's relations with his middle-class allies in Ayrshire were not a matter of either bonhomie or trust in the years 1884 to 1886 during which he was drawn most closely into Liberal politics. He was often uncomfortable with them, thinking that they gave themselves airs and condescended to him as a man of the working class. He felt that they were trying to use him for their own ends. Thus on the night of his great local triumph in 1884, when he seconded the motion to establish a Junior Liberal Association in Cumnock, making what was considered '*the* speech of the evening,' he confided to his diary:

> Only got notice a few minutes before meeting that I was expected to do so and only then because no other one could be got. Unfortunately I belong to that class of men who do not and cannot push themselves forward or seek for favour by currying. Believe it would be to my interest to make friends but cannot bear to do so unless the approach be mutual.[1]

Other diary entries show that he hated the stiff conventionality of the free breakfasts for the poor. He writhed under the condescension of ministers who lectured them on temperance and then hurried home to enjoy a glass of wine at dinner. The petty-mindedness and intrigue of people in the Good Templars Lodge irritated him. He stiffened when he felt praise to be insincere and so his allies often accused him of being prickly and difficult to work with.[2]

For his part, Hardie doubted their enthusiasm for radical politics. Gladstone's government had not made a very good showing in radical legislation since he had taken office in 1880. True, it had passed the Irish Land Act, which Hardie had described as 'the greatest achievement of modern statesmanship,'[3] but its radical momentum had then seemed to flag. The extension of the franchise to the counties had been delayed by opposition from 'Whig' elements in the Cabinet. Local veto was still not on the statute book, in spite of strong pressure from Scottish and Welsh temperance Members. The government seemed to pay more heed to its Conservative opponents than to its radical supporters. Gladstone was still the hero of the Midlothian campaign in Hardie's eyes, but he felt that Gladstone could and would do little without powerful pressure from radicals in the party out of doors.

Gladstone's performance on temperance, for instance, was acutely disapointing to Hardie in 1884. One evening, he opened his paper on a train to read that the government intended to enact local veto in the coming session of Parliament:

> the floodgates of joy were opened and I shed tears of joy while my heart went out in praise to Him from whom all blessings flow. If W.E.G. gives the people the power to deal with this licensed traffic by majority it will prove the crowning deed of a glorious record.[4]

When, however, Gladstone announced that temperance reform must await the settlement of both the parliamentary franchise and county councils questions, Hardie wrote angrily to the press, invoking memories of the Anti-Corn Law League: 'Something out of the ordinary course may be necessary in order to bring home to the minds of the members of the Government the necessity for immediate action.'[5] It was this letter which led him to cooperate with the local Cumnock ironmonger, Adam Drummond, in the establishment of a Total Abstinence League to register voters for the temperance cause.

Drummond was an influential figure in Cumnock. Soon to be a member of the town council, he was a moving force in the Junior Liberal Association and a deacon in the Congregational Church, which Hardie had joined in 1881. The Cumnock Congregationalists were an old established sect, prosperous and in many cases ultra-respectable. Hardie soon found himself drawn into a quarrel between Drummond and the other deacons on the one hand and the new minister, Andrew Noble Scott on the other. Scott seems to have taken some pains to encourage some of the less prosperous members of the congregation. As we have seen, he was friendly with the Hardies and he opposed the decision of the deacons to discipline another of their friends, Elliot, who had got drunk at the New Year.

Hardie's diary fragment and the minutes of the Congregational Church give a vivid record of the private tensions that lay behind public collaborations. At first Hardie tried to hold aloof:

> 18 Feb. 1884.—Did not go to Church on Sunday. I have heard it was proposed to put me on a deputation to Mr Elliot who got drunk at the New Year time. I object to mode of doing this kind of work being unscriptural. There has been great row at Church over the matter. The Minister had to fight single-handed so far as speaking was concerned against Deacons etc. Never was a good man so

persecuted as Mr Scott. I have not yet taken any decided stand as wish to keep aloof.

Whether Hardie's wish to keep aloof stemmed more from doubt as to the scriptural validity of the method of discipline or to concern for the work of the Total Abstinence League it is impossible to say. What is clear is that he could not avoid being drawn in. He seems to have felt that the deacons treated him and other newcomers to the congregation as outsiders, even upstarts. At least this is the impression given by the next diary entry, which gives an account of a prayer meeting at the church, which the minister asked Hardie to lead. He chose as his text the second chapter of the Epistle of James, which seems to warn the early church against class division:

> For if there come unto your assembly a man with a gold ring, in goodly apparel, and there come in also a poor man in vile raiment; And ye have respect to him that weareth the gay clothing, and say unto him, Sit thou here in a good place; and say to the poor, Stand thou there, or sit here under my footstool: Are you not then partial in yourselves, and are become judges of evil thoughts?[6]

Hardie's preaching on this text greatly annoyed Mr Adam Drummond:

> 20 Feb. 1884. Was asked to take the weekly Prayer Meeting for Mr S. who is ill, the abuse he received on Sunday having been too much for him. A.D. was present and I read Second Chapter James which it seemed had formed the subject of dispute between him and Elliot though I knew it not. Then I spoke of going forward in brotherly love and kindness and he seemed to think from the way he looked that I meant him and I got agitated and made matters worse by stopping at this point. Of course it will be said that the whole thing was planned, but it was not.

The quarrel became so bitter that Hardie and Scott appealed to the leaders of the Congregational Church in Glasgow, but in a church which prided itself in having no centralised discipline it was easy for the Glasgow people to deny responsibility. Hardie understood them to advise that the whole matter be allowed to drop, lest the deacons withdraw from the Church with their financial support, a serious enough matter when the congregation had just undertaken the building of an expensive new church. Hardie was furious and scrawled over two pages of his diary: 'Nice teaching that. Principles to be thrown overboard to suit Mammon. This may be Christianity but I will have none of it.'[7] The upshot was that Scott was forced to resign as minister by the deacons and Hardie led thirty-eight members in a walk-out from the congregation, after making what the Church minutes describe as an 'inflammatory speech'.[8]

II

This bad feeling between Hardie and the Cumnock middle-class radicals soon appeared in public issues. Gladstone's government introduced a Bill to extend the Parliamentary franchise to the counties in 1884. It passed all its stages in the Commons, only to be held up by the Lords, who refused to pass it unless a Bill for the redistribution of seats were introduced and carried simultaneously. This was a piece of shrewd tactics by the Conservative leader, Lord Salisbury, who wanted to ensure that his party would not suffer under redistribution after it had strengthened the popular party by extension of the franchise.

Hardie saw this as an opportunity for the Liberals to raise the radical question of abolition of the House of Lords. The Cumnock Liberals, on the other hand, saw abolition only in terms of a threat to help the government force through the franchise measure. Gladstone, in fact, had no wish either to strike at the Lords or threaten them and was quite ready to settle the redistribution issue amicably with Salisbury. The Cumnock Liberals summoned a public meeting and contented themselves with a moderate resolution which warned that any delay in passing the Reform Bill would tend to encourage the demand for Lords reform. Hardie rightly suspected that neither they nor Gladstone had any stomach for a fight with the Lords and urged that the country was ripe for a great agitation on this question.[9]

His complaints against the Cumnock Liberals went further. He wanted them to take the opportunity to work up an agitation among the Ayrshire miners on the franchise issue itself. He believed that the miners in iron companies would be subjected to intimidation when they exercised the vote and he wanted them to feel that they had been involved in the struggle to obtain it so that they would prize it highly enough to exercise it in spite of company pressures. The Ayrshire Liberals organised a countrywide demonstration in favour of the Reform Bill, but the Cumnock Liberals sent only a small contingent of local men and made no effort to involve the miners of the surrounding company towns—'very callous and lukewarm' Hardie thought them.[10] He decided to organise a scratch demonstration for the miners of south Ayrshire to show their support for the Bill. It was arranged to take place in Cumnock a week after the county affair. The miners of New Cumnock turned up in some numbers, but those from the iron company towns stayed away. So did the Cumnock Liberals. Hardie was bitterly disappointed and accused the Cumnock Liberals of betraying the iron company miners, who needed to be given confidence by seeing the support of people of standing in the community. The Cumnock Liberals, he wrote, thought it 'infra dig. to have anything to do with a gathering of colliers'.[11]

Meanwhile Gladstone continued his private negotitations with Salisbury over tea at Number Ten and, the issue settled, the Lords passed the Reform Bill quietly enough. Hardie commented tartly: 'Once more Mr Gladstone has proved himself the true friend of the Constitution as it at present stands and has outwitted both Peers and People.'[12]

As the general election approached, however, Hardie sank his differences with the Cumnock Liberals and fell in staunchly behind the Gladstonians. He warmly supported Gladstone's inactivity in the Sudan in 1884-5, though perhaps with just a tinge of ambivalence. Gordon's fate seemed, he wrote: 'bad enough, but what. . .[it] . . .would have been under a Tory Government is past imagining'. Gladstone might be accused of following an 'over-cautious' foreign policy, but on the whole it seemed best calculated to:

> preserve the prestige of the Nation, while at the same time preserving us from that policy of revenge of which we hear so much at present from the Jingo element, as if the honour of Great Britain depended on the slaughter of so many thousands of half-naked Arabs fighting for home and liberty.[13]

The general election of 1885 saw a number of defections of radicals from the Gladstonian camp in Scotland.[14] The Henry-Georgeite-cum-socialist body, the Scottish Land Restoration League, ran five independent candidates in Glasgow. In the Highlands, the 'Crofters' Party' ran candidates against the Liberals in protest at Gladstone's handling of the 'Battle of the Braes'. Hardie, who gave a general support to land reform in principle, gave no countenance to these tactics. He believed that the best chance of getting a miners' eight-hour Bill was to give loyal support to the Liberal party. During the 1884 franchise demonstrations, Hamilton miners had refused to march behind a huge block of coal supplied as a spectacle by a Liberal coalmaster. The coal, they stated, represented part of the wages of which they were robbed by false weighing at the pit-head. Hardie deprecated these remarks in his mining notes as injudicious and 'not the way to encourage good feeling'.[15]

Hardie was hopeful that a victorious Liberal party would remember the loyal support of the miners of Ayrshire. He drew up a miners' programme which included the legal eight-hour day and a set of well-established proposals for amending mining legislation. This he presented to the Liberal candidates for north and south Ayrshire, who agreed readily enough to support it. Hardie then moved a motion for the adoption of the south Ayrshire candidate, Eugene Wason, at the Cumnock Junior Liberal Association.[16] Two weeks before the poll, he addressed a manifesto to miners which contained the following fulsome tribute to the Liberal party and the Grand Old Man:

> it [the Liberal Party] has fought for you and won for you the right of citizenship. They have given you cheap bread to feed the body and a cheap Press to feed the mind. They have always stood up for the Rights of Man, no matter what his creed or colour. They recognise the doctrine of the Brotherhood of Man and the Fatherhood of God. They seek, by means of wise and just legislation, to make it easy to do right and difficult to do wrong. They desire the greatest good to be secured for the greatest number. . .Abroad, they are in favour of justice being done to all, even the weakest, of the nations of the world. The great and venerated head of this Party is William Ewart Gladstone, a man revered not only at home but abroad for his large-heartedness and sympathy with the weak.[17]

The two Liberal candidates won comfortably in Ayrshire and Hardie lost no time in claiming a share of the credit for the miners. 'The mining vote has won North and South Ayrshire', he claimed, and went on to express his confidence that the solicitude of the new Members would more than repay the men who, on this occasion, 'have done such signal service in the good cause of Liberalism'.[18] He was glad that warnings in the radical press against attempts at intimidation by iron companies had been effective. Another source of satisfaction was the return of the largest number of labour candidates ever. He felt sure, he wrote, from what he knew of the men elected that 'They will never do anything to disgrace the class from whose ranks they have risen.' He could not, however, refrain from noting that one of their number, Henry Broadhurst, was not a total abstainer. Hardie and Broadhurst were soon to be locked in single combat and his opinion of these other Liberal-Labour MPs was also to change.

Viewed from the wider national standpoint, the election offered fewer grounds than Hardie thought for optimism about the future of the Liberal party. Their electoral support had fallen away badly in English urban constituencies, reflecting the contemporary flight of property from the party of Chamberlainite radicalism. There was trouble brewing in the party in Parliament. Many were determined not to support Irish Home Rule, to which Gladstone was soon known to be committed. Chamberlain himself was determined not to support major concessions to Irish nationalism. Gladstone, however, could not hold office without the support of Parnell's Irish party and a bitter wrangle seemed inevitable. Even if Gladstone could succeed in holding his party together, there was still the House of Lords to bar the way.

Hardie had no great love of the Irish miners in Ayrshire. Immigrant labour from whatever quarter always offended his independent collier's instincts and we have seen his expostulation against Irishmen who would not follow trade union rules. But he shared the general radical view that a nation was best governed by its own people and he was inclined to think that good government in Ireland was one of the surest ways of preventing Irish agricultural workers from blacklegging on Scottish miners. Moreover, he valued the Irish demand as setting a precedent for 'Home Rule All Round', including a separate Parliament for local Scottish affairs. Scotland, he believed, was far more ripe for radical government than England and should not be held back by the conservatism of the southern kingdom. He therefore expressed strong support for Gladstone's efforts to unite the warring Liberal factions and hoped that popular sentiment would come to his aid: 'The heart of the nation. . .beats kindly to its Grand Old Man and its voice should be heard, cheering him in his loneliness, holding up his hands in his hour of conflict.'[19]

The outcome, however, was otherwise. A combined group of 'Whig' and radical Unionists defeated Gladstone's Home Rule Bill on second reading and sent the country back to the polls in 1886. With the Irish Question now starkly before the electorate, the tide of property and British sentiment away from the Liberals was strongly confirmed. The Conservatives shrewdly refrained from standing against dissident Liberal-Unionists, intensifying the party split. Anti-Irish sentiment was strong in the west of Scotland. In north Ayrshire the sitting Liberal went over to the Unionists, but in south Ayrshire the Liberal party held together and Wason was again returned. Hardie once again campaigned on his side. In the country as a whole, the Liberals went down to defeat. Their strength in Scotland was broken, while their position in English urban constituencies was still further weakened. Lord Salisbury formed a Conservative government with the support of Liberal-Unionists.

All this strengthened Hardie's belief that the radicals were untrustworthy. Only strong popular pressure would keep them up to the mark. He remained hopeful, however, about the possibilities of mounting this pressure from within the Liberal party. In common with many radicals in 1886, [20] he was inclined to view the 'Whig' secession from the party as a health-giving purge which would leave the radicals 'a free hand to deal with the questions which affect ourselves'. [21] Nor did he think of the Conservatives as the monolithic 'stupid party' which Liberal electioneering represented it to be. He thought the Conservatives would be anxious to consolidate their victory over the Liberals by wooing the popular vote, and he was soon to be found writing to Lord Randolph Churchill, the Tory Democrat, and Joseph Chamberlain, the Liberal-Unionist, canvassing their support for a miners' eight-hour Bill. [22]

Hardie was too sanguine. The Liberal party was not purged of property interests by the split of 1886—indeed, it was even more dependent than ever on the financial contributions of those who remained. The radicals were still a widely disparate group with many different priorities. Some would give nominal support to labour measures such as the legal eight-hour day, but few would treat it as an issue on which they were prepared to endanger the existence of a Liberal government. In the famous Newcastle Programme, drawn up by the National Liberal Federation in 1891, labour measures came last in a very long list of radical demands. [23]

Within twelve months of the 1886 election, Hardie had completely changed his mind about the Liberal party as the vehicle for labour measures. By the middle of 1887, he had joined those who were agitating for the creation of a new, independent Labour party. It is important to describe what happened to him in this way since Hardie is too often seen in isolation from those who preceded him in the formation of such a strategy. [24] In reality, Hardie was caught up in a socialist agitation among the Ayrshire and Lanarkshire miners which helped to change his political consciousness. He was also encouraged by contacts with London socialists, which made him realise that there was a stronger basis for agitation within the labour movement than he had supposed. By the middle of 1887, therefore, he had abandoned his former Liberal-labourism and had adopted a political outlook which can best be described as socialist labourism, because it looked to the organised labour movement to press for those social changes which, in Hardie's view, would lead Britain to socialism. In the remainder of this chapter we shall examine how this change was brought about and analyse the character of Hardie's maturing socialism.

III

Between 1884 and 1886, the younger leaders among the miners in the Hamilton district of Lanarkshire were gradually evolving a socialist approach to the problems of the mining industry. They received help from William Small, a draper in Blantyre. Small, the son of a jute manufacturer in Dundee who had set up a small business in Blantyre after quarrelling with his father, was drawn to the miners' cause by his belief that the Bible enjoined sympathy for those who laboured to produce man's worldly needs. His favourite Biblical text was 'Thou shalt not muzzle the ox that trampleth the corn.' He began to study mining legislation with a view to getting more of the corn for the miners, and he fastened on the large revenue made in the form of mineral royalties by land owners who owned the coal under their soil. After some time spent in the British Museum, researching old Scots laws on mineral leases from the Crown, he became convinced that Crown grants in the seventeenth century had laid down provisions for the welfare of miners. About the same time, he came into contact with land nationalisers in Scotland and soon he was advocating nationalisation of mineral royalties to provide funds for a scheme of state insurance for miners. In 1884 he held a conference in Hamilton, attended by some of the younger trade union activists such as Robert Smillie, the future president of the Miners' Federation of Great Britain. To it also came J. Shaw Maxwell, later to be first secretary of the Independent Labour Party and J. Bruce Glasier, its future chairman. Small laid before the conference a letter from Michael Davitt, the Irish nationalist and land campaigner, who proposed the establishment of a Miners' National Labour League in Scotland, to campaign for nationalisation of mines and royalties and state insurance for miners. Maxwell and Glasier wanted the conference to form a branch of the Scottish Land Restoration League which they represented, but the miners' leaders were unwilling to go so far beyond miners' questions. Finally, it was agreed to set up a Scottish Anti-Royalty and Labour League.[25] Before this new organisation was formed, however, Small was drawn directly into the socialist movement.

In 1884, a new socialist party was formed in London, called the Social Democratic Federation. The SDF has long been the butt of

British historians, who content themselves with reiteration of its many and undoubted shortcomings while denying it the ordinary respect due to historical subjects of sympathetic evaluation in its own terms. For at least twenty years after 1884, it represented something new in British politics, the theory of social democracy. It propounded a belief in the necessity of the nationalisation of the means of production as a precondition of abolishing the poverty and exploitation of the working class. It insisted on the need for a workers' political party for this object. It produced the first socialist critique seen in England of trade unions as bastions of privileged workers whose organised interests could and often did diverge from the interests of the working class in emancipation from insecurity and poverty. For many years, the SDF remained the only socialist party in England which judged policies by the standard of their effect on the conditions of life of the working class as a whole. In the 1880s it applied that standard to issues of the day, demanding the abolition of unemployment by the organisation of production for use rather than profit, and it made the first experiments in organising the unemployed for political action.

The achievements of the SDF, real as they were, were limited by the tendency of its leaders to over-estimate the economic instability of British capitalism. They mistook the first provincial difficulties of an archaic industrial economy for the storm-clouds of revolution. Consequently, they underestimated the role of a socialist party in the political processes of the working class in an on-going capitalist society and a partially democratic parliamentary system. They persisted in denouncing, in and out of season, all working-class organisations such as trade unions and radical clubs which did not share their own belief in the imminence and desirability of socialist revolution. The personality of its national leader, H.M. Hyndman, reinforced this tendency in the SDF and also helped to stamp it with a secularist, anti-Christian tinge which made cooperation with religious-minded socialists difficult. Hyndman quarrelled from the first with some of his best colleagues in the Federation, including William Morris and Edward and Eleanor Marx-Aveling. Partly under the guidance of Engels, who wanted British socialists to take a more flexible approach, these dissidents left the SDF and formed a new party, the Socialist League, in 1885. Shortly after, Hyndman succeeded in alienating men who had supported him in this quarrel, such as Tom Mann, a young trade unionist in the Amalgamated Society of Engineers, and H.H. Champion, an ex-Conservative turned socialist journalist, who wanted to tailor the socialist programme to the needs of trade unionists.

The earliest effect of the formation of the SDF, however, was to stimulate local agitations for independent working-class politics on socialist lines. In Scotland, such propaganda was vigorously pursued in the coalfields by J. Bruce Glasier, who joined the SDF after involvment in land politics, and Andreas Scheü, an Austrian who helped set up a broad organisation in Edinburgh called the Scottish Land and Labour League. Both Glasier and Scheü sided with Morris when the Socialist League was formed in 1885 and it was about this time that William Small made contact with them. [26]

Glasier met Small at meetings of the Scottish Land and Labour League in Edinburgh. These were held in the improbable location of the manse of the minister of Greyfriars Kirk in Edinburgh.[27] These early Scottish socialists had often come from enthusiastic Christian backgrounds and their socialism had correspondingly an apocalyptic tinge. Small, Glasier and others could accommodate their Christian beliefs to the socialist doctrine of class struggle. In this they differed from the better-known tradition of Christian socialism which stressed self-help and class collaboration. Thus, when Small launched the new political organisation of miners at Hamilton, he promulgated it as a branch of the Scottish Land and Labour League.[28] In 1885, he began to address miners' meetings, often joined by Glasier from Glasgow. He urged the miners to refuse to vote for any Liberal candidate who was a coalmaster or ironmaster and to imitate the crofters by running their own candidates at the general election. [29] Although he sometimes encountered heckling from his audiences he won support from some of the rising new miners' leaders like Robert Smillie. At the election in 1885, he openly supported the candidates of the Scottish Land Restoration League in their fight against Liberals, and even considered putting up himself as an independent miners' candidate in mid-Lanark against the sitting Liberal, whom he attacked for stating that miners must be prepared to work longer hours during times of depression.[30]

Hardie had set his face against class conflict in politics. Watching Lanarkshire developments through the local press, he was completely opposed to Small's attacks on the Liberals. When Small wrote requesting his support for the proposed anti-royalties conference he replied that, while he favoured nationalisation of royalties, he could not see how it would improve the miners' wages. The miners would get no benefit unless they had strong unions to press for their share of the reduced costs. He drew satisfaction from the small attendance at the anti-royalties conference:

This was just what was to have been expected, as men are not so foolish as to trouble themselves about a matter that scarcely concerns them. Had the demonstration been purely and simply a wages one, then the likelihood is it would have been a success, and the employers have reason to thank the Land Restoration Leaguers for taking the men off the scent.[31]

In the ensuing months, Hardie's comments on Small and his campaign became noticeably acid. When, however, Ayrshire Liberals got up their own agitation on the royalties issue, Hardie took the question up vigorously in his mining notes, though without raising in any way the question of what the nationalised resources should be used for.[32]

Clearly, Hardie was working within a Liberal-Labour framework at this time. His antagonism to Small did not rest merely on personal sentiment against a middle-class incomer. What was at stake was the threat posed by Small's campaign to Hardie's policy of mutual aid between middle-class Liberalism and the miners in the west of Scotland. Small, of course, was carrrying further the policy with which Hardie had flirted in 1880, appealing to the state to maintain the standard of living of miners and claiming the savings in royalties for the men rather than the masters through the redistributive agency of the state.

As a journalist on a Liberal paper, Hardie had left all that behind him. He now filled his mining columns with the blandest sentiments of John Stuart Mill:

I express no hastily formed opinion, but the result of mature and deliberate consideration of these questions when I say my opinion is that the Temperance and Co-operative Movements are destined to be the forces which will eventually elevate the working classes of this country into a position of high social comfort and comparative independence, when the profits accruing from labour shall be paid to the labourer and not, as is the case at present, go to make million-aires of those who neither toil nor sweat and who usurp to them-selves all the good things of this world, while the poor horny-handed son of toil is compelled to drudge on from year's end to year's end, living in the most uncomfortable dwellings, forced to be content with the coarsest and meanest of food, denied everything in the shape of luxury and at length, when his days of toil are over, have to eat the bread of charity from relatives or, mayhap, having to end his days in the workhouse.

I am no demagogue Mr Editor, else your columns would be closed against me. I don't wish to see any levelling down, but I do aim at a levelling up. I have no wish to take from those who have, I only wish that those who have not should, by natural means, be placed in the ranks of those who have. [33]

The turgid, contorted prose of this extract strongly suggests a tongue-in-cheek tone, but the sentiments are not entirely the product of political calculation. They have their root in the evangelical distrust of the lower strata which we have already noted. Nowhere in Hardie's journalism before late-1886 is there any indication that he believed that a change in property relationships offered a means to working-class emancipation. Rather, the thrust of his convictions is towards the view that the cooperative future will come about only after the working class has been moralised and elevated by self-help and the disciplining power of the state. His attitude to Henry George is interesting in this connection and because Hardie later claimed that George converted him to socialism. The American propagandist for land reform toured Britain in 1884. Hardie could easily agree with George that recent industrial progress, though remarkable, had not been accompanied by a diminution of poverty. Hardie, believing, albeit mistakenly, that George advocated land nationalisation, commented: 'I am not one of those who believe that this scheme would do much for the people, so long as the traffic in intoxicating drinks is allowed to remain.'[34] Hardie quoted extensively from the statistical evidence of Robert Giffen, who attempted to refute George's argument by showing that the wages of certain categories of workers had risen markedly over the previous fifty years while the price of commodities had fallen. Hardie summed up:

If we accept these conclusions as correct that the income of the working classes has increased over one hundred and fifty per cent but the cost of living is not greater, why is it that there is so much bare poverty still in the land. Why is it that so many of our working classes have not one week between them and starvation. To my mind, the answer is clear as the noonday sun. The people are pouring it down their throats in intoxicating drink. . .If the money now spent on drink were spent on the purchase of manufactured goods, it would give employment not to five hundred thousand as at present, but to four million men. Think of it, ye working men who are crying out that the country is over-populated. Try to imagine what a change for the better would be effected were only one-fourth of this money put to its proper use. Think of employment being found for another million of workmen. There would be no over-production then. What the Nation suffers from is not over-production but under-consumption.[35]

Hardie urged employers of good will to set an example to the wastrels among the working class, rewarding the respectable men by associating them in the running of industry through profit-sharing schemes. He frequently referred to contemporary experiments with profit-sharing in the Scottish cooperative movement, arguing that men who were given an interest in the running of their industries became sober and thrifty:

As soon as a man has learned not to waste his money on drink, he turns his attention to the problem of how to increase his earnings by every legitimate means. Co-operation offers advantages over all other means as a man has simply to eat himself into a fortune by dealing at the store and allowing his profits to accumulate.[36]

Hardie urged employers to experiment cautiously with profit-sharing schemes along the same lines as those the cooperative movement was introducing:

I am quite free to admit that, at present, owing to the want of education which prevails, it would in many cases be unsafe to share the profits with the workmen because if they got a portion, they would, in all probability be wanting to strike for more still; an employer prepared to give the principle a trial could easily select men from amongst the most intelligent of their class and the success which would immediately attend his efforts would be the means of educating others. [37]

Such experiments would be 'perfection itself as a preventive of strikes and all similar disputes'.

Thus Hardie saw enlightened employers and respectable workmen as engaged in a common task to improve and elevate the mass of the working class. As moral discipline extended, so production could be organised on increasingly cooperative lines. 'I fail to see,' he commented,

wherein the honest, upright employer has anything to fear from the change which is slowly but surely coming. Brains will always command a premium. There must always be some born to rule, just as the great majority of us are born to obey, and the employer who cannot occupy this position of command is out of place at present, and must inevitably go to the wall in the coming struggle for existence between mind v. money among the people of this great nation.[38]

It is thus quite wrong to see Hardie's political outlook at this time entirely in terms of trade union action to improve the miners' working and social conditions. His labourism extended to encompass a vision of the emancipation of his class. It was a vision of the working man's ascent from serfdom to complete freedom, industrial as well as political. The struggle for such emancipation was a battle not between economic classes but between idlers and labour, managing employers being included in the term 'labour' along with the workmen. In this battle, the state was to have its role. Self-improvement could not be left to *laissez-faire*. The state should make it 'easy to do right and difficult to do wrong', as the Covenanters and the evangelicals had taught. It should shut up the public house and regulate the hours of labour. It should make it easier for poor men to acquire land and minerals on which to organise cooperative production. Hardie saw himself as making war, not on a class, but on a system. That system was not at this time capitalism, but *laissez-faire*, castigated by Carlyle as 'the do-nothing philosophy'.

Hardie's general political outlook was widely shared among the independent colliers of the Scots coalfield. It harmonised easily with the outlook of small coalmasters and radical journalists. In Hardie its intellectual roots were diverse. As we have seen, Carlyle had much to do with it. So also did the Millite economist, Henry Fawcett, whose work Hardie sometimes quoted. His wide reading in the press of both sides of the Atlantic kept him abreast of 'advanced' radical developments. His views at this time were closest, perhaps, to the tradition of Christian socialism. Like Maurice and Kingsley, he looked forward to a cooperative Utopia ensuing upon the moral elevation of the working class. Like them, he looked to the collaboration of superior workman and Christian philanthropist in the work of social regeneration. But he imported into the tradition the new ambitions of the labour movement, grown in stature since the days of the Christian socialists. Labour would need a larger say in any partnership of which Hardie would be a part. A far greater role would have to be accorded the state than Maurice or Kingsley were prepared to imagine. Hardie was thus in harmony with the 'Christian Socialist revival' which one historian has detected as beginning in the late 1870s.[39]

As the year 1886 advanced, however, Hardie came under social democratic pressures which gradually began to modify his views. James Patrick, a Cumnock miner, had visited London and had heard Hyndman speak. On his return, he discussed the new socialism with his friend, James Neill, also a miner. They decided to order copies of *Justice,* the SDF paper, and proceeded to get up an agitation among miners in the Cumnock district for trade unionism and socialism.[40] Hardie's mining notes show a growing acquaintance with social democratic ideas in the autumn of 1886. He read with approval a pamphlet by James Young entitled 'The Organisation of Labour'. This was the SDF slogan meaning nationalisation of the means of production, and Young, a mining engineer, put forward a scheme for nationalising mines, iron works and railways.[41] About the same time, when he drew up rules for a new Ayrshire Miners' Union, he prefaced them with some economic definitions which have an unmistakable SDF origin:

All wealth is created by labour. Capital is part of this wealth which, instead of being consumed when created, is stored up and used for assisting labour to produce more wealth.

Interest is a charge made by those who own capital for the use of it made by those who labour. . .

Capital, which ought to be the servant of labour and which is created by labour, has become the master of its creator. The principles of trade unionism, properly understood and applied aim at a reversal of this order of things. [42]

Such utterances were still only adjustments of his Liberal-Labourism. Socialism, whatever its form, remained for him a remote contingency, the final outcome of the radical programme. He read a paper to the Cumnock Debating and Literary Society on 'Socialism' and the meeting afterwards passed a mild resolution stating: 'In the opinion of this meeting, the legislation of the future must advance on the lines of Socialism until the people are in possession of the land.' [43] There was nothing here to prevent him working within the Liberal party. At the end of the year, he attended a conference which re-formed the Scottish Liberal Association, where he pressed for a seat on the Executive to be allotted to the Scottish miners.[44] Although no formal agreement was accorded to this request, he seems to have hoped that his wish would be conceded.

Within two months of this conference, Hardie's political outlook had changed in two important respects. First, he had become convinced that the poverty and exploitation of the workers could not be ended without the abolition of private ownership of the means of production. Second, he had decided that an independent party of labour, entirely separate and distinct from the Liberal party, must be created, and committed to replacing the Liberals as the alternative party to the Conservatives. Both ideas came from social democracy, and we must turn once again to the pressure of the rank-and-file miners to see how Hardie was converted to two central propositions of socialism which hitherto he had resisted.

IV

In the deep economic depression of 1884-6, downward pressure on Scottish miners' wages continued relentlessly. Wage reductions in the autumn of 1886 sparked off renewed efforts to form a union in Ayrshire. Hardie accepted an invitation to become its secretary and drew up its rules. [45] In Lanarkshire, a new attempt was being made to organise a county union with William Small as its secretary. Even in Stirlingshire, on the remote north-west fringe of the Scottish coal-field, an energetic young mining engineer, Robert Chisholm Robertson, was conducting a militant campaign for organisation. The Fife Miners' Association, formed in 1871, was still in existence.

The end of 1886 saw an upward movement in coal prices without any accompanying improvement in iron prices. In November, the sale masters of the west of Scotland conceded a wage increase, but refused to meet a further demand in December unless the ironmasters also advanced wages. The response of the Lanarkshire miners was militant and, by the end of the year, the whole county was on strike. The Lanarkshire leaders urged the extension of the strike to the whole of Scotland, but were met with strong moderate opposition from the Fife miners and from Hardie in Ayrshire. He had been against strike action from the outset of the movement. He believed that the sale masters could be induced to open a wide and permanent gap between their wages and those of the ironmasters. This, he argued, would attract younger men away from the iron companies, forcing them in the end to raise their miners' wages. He urged restriction of output in order to create the best conditions for sale masters to increase wages.[46] In reality, his policy was quite unworkable. Not only had the separate county unions failed to agree on a common method of restriction at a conference earlier in the year, but the larger sale masters had joined forces with the iron companies to resist any restriction policy which might be adopted.

Desire for unity was, however, growing among miners' unions. Out of a series of conferences in Glasgow, there grew a Scottish Miners' National Federation.[47] Hardie was elected secretary of it, defeating William Small, apparently by combining the votes of the moderate districts against the Lanarkshire socialist.[48] In England there was a renewed spate of miners' delegate conferences. Hardie attended several of them with Scottish delegations in the years 1886-9. In January 1887, he extended his influence by launching a monthly paper, the *Miner*, addressed to the members of the new Scottish Federation to 'ventilate their grievances', as Hardie put it, 'and teach them the duty they owe to themselves'.[49] The cost of the new paper seems to have been covered by a guaranteed order from the new Ayrshire Miners' Union.[50]

In pursuit of his moderate policy, Hardie desperately sought a method of restriction that would be suitable to all districts, but it proved totally impractical to get agreement either in Scottish or English conferences.[51] Seeing the danger of an uncoordinated strike in Scotland, he at last modified his policy. He tried to combine strike action with restriction by proposing that all the districts in the Scottish Federation take a week's 'holiday' to push up the price of coal.[52] No doubt he hoped by this means to get the unofficial strikers in Lanarkshire back to work. But matters in Lanarkshire had gone too far for that. During the 'holiday' agitation they rose to a climax. William Small brought Bruce Glasier and other members of the Glasgow Socialist League to speak at mass meetings in the county. At the end of the week, Smillie, the Lanarkshire delegate, persuaded the Scottish Federation to stay out until the wage increase was conceded.[53] Hardie was furious:'The holiday movement has not turned out as intended [he groaned]. It was to be a week and no more, win or lose. This, however, did not suit certain leaders, who dinned into the men's ears to remain out until the advance was conceded.'[54] He sent the Ayrshire miners back to work. The Fife miners also returned, leaving Lanarkshire and the other new districts to battle on alone. He seemed, at this point, to have nailed his colours to the mast of a restrictionist policy, when the action of the combined ironmasters and sale masters suddenly and drastically made the whole restrictionist outlook irrelevant.

Lanarkshire had by this time been on strike for five weeks. The situation in many districts was tense. Masters had brought in blacklegs who had been stopped at the pit-heads by strong forces of pickets. The masters were in danger of losing winter orders as the result of the most solid strike in the county for a generation. They therefore asked for and obtained a force of mounted police from Glasgow to escort the blacklegs to work. There was shortage of food in the mining villages and men were forced to go begging in the streets. During the 'week's holiday', a rumour flashed around that a child had been killed in a clash between pickets and mounted police escorting blacklegs to work. This untrue report sparked off a serious incident. Miners returning to Blantyre from a mass meeting where they had heard the false report held up some food vans and seized their contents. Next day, an excited crowd in Blantyre looted shops and stormed the jail, releasing prisoners. William Small went among the crowd, pleading with the men to refrain from senseless violence. Glasgow magistrates met hurriedly and rushed off police and troop reinforcements. They raided the miners' rows at Blantyre in the middle of the night, arrested fifty-two men and seized food and whisky found in the houses.[55]

Hardie never at any time opposed the principle that the civil magistrates had a duty to keep the peace during industrial disputes. But he was vehemently opposed to the practice of employers bringing in blacklegs during a strike, and then appealing to the authorities for protection for them when they encountered the resistance of pickets. As he rightly saw, the basic freedom to organise a union was at stake here and even the most moderate trade union policy could be defeated by these heavy-handed tactics. Hardie was drawn personally into the affray in Ayrshire. Pickets there had taken to marching round the miners' rows, urging the men not to report for work. At the request of the companies, police had been stationed at the entrances to the rows to deter the marchers. It is a measure of Hardie's outrage at these tactics that he personally led a march in the early morning. When his column arrived at the rows, the police inspector in charge tried to forbid them entry. A heated argument ensued between Hardie and the officer, after which the column was allowed to proceed, Hardie having given assurances regarding the keeping of the peace.[56] To Hardie, the right to picket was a fundamental part of the right of trade union organisation. Remove it, and trade unionism would be only a hollow sham. In its defence, he was prepared to drop all evasive language and make the blunt assertion: 'Miners are prepared to render a fair day's work to the employers, in return for which they demand a fair day's pay, with all the rights of freedom to boot.'[57]

The Blantyre incident and the confrontation of police and pickets had the opposite effect on the radical press in the west of Scotland from their effect on Hardie. Where he became more openly a working-class radical, they presented more openly a middle-class viewpoint. The most prominent radical editor in Glasgow was Dr Charles Cameron, MP, owner-editor of two newspapers. Cameron stood as an advanced radical, supporting the crofters, the Irish tenants and professing a concern for labour causes. On the day of the 'Blantyre Riots', he had initiated a debate in Parliament in which he had accused the government of using troops and police to intimidate the Skye crofters 'for the purpose of exacting unjust rent'.[58] By contrast, his attitude towards the Lanarkshire miners was much less sympathetic. His newspapers stigmatised the incident at Blantyre as 'lawless proceedings of the lowest section and population in the central mining districts of Lanarkshire'.[59]

This was precisely the kind of stigmatisation of miners which Hardie felt most keenly. He argued that the incidents at Blantyre had been caused by the behaviour of the masters in bringing in police long before anyone had threatened violence or intimidation. Even the looting of the food vans, he claimed, had been nothing but the work of a few misguided youths. It was just like so many radicals to weep over the fate of tenant farmers and to desert the miners in their moment of crisis. What was the difference, he reasoned, between the unjust rent exacted by landlords from defenceless tenants and the unjust profits exacted by mining companies from defenceless miners? The desertion of the miners by the Liberal press was a powerful reinforcement to his long-standing distrust of middle-class radicals: 'Newspapers can devote page after page to the sufferings of the Irish tenants, whilst they are completely silent about an even greater amount of suffering which is being endured at their door.'[60]

Meanwhile, the associated coalmasters and ironmasters were following up their advantage. They offered to meet a deputation of their workmen, unaccompanied by trade union representatives, if the strike were called off. Overwhelmed by main force, the Lanarkshire miners were already drifting back to work. They now agreed to Hardie calling off the strike as secretary of the Scottish Federation. Hardie was unhappy about raw, inexperienced workmen going into negotiations with the masters and laid it down in advance that there could be no bargaining away of the miners' right to work a shortened week and an eight-hour day. His aim was thus to gain recognition for the union and for the right to restrict output. This however, was precisely what the triumphant ironmasters and coalmasters did not intend to concede.[61] When they met the men in conference under the chairmanship of the Lord Provost of Glasgow, they offered them a sliding scale, provided they would agree to keep the mines working six days a week and sign an agreement not to operate any other form of restriction. These terms would have put an end to all forms of trade unionism as Hardie and the Scottish miners had hitherto understood it. The men spurned them at once. The masters, no doubt well satisfied, broke off the talks, placing the blame on their opponents.[62] Hardie's policy of working for an agreement with the coalmasters to restrict output had reached the limits of credibility.

The defeat of the Lanarkshire men was, of course, a severe blow to miners' trade unionism in Scotland, but its severity should not be exaggerated. Permanent gains arose from the agitation of that winter. The new county union formed in Ayrshire proved permanent. That in Lanarkshire broke up, but several districts, including Larkhall and Blantyre, maintained permanent and effective organisation. The Scottish Federation had pointed the way towards a common wages policy, a legal eight-hour day and Parliamentary action to return a Scottish miners' representative to Westminster. It did not survive the strike in its 1887 form by more than twelve months, but the leaders who had helped in its formation were soon to be involved in reviving it in 1893, and in 1894 led the Scottish miners to their first successful national strike without ruining the Federation. Out of defeat in 1887, therefore, came gains in organisational strength and clarification of the task that confronted the Scottish miners.

The defeat of the strike served to intensify Hardie's sense of the urgency of winning an eight-hour law for Scottish miners. As it happened, the very weeks of the crisis coincided with an opportunity to try to win one. The new Conservative government had taken up a Bill to improve the regulations governing mining which their Liberal predecessors had had in hand in 1886. The Scottish Miners' National Federation was ready with a draft Bill to limit the working day underground to eight hours and they now sought to have this incorporated into the new Mines Regulation Bill. They had the support of several Scottish Liberal MPs who sat for mining constituencies, as well as that of Parnell and the Irish nationalists. But they had failed to win a majority for the proposal at successive conferences of miners held in England during the winter of 1886-7.[63] These conferences were still dominated by the unions of Northumberland and Durham, where the hewers worked a seven-hour shift system and were consequently opposed to a legal workday of eight hours. In parliament, the northeast miners were strongly represented by the veteran, Thomas Burt, who agreed,however, that he would not oppose an eight-hours amendment applying only to Scotland. When the debate came on, he spoke formally in support of the amendment, but his sentiments were lukewarm and he dwelt heavily on the practical difficulties of applying the measure in one coalfield alone. William Abraham made a similar speech as leader of the South Wales miners. Hardie was furious at these betrayals, as he saw them, but perhaps the most galling speaker to him was Henry Broadhurst, secretary to the Trades Union Congress. He expressed doubt as to whether the Scots miners really wanted the measure and stated that they had not presented the demand to him in 1885, when, as an Under-Secretary in Gladstone's government, he had been in charge of preparing a new Mines Bill. Outside Fife, which already had the eight-hour day, there had been no unions in Scotland in 1885.[64] Hardie, sitting in the Strangers' Gallery, saw the Scots clause rejected in a division and the legislative prospects of the Scots dimmed with their industrial hopes.

V

Hardie recognised that the strike of 1887 had brought miners' trade unionism in Scotland to a crisis point. 'We are passing through a severe crisis at the present moment', he wrote in the *Miner*.[65] A conjunction of the ironmasters with the largest sale masters to impose contract rules on their men preventing restriction in any form, completely undermined the strategy which he had been preaching since 1882. The use of the coercive forces of the state to enable the companies to replace trade union labour by blackleg labour recalled the worst conflicts of the 1840s and 1850s and threatened to block all progress by the respectable men for a generation. On the Parliamentary front, the Scots miners' weakness in Liberal-labour politics had been clearly exposed.

These developments reawakened in him the sense of the need for state intervention which he had felt so urgently in 1880, but temporarily suppressed between 1882 and 1886. In speeches to miners during the strike, he boldly revived his earlier demands, urging the establishment of state arbitration to fix miners' wages. To this he added Small's demand for state insurance for miners and the legal eight-hour day.[66] These henceforth became the nucleus of his miners' political programme. The state must step in to do for the miners what the systematic opposition of the masters was making it impossible for them to do for themselves.

The strike had driven home another lesson. If the miners were to carry their programme they must step outside the framework of the Liberal party. The sense of urgency engendered by the defeat of 1887 made it impossible for Hardie to go on thinking of the miners occupying a place in the queue of church radicals, land radicals, nationalists, temperance reformers and all the other so-called 'faddists' who jostled for position within the Gladstonian Liberal party. Instead, the miners must turn themselves into the advanced guard of labour politics, generalising their own grievances and demands into those of organised labour as a whole and rallying it to the task of creating a separate Labour party with a distinct political programme: 'We want a new Party', he wrote in the *Miner* of April 1887, only a fortnight after the final defeat of the Lanarkshire miners, 'a Labour Party pure and simple—and trades unions have the power to create this.'[67]

In the three months following, he widened his political differences with the Liberal party and began to develop the argument that it had reached a historic crisis. In the *Miner* of July 1887, he published a programme for a Labour party, prefacing it with the comment:

> We require a new Party to carry it out. The Liberal Party has done noble work in the past in securing civil and religious freedom. It is, I believe, prepared to carry this part of the work forward to completion. But there, it seems to me, its work ends, as in all matters affecting the rights of property or capital or interfering with 'freedom of contract' there is not, nor has there ever been, much to choose between Whig and Tory.[68]

He was beginning to discern the strategy which guided him for the rest of his political career, through many vicissitudes and apparently baffling set-backs. As he conceived it, agitation by the trade unions for increased state intervention to alleviate the poverty of working people would begin to attract to itself all the dissident collectivist and democratic forces within the Liberal party. If only labour pressure could be sufficiently strong, the Liberal party must either shed its own reactionary elements such as the great landowners and capitalists, adopting the labour programme, or its collectivist and democratic elements must come out and group themselves in alliance with labour. Either way would bring progress for the miners and the working classes generally. But such pressure could not be generated by the existing leaders of the labour party, as their conduct over the Scottish eight-hours amendment had revealed. It would require a long, hard process of agitation to teach trade unionists by example what independent political action could achieve. Of all those who were in a position to lead such an agitation in 1887, most were socialists. If their vital energy and commitment were to be involved, the new party would have to include socialism as one of its objectives. Further, only a commitment to socialism could provide a clear indication that the independence of the Labour party was complete and that, henceforth, the Liberals must treat it as a separate entity with which they had to bargain.

This point is crucial. Of all the dissidents from Gladstonianism, only the socialists were not prepared to be reabsorbed provided this or that measure were conceded to them. Herein lay one of the new-found attractions of socialism for Hardie. It seemed to give to organised labour the primary social role which he felt it entitled to. It would accept the organised workers as the controlling constituency of the new party and place their interests at the top of the political agenda, instead of putting them behind Irish Home Rule or any other cry of the hour.

Hardie's sense of the claims of socialism for labour was growing throughout the winter of 1886-7. If William Small's daughter can be trusted, he was now a regular visitor at their cottage in Blantyre, where he and the draper argued out the principles of socialism. [69] Valuable also were socialist contacts made in London while lobbying at Westminster. He was far from impressed with a meeting of the SDF which he attended. It was on the evening of Queen Victoria's Jubilee, and he heard socialist speakers denounce the Queen as:

'that old woman who had never so much as spent ten minutes washing a shirt for her husband in return for all the money she had received.' His audience cheered him to the echo and, after the meeting was over, robbed themselves of their manhood by swilling in a public house. I took the opportunity of stating a few wholesome truths and reminded the meeting that, before we could have Socialism, we must have a fit and prepared people. Had I to choose between the autocratic rule of the Emperor of Russia and the democratic rule of an unprincipled, ignorant mob, I would by preference, choose the former as the better of the two—and I speak as an extreme Democrat. [70]

But he met other socialists in London, including Tom Mann and H.H. Champion. Mann made a favourable impression on him, because he envisaged socialism coming about by constitutional means rather than physical force revolution. He gave Hardie a copy of the pamphlet he had just written, advocating a legal eight-hour day for all workers as a palliative for unemployment. [71] Mann introduced Hardie to H.H. Champion who had broken with Hyndman and the SDF over the latter's dogmatic resistance to socialist collaboration with trade unionists. Champion was launching a new paper, the *Labour Elector,* to campaign for a National Labour party with a collectivist programme. He gave Hardie to understand that he had funds to help working men who were prepared to run independently against Liberals.[72]

One other important contact in London was with the Marx-Engels family circle. Eleanor Marx, daughter of Karl Marx, introduced to Hardie by Mann, took him to visit Engels. Hardie was pleased when the German philosopher criticised the SDF for its sectarianism. There is no evidence of any mutual antagonism between the two men at this time. Although distrust developed between them after 1892, when Engels suspected Hardie of working with the Conservatives, they seem to have cooperated on friendly terms in 1888 and 1889 to promote British trade union participation in the foundation of the Second International.[73]

Champion's finances, Engels' international contacts, Mann's propagandist flair—these were all elements which Hardie put into the agitation to get the trade unions to form a separate Labour party with its own programme. After the early months of 1887, he knew he would not be on his own, but would have influential socialist backers. When he published his Labour programme in July 1887, therefore, it included far-reaching socialist demands for the nationalisation of mines, railways and minerals. This fact has been overlooked by a recent biographer, who writes: 'Socialism did not mean the same thing to Keir Hardie in 1886 as to us today. In Hardie's mind, Socialism was linked with a Georgeite campaign for land nationalisation; the word had no particular implications about attitudes to industrial organisation.[74]

As we already know, this is not an adequate representation of Hardie's mind even in 1886 when he had already given a warm welcome to proposals for nationalising mines, iron works and railways. But a more serious objection is that this emphasis leads to an important underestimation of what Hardie was doing when he wrote socialist demands into the 1887 programme, which was otherwise a mixture of labour collectivism, republican land radicalism and constitutional reform.[75] By writing these nationalisation measures into the programme of the proposed new Labour party, Hardie was proposing to draw a sharp and irrevocable dividing line between it and the Liberal party. In this respect he clearly pointed the way to the Labour party of the twentieth century.

Recent biographers have attempted to cast doubt on Hardie's conversion to socialism in 1887.[76] They would prefer to think of that year as witnessing only a development of Hardie's labourism. They disregard the evidence, however, that the crisis of January to February

1887, and the contacts with socialist agitators which it entailed, introduced into Hardie's journalism two lines of policy which he had explicitly rejected before 1887. One was the view that the Liberal party was nearing the end of its historic work and must be replaced by a new party relying on organised labour. The other was the belief that there could be no complete solution to the poverty of the working class without the abolition of capitalism. The former view we have already analysed in Hardie's writings and reported speeches. The second appeared for the first time in a vigorous editorial in the *Miner* in May 1887. There, Hardie completely inverted the social views he had advocated with such apparent conviction in the columns of the *Ardrossan and Saltcoats Herald.* Once again he took up the question raised by Henry George: how could so much poverty and so much wealth coexist in a country like Britain?

Over-production, say some, is the cause. Produce less and there will be plenty for all. Surely this is contradictory reasoning, even in this world of contradictions. To say that people must starve because Nature has been kind, or because men have been industrious, is so outrageous as almost to pass belief. . .
There are those who, and not without reason, lay the blame at the door of our expenditure on intoxicating drink. . .
There can be no doubt whatever but that the traffic in strong drink has a good deal to do with the poverty which exists. We are far from saying, however, that it is the only cause. Suppose the money now spent on drink to be divided equally among the working men of Great Britain, it would only increase their present earnings by about five shillings a week and, while this no doubt would do much to relieve the gloom which now hangs over many a home, it would not remove poverty from our midst. We do not complain of the drunkard being poor – he has a right to be poor and to suffer all the pangs which poverty brings. What we complain of is that the honest, industrious, sober toiler is kept from year's end to year's end with only one step between him and pauperism. . .
    The remedy is a simple one, if only the nation had sense enough to apply it. Get rid of the idea that the capitalist is an indispensible adjunct of an industrial system and the problem is solved. Capital is a necessity, but not the capitalist. . . The capitalist has done good service in the past by developing trade and commerce. His day is now nearly past. He has played his part in the economy of the industrial system and must now give way for a more perfect

order of things, wherein the labourer shall be rewarded in proportion to his work.[77]

This is a new, urgent Hardie, with a sense of history in which the capitalist is fast becoming an irrelevancy in the social relationships of production, rather than an unfortunate necessity who may, at some remote time, bring labour into association with himself in cooperative production.

This *volte-face* is so sudden and dramatic that it seems to justify the term conversion. The strike of 1887 forced Hardie to drop the mental habit of deference towards the susceptibilities of middle-class allies such as his editor. From the foundation of the *Miner,* his links with the *Ardrossan and Saltcoats Herald* became increasingly sporadic, and he resigned his post on it in 1890 in order, as he said, to obtain more liberty of self-expression. His pent-up resentment at the lowly position allotted to him and his class boiled over in 1887 into a fierce, righteous anger against the Mammon-worshippers who blocked the path of progress. Henceforth he would be the heroic leader of his class heading its crusade for a new moral world in which the ethic of cooperation would replace the ethic of competition.

We should not deny the force of this emotional liberation merely because Hardie carried through his conversion a great deal of his old self-help luggage. Paul's experience on the Damascus road did not mean that he forgot everything he had ever learned about Judaism. To say that Hardie was converted to certain socialist tenets in 1887 is not to deny that there were important continuities, far less to say that he became a Marxist. He retained his faith in self-help as the means by which the workers would contribute to their own fitness for power. He continued to believe that socialism would come about by class-collaboration, once the power of labour had convinced enough of the middle class that socialism was in their interests as well. He would always be highly flexible in accommodating labour policy to the views of non-socialist radicals who were prepared to make concessions to labour demands. In this respect he never departed fundamentally from the Christian socialism he had come to understand by 1886. But the year 1887 left in his thought the permanent marks of social democracy. Henceforth he would champion the power of organised labour as the generating power of social progress. Henceforth also, he would regard measures for the nationalisation of the means of production (especially mines and land)[78] as integral and necessary parts of a political programme for the emancipation of labour. Liberal-labourism had given way to socialist labourism.

Notes

1. Diary Fragment, 11 March 1884.
2. Ibid., e.g., 4 January, 7 January, 12 January 1884.
3. *Ardrossan und Saltcoats Herald*, 3 December 1881.
4. Diary Fragment, 6 January 1884.
5. *Ardrossan and Saltcoats Herald*, 15 February 1884.
6. *The Bible (Authorised Version)*, The Epistle of James, ii, 2-4.
7. Diary Fragment, 17 March 1884.
8. Minutes of Cumnock Congregational Church, 28 March 1884, ms., Cumnock.
9. *Ardrossan and Saltcoats Herald*, 25 July 1884.
10. Ibid., 15 August 1884.
11. Ibid., 30 September 1884.
12. Ibid., 12 December 1884.
13. Ibid., 20 February 1885.
14. D.W. Crowley, 'The Crofters' Party, 1885-95', *Scot. Hist. Rev., xxxv*, 1956, 109-26; D.C. Savage, 'Scottish Politics, 1885-6, *Scot. Hist. Rev.,* xi, 1961, p.118.
15. *Ardrossan and Saltcoats Herald*, 22 August 1884.
16. Ibid., 27 October 1885.
17. Ibid., 20 November 1885.
18. Ibid., 11 December 1885.
19. Ibid., 26 March 1886.
20. D.A. Hamer, *Liberal Politics in the Age of Gladstone and Rosebery* (Oxford, 1972), p.124.
21. *Ardrossan and Saltcoats Herald*, 26 March 1886.
22. Hardie to Lord Randolph Churchill, 6 December 1889 (Nat. Lib. of Scotland, Emrys Hughes Papers, Dep.176, Box 1).
23. H.V. Emy, *Liberals, Radicals and Social Politics, 1882-1914* (Cambridge, 1973), pp.1ff.
24. McLean, *Keir Hardie*, pp.33ff; cf. Morgan, *Keir Hardie*, pp.23ff.
25. *Hamilton Adv.*, 9 September 1884. For William Small see Bell Small's Paper Concerning Her Father, Nat. Lib. Scot., ms. acc.3359, esp. inscription in Small's Presentation Bible, and cuttings from *Forward*, 31 January 1953, *Scottish Co-operator*, February 1903; also ms. memoir by William Small; and ms. memoirs by his daughter and Andrew McCowie.
26. J. Mavor, *My Windows on the Street of the World* (1923), p.178; L. Thompson, *The Enthusiasts* (1971), *passim;* Lowe, *Souvenirs*, p.12; R.P. Arnot, *William Morris, the Man and the Myth* (1964), pp.72ff.
27. Ibid.
28. *Hamilton Adv.*, 15 November 1884.
29. Ibid., 20 June 1885.
30. J.G. Kellas, 'Highland Migration to Glasgow', *Bul. of the Soc. for the Study of Lab. Hist.,* 12, 1966, p.9.
31. *Ardrossan and Saltcoats Herald*, 26 September 1884.
32. Ibid., 10 October 1884.
33. Ibid., 22 July 1882.
34. Ibid., 22 February 1884; for George see E.P. Lawrence, *Henry George in the British Isles* (Michigan, 1957), p.35.
35. *Ardrossan and Saltcoats Herald*, 7 March 1884.

36. Ibid., 22 July 1882.
37. Ibid., 19 January 1883.
38. Ibid., 22 July 1882.
39. P. d'A. Jones, *The Christian Socialist Revival, 1877-1914* (Princeton, 1968), *passim*
40. J. Neill, 'Memoirs of an Ayrshire Agitator', *Forward*, 1,11, July 1914.
41. *Ardrossan and Saltcoats Herald*, 10 September 1886.
42. *Rules of the Ayrshire Miners' Union (1886)*, Scot. Rec. Off. FS 7/18.
43. *Ardrossan and Saltcoats Herald*, 19 November 1886.
44. Minutes of the Scottish Liberal Association, 22 December 1886.
45. *Ardrossan and Saltcoats Herald*, 6 August 1886, 22 July 1887, 28 November 1889.
46. Ibid., 27 August 1883, 6, 13 August, 10 September 1886.
47. *Hamilton Adv.*, 14 August 1886.
48. Ibid., 4 September 1886.
49. *Miner*, January 1887.
50. *Ardrossan and Saltcoats Herald*, 5 October, 24 December 1886; *Miner*, January 1887.
51. *Ardrossan and Saltcoats Herald*, 22 October, 12 November 1886; *Conference of Miners' National Union, Manchester, November 1886, Proceedings*, p.17. Webb T. U. Col.
52. *Ardrossan and Saltcoats Herald*, 28 January 1887.
53. *North British Daily Mail*, 5 February 1887; *Miner*, February 1887; *Commonweal*, February 1887.
54. *Ardrossan and Saltcoats Herald*, 5 February 1887.
55. *North British Daily Mail*, 8-10 February 1887; *Labour Tribune*, 22 February 1887; *Commonweal*, 26 February 1887.
56. *Ardrossan and Saltcoats Herald*, 28 February 1887.
57. *Miner*, February 1887.
58. *North British Daily Mail*, 16 February 1887.
59. Ibid., 11 February 1887.
60. *Miner*, February 1887.
61. *North British Daily Mail*, 24 February, 5 March 1887.
62. Ibid., 9-12 March 1887.
63. *Ardrossan and Saltcoats Herald*, 25 October 1886; *Miners' Conference, November 1886, Proc.*, Webb T.U. Col; *Labour Tribune*, 15, 22 January 1887.
64. *Ardrossan and Saltcoats Herald*, 18 February 1887; *Miner*, March 1887; *H.C. Debs.*, 3rd Ser. CCCXVI, 62; CCCXIX, 90ff.
65. *Miner*, April 1887.
66. *Ardrossan and Saltcoats Herald*, 28 February 1887.
67. *Miner*, April 1887.
68. Ibid., July 1887.
69. B. Small's annotation on p.21 of Lowe, *Souvenirs* and on *The Independent Labour Party, 1893-1943, Jubilee Souvenir*, Nat. Lib. Scot., ms. acc.3359.
70. *Ardrossan and Saltcoats Herald*, 24 June 1887.
71. Ibid., 27 May 1887; T. Mann, *What a Compulsory Eight Hour Working Day Means to the Workers* (1886).
72. H.M. Pelling, 'H.H. Champion, Pioneer of Labour Representation', *Cambridge Hist. J.*, VI, 1952, p.222.
73. See *Labour Leader*, 24 December 1898 for Hardie's first meeting with Engels. Hardie to Engels, 1 April and 21, 27 May, 1889, Engels Papers, Int. Inst. Soc. Hist., Amsterdam. K.O. Morgan suggests that Hardie and Engels made an unfavourable impression on each other at their first meeting, but cites no evidence in support of this contention: *Keir Hardie*, p.16.
74. McLean, *Keir Hardie*, p.22.
75. *Miner*, July 1887.

76. McLean, *Keir Hardie,* p.22; Morgan, *Keir Hardie,* p.20.
77. *Miner,* May 1887.
78. *Rules and Report of the Scottish Miners' National Federation* (Ardrossan, 1887), p.6.

5 THE SCOTTISH LABOUR PARTY

Many of Hardie's socialist contemporaries found him difficult to understand. Engels, who began by cultivating him after their first meeting in 1887, ended by distrusting him.[1] David Lowe, who was Hardie's assistant-editor on the *Labour Leader* from 1894 to 1906, recalled him with an ambiguous respect: 'He was a difficult man, reticent, stable in his mission, trusting few, friendly to the mass . . . and ever carried onward by a deep, broad under-current of duty, with an implacable determination to win well-being for the working class'.[2] In the years after 1887, socialists would often question whether Hardie followed any principled course of action whatever and, if he did, what it was.

Recent historians and biographers have laboured under a similar difficulty, and in no period of Hardie's life is it more acute than in the years between 1887 and 1892. Hardie's personal papers, always fragmentary, are almost at their thinnest for this period and rarely throw illuminating light on his political convictions. The public record is also obscure and tantalisingly interrupted in 1889 by the collapse of Hardie's *Miner* (renamed the *Labour Leader* in that year). Publication was not recommenced until 1893. His Parliamentary candidatures for Mid-Lanark in 1888 and West Ham South in 1892 exposed him to considerable press publicity, but between these dates we are obliged to follow him through sporadic newspaper reports of his work as secretary to the Scottish Labour Party. The party attracted only intermittent attention, as when a by-election or industrial dispute allowed it to win publicity.

It is hardly surprising, then, if Hardie's biographers encountered most difficulty in defining his political strategy in these years. Morgan seems to play down the significance of the Scottish Labour Party as precursor of the 'Labour Alliance' of 1900, and to see Hardie as seeking only to increase pressure on the Liberals for labour demands. [3] McLean, on the other hand, fully acknowledges the class character of the Scottish Labour party, but believes that Hardie intended it to have no more to do with socialism than was necessary to win the support of socialist activists for a party based on trade union interests. [4] Neither makes any serious attempt to reconstruct Hardie's personal development in these difficult years. His important interventions in Scottish by-elections in 1889 and 1890 are passed over, as are his efforts to win trade union support for the new party. As a result, the inner consistency and continuity of Hardie's aim (sensed by those who, like David Lowe or Joseph Burgess, knew him best in these years) are obscured or mis-construed.

In the following chapter, an attempt will be made to reassemble all the evidence. Such detailed treatment is justified, since it will enable the reader to assess for himself the validity of the argument. This proceeds from the position taken up in chapter 4, that Hardie was converted to socialism in 1887, a socialism which committed him to class politics and to nationalisation of the mines, railways and land. It will now be argued that Hardie had to pursue his vision cautiously, even deviously, in the Scottish situation, where there were as yet few socialists who were not 'extremists', few trade unionists who trusted Hardie and few radicals who wanted a clean, permanent break with the Liberal party. Thus we shall see Hardie begin the Scottish Labour party with a weather eye on the socialists, keeping their influence out of the party's propaganda as much as possible. Later, he will lean his weight to the other side, as the SLP cockle-shell lists to a strong wind of compromise from the Liberal party managers, a wind which its crew of ex-Liberals found hard to resist. Hardie's public statements on socialism will become more sympathetic, even enthusiastic, as he senses the need to emphasise the implicit class character of the party's political position. The Labour party, he will be asserting by 1892, did not aim merely at winning a few seats in the House of Commons or at this or that reform. It cast itself for the role of government. This, quintessentially, was what socialism came to mean to Hardie. It was an inner sense of labour's destiny, nourished by the struggle to keep the SLP afloat, which provided a fixed bearing for the Labour party's relationship to trade unionism, socialism and the Liberal party. Eventually, in 1894-5, it would become the starting-point for him to develop an alternative version of socialism to that of the Social Democratic Federation.

I

Hardie's decision to form the new Labour party in Scotland was hast-ened by his growing disillusionment with the English miners' leaders in Parliament during the crisis which overtook the Scottish miners in February 1887. Their failure to support the demand of the Scottish Miners' National Federation for a legal eight-hours amendment to the Coal Mines Regulation Bill of that year made him feel the isolated weakness of the Scots keenly. 'One thing I feel very much ', he wrote a few days before the debate in Parliament, 'the Scotch miners have no one in Parliament to speak in their name and from their standpoint. The English miners have such members, but they are out of touch with Scotch thought and feeling.'[5] After the debate, when introducing his programme for a new Labour party in the *Miner,* he singled out the Liberal-Labour members for attack: 'what difference will it make to me that I have a working man representing me if he is a dumb dog who dare not bark and will follow the leader under any circumstances?'[6]

Before anything much could be done, however, to start a Labour party in Scotland, the Trades Union Congress met at Swansea in September 1887. Hardie was the delegate of the Ayrshire Miners' Union and this gave him an opportunity to express his criticisms of the Liberal-Labour MPs in a very public way. He singled out Henry Broadhurst as the main target of his attack. Broadhurst had never impressed him much as a representative of labour and he felt none of the personal respect for him which he felt for the veteran Northumberland miners' leader, Thomas Burt. It had been Broadhurst who speciously queried the authenticity of the Scots miners' demand for a legal eight-hour day. Champion and Mann had told Hardie that Broadhurst had supported Sir John Brunner's Liberal candidature for Northwich and that Brunner was a chemical manufacturer who kept men working twelve hours a day in dangerous conditions. Broadhurst, Champion pointed out, had shares in Brunner's firm. It was, therefore, Broadhurst who, as secretary to the Parliamentary Committee of the TUC, seemed to represent most clearly the commitment of organised labour to the *laissez-faire* principle that the state should refrain from doing for trade unionists what trade unionists ought to do for themselves.

In reality, Broadhurst seems to have had no deep objections to state intervention. In 1872, he had been involved in discussions between trade union and Conservative party leaders as to the possibility of the latter introducing a legal eight-hour day for all workers.[7] It seems likely that the dogmatic self-help opinions which he voiced in the 1880s were a tactical interlude, occasioned by the opposition of Gladstone and other Liberal leaders to state interference with the hours of adult male workers. Broadhurst hoped, by close and friendly cooperation with the Liberal leaders, to go on increasing the numbers of Liberal-Labour Members of Parliament.

Craft unions had long been a byword for complacent self-assurance and suspicion of state assistance, but the severe unemployment of 1884-7 hurt even the strongest of the craft unions and generated support for a new collectivist approach. In engineering, printing, bootmaking and shoe-making, for instance, technological innovation was already undermining the position of the time-honoured craftsman and from these trades came support for Tom Mann's demand for a legal eight-hour day to spread work among the unemployed.

The Parliamentary Committee, which formed in the TUC a kind of steering group of the top trade union executives of the day, was aware of these new currents of opinion at Swansea. Its annual report, therefore, took a firm line against state assistance:

> If Labour holds steadily on the course it has hitherto maintained, by showing self-reliance and independence in trade matters and by refusing State assistance, helping those who can help themselves, providing for their own wants and keeping a firm grip on all it has gained, it cannot fail to increase its dignity and importance.[8]

The growing opinion in support of seeking state assistance was indicated, on the other hand, by a motion on the agenda from the Steam Engine Makers' Society, calling on the government to introduce an eight-hour day in all its workshops. The London Cabinet Makers had put down an amendment calling on the Congress to press for a general eight-hours enactment to counter unemployment.[9]

There was also division of opinion in the Congress over the issue of increasing labour representation in Parliament. In 1886 it had been agreed to set up a Labour Representation Committee, but it was left to individual unions to decide whether to join or hold aloof. The secretary to the Committee was T.R. Threlfall, who, although a Liberal, was keen to see the committee develop into a separate party, backed by the unions. At Swansea in 1887, he gathered together a conference of TUC delegates to draft a constitution for such a party under the new name of the Labour Electoral Association. The programme as drafted, however, reflected Threlfall's own ambiguity about the independence of a Labour party from the Liberals. It said nothing about legislation on the hours of labour, though Threlfall himself supported the legal eight-hour day, and confined itself to radical political reforms such as state payment of Members of Parliament and adult suffrage. On social questions, it called vaguely for land reform and reform of the Poor Law. [10]

Hardie attended Threlfall's conference, but felt that its approach was too timid. The Labour party should stop demanding only those measures to which the Liberal Party was thought likely to agree and boldly put forward its own programme for dealing with unemployment and low wages, and it should give clear warning that it would support no Liberal who refused countenance to such measures. This was the reason why Broadhurst's opposition to the legal eight-hour day and support for Brunner were so important to him and he set out to cleanse the Augean stable of trade unionism with all the energy and determination of a hero.

On the first day of the Congress's formal proceedings, he took the unusual step of moving an amendment to the report of the Parliamentary Committee, calling attention to the fact that Broadhurst had spoken and voted against the legal eight-hour day for Scottish miners. The amendment was heavily defeated by eighty votes to fifteen. But this did not silence the new Scots delegate. He was immediately on his feet again, trying to move the reference back of that section of the report which adjured unions to reject state assistance. This was defeated by a similar majority. Later in the day, he again clashed with Broadhurst, this time challenging the opinion of the established authority on a point of interpretation regarding the law of employers' liability. [11]

Delegates to the TUC in those days were highly respectable men. They liked to think of their Congress as a dignified and worthy display of the intellect and responsibility of the best representatives of the working class. They shifted uneasily at these unbusinesslike interruptions and craned round to see the newcomer who behaved in this upstart fashion. They saw a stocky figure, rather under medium height, with a thick mane of long brown hair. His eyes glared penetratingly from beneath shaggy brows and he looked and spoke as though all the suffering and sin of the world rested on his shoulders. Clearly not the kind of man to be trusted for cool, level-headed assessment of a situation. [12]

But they had heard nothing so far. During the debate on labour representation, Hardie rose to speak after William Pickard, the Lancashire miners' leader, had opposed Threlfall's view that working men should stand for Parliament as Labour candidates rather than Liberals or Conservatives. Brusquely, Hardie went straight to the gravamen of his charge against the existing leadership. He denounced candidates like Brunner, who presented themselves as Liberals to working-class constituencies while conducting their businesses in direct antagonism to their workers' interests. Then he rounded on Broadhurst for supporting Brunner. Giving details of the long hours worked and the low wages paid in Brunner's chemical works, he concluded:

Little wonder that there was difficulty found in forcing the programme of the Congress on the country. They wanted a Democratic party, which should embrace men of every line of thought. There should be a programme and every candidate for Parliament should know that unless they could support it he must look elsewhere for a seat.[13]

The Parliamentary Committee was not prepared to take this meekly from a new delegate representing only fifteen hundred members. Hardie seemed to them not merely an upstart, however. He also seemed representative of the socialist agitation that was spreading among their own members. They believed this agitation to be inspired by the SDF and H.H. Champion, men who had taken Conservative funds to run breakaway socialist candidates in the election of 1885. Hardie, therefore, must be squashed, firmly and finally. In his reply, Broadhurst played skilfully on the prejudices of the delegates. Who was this newcomer, he asked, to lecture him on his duties as a trade unionist and Labour MP? Where had Mr Hardie been until this year in trade union struggles, while George Howell and the other great names of craft unionism had built up the movement? 'I was not born', shouted Hardie. Pretending not to hear, Broadhurst repeated the question. Hardie again called out, 'I said I was not born'. 'What', gasped the ready debater, 'not born only ten years before!' This was marvellous indeed: 'He had heard of children being born with full sets of teeth, but he had never heard of one being born with such magnificent development of manly appearance about the head.' The audience roared with laughter and Broadhurst went on to say that Brunner had always supported the labour members in parliament and to accuse Hardie of fishing in the Tory press for charges against him.

On the following day, during the continuation of the debate, Charles Fenwick spoke and referred to the efforts which, he said, were being made in the constituency of every labour Member 'to unbind the confidence and sap the good will of the constituents towards the Members', merely, he alleged, on the ground that the latter were not prepared to accept 'certain revolutionary measures that had been submitted to them.' He went on:

The policy of this Congress and of the working class as he had hitherto understood it, had been a policy of reform and not revolution [cheers] and as an humble individual he refused to take his instruction from one who, like Jonah's gourd, sprang up in the night only to collapse as soon [laughter].[14]

The sharpness of these replies from the 'Front Bench' is not difficult to understand. Hardie, in a sense, had been very unfair to Broadhurst. Congress was not at that time committed to an eight-hours law for miners or anyone else, so, presumably, Broadhurst was free to speak and vote on it as he thought fit. To the platform and most of the delegates, Hardie seemed to be yet another of those wild young men of the eighties who were trying to make trouble between labour and the Liberal party by raising socialist demands. Such action could only benefit the Conservatives, the enemies of true progress.

But if Hardie's attack appears inept in its over-attention to Broadhursts' personal motives and its shaky grounding in Congress decisions, it was nonetheless prophetic.

It drew the line that was to differentiate him, not only from Broadhurst and the 'Lib-Labs', but also from Threlfall and that middle opinion which thought it would be enough merely to strengthen labour representation in Parliament and argue later about what it was there for. Hardie insisted that these demands should be made clear in advance and electoral support should be conditional on their acceptance. Already, in Hardie's vision of the future, governments were to act at the behest of labour, and not as sovereigns condescending graciously to a supplicant. It was this enhanced claim on behalf of organised labour which made Hardie seem so novel in 1887 and so dangerously close to the socialists.

Hardie, for his own part, had avoided too overt an association with socialists in the Congress. He took no part in the debate on the general eight-hour day. He had not yet called himself by the name of socialist and would not do so until about 1890. He was still very wary of the damage which could be done to his cause by branding it with a term which awakened all the conservative opposition of trade unionists to extremism and revolution. He was coming to believe that labourism could develop into socialism in the trade union movement, but this development could not come about by lecturing. Trade unionists had never been used to think of themselves as a solid class with common political objectives. They must be taught to do so by being engaged in the class struggle. What was needed at this moment was a heroic pioneer who would carry the labour cause into the electoral arena and Scotland would afford an early opportunity.

II

Hardie had probably nurtured the ambition to succeed Alexander McDonald as the Scottish miners' representative in Parliament from a very early stage.[15] His view of his Parliamentary role began to crystallise, like so much else, at the beginning of 1887. In February of that year, he paid his first visit to the House of Commons to lobby for the legal eight-hour day, and was shocked by the way he found the people's business being conducted. Crossing the precincts of the Palace of Westminster he 'felt as excited as if I had been going to get married or executed (which, I suppose, amounts to much the same thing)'. Once in the Strangers' Gallery, however, his excitement quickly diminished. The lounging forms of Liberal leaders on the Opposition Front Bench bespoke only boredom. Honourable Members who addressed the House seemed more concerned to score points off each other than to get something done about the problem confronting them. In his mood of impatience about the miners' eight-hours measure, his anger grew. 'Any man in earnest would either kick up a dust or resign his seat', he wrote later.[16]

As he looked down on the chamber, he could pick out the celebrated radicals and was shocked to see how completely they had conformed to the style of the establishment: there was Charles Bradlaugh, his father's hero, whose 'display of shirt-front was only equalled by the wealth of face with which it was surmounted'. There too was John Morley, another celebrated agnostic radical 'who lounged and lolled on the Front Bench as if he had been out in a picnic party'. The place seemed stifling with conventionality, conformity to which robbed all would-be reformers of their will to see great changes brought about. Only one Member in that 1887 Parliament seemed to Hardie capable of resisting that atmosphere. He was Robert Cunninghame Graham, Laird of Gartmore, and Member for North-West Lanark. Graham had come into politics after a career of adventures in South America.[17] He was shocked at the urban poverty he found in 'civilised' Britain after his life among supposedly more primitive peoples, and he made himself the Parliamentary spokesman of all those who were trying to regenerate the Labour party for a campaign against working-class poverty. Hardie appreciated his aristocratic contempt for the forms and petty dignities of Parliament and quoted with approval Graham's ideas on how a true labour representative should behave towards the House:

A working man in Parliament, to do any good at all should be paid the current wages for the district he represents and for the trade he has been accustomed to work in. He should go to the House of Commons in workaday clothes, no matter if he has to leave his basket of tools in the dressing room. He should address the speaker

on labour questions, and give utterance to the same sentiments, in
the same language and in the same manner in which he is accustomed to address the President of the Radical Club. Above all, he
should remember that all the Conservatives and the greater proportion of the Liberals are joined together in the interest of capital
against labour. [18]

Before this was being written, February 1886, Hardie was allowing his
name to be canvassed as Liberal candidate for south Ayrshire. [19] By
September, his name was before the Liberal Association in north
Ayrshire as a miners' nominee. In November, however, the north
Ayrshire Liberal Association adopted as its candidate Sir William
Wedderburn. [20] By this time, definite moves were afoot to form a
Scottish Labour Party. Hardie had announced in July 1887 that the
Scottish miners had decided to form a new political organisation and
to run three candidates for Scottish constituencies. In October, the
well-informed Championite, J.L. Mahon, reported from the British
miners' conference at Edinburgh (where, of course, he met Hardie)
that the formation of a Scottish Labour party was imminent. [21]
It may seem strange at first sight that Hardie should be seeking
Liberal nominations while trying to form a new party. In fact, such
a course of action was perfectly compatible with the way in which
he thought a new party would have to be created. Working men were
not going to switch suddenly from voting Liberal to voting for a new
party just because a few young leaders told them to do so. It would
have to be demonstrated to them that they could not get increased
working-class representation through the Liberal party. Throughout
the next five years, Hardie's tactics were designed to put the Liberals
on the wrong foot. He would give them every opportunity to demonstrate their good will towards labour. If, as he expected, they proved
unwilling or unable to make the concessions demanded of them, he
would raise the standard of revolt. Thus, when north Ayrshire spurned
his advances in November 1887, he was immediately ready with his
reply. A middle-class candidate like Sir William, however radical, was
no candidate for a mining constituency. Let the Liberals test the
question by taking a plebiscite of their supporters and so ensure that
the Liberal candidate was the choice of the working people. [22]
While Hardie was thus squaring up for a fight at north Ayrshire, a
better opportunity to demonstrate his point arose at Mid-Lanark when
the resignation of the sitting Member occasioned a by-election. Hardie's
home town, Hamilton, was situated in the constituency, which

also contained the chief coal and iron centres of the county. In Larkhall, there was a well-organised miners' union which submitted Hardie's name to the Mid-Lanark Liberal Association in March 1888. Hardie knew from the outset that he had virtually no chance of obtaining the nomination. H.H. Champion, his ear close to well-informed sources at Westminster, informed Hardie that the Liberal Chief Whip wanted the seat for a nephew of Lord Aberdeen. On receipt of this intelligence, Hardie withdrew his name from the Liberal selection list and announced that he would run as a Labour and Home Rule candidate, unless the Liberals held a plebiscite of their voters.[23]

The Liberal Association, as it happened, wanted neither a miners' candidate nor a nominee of the Chief Whip, but a middle-class candidate of their own choosing, who would be able to finance his own candidature and be tinged with enough radicalism to suit their needs. After considering a number of possibilities among local men, but without finding an obvious candidate, they settled for a Welsh barrister, J.W. Philipps, then at the beginning of a long political career that was to lead eventually to high office.

The contest which ensued between Hardie and the Liberals provides many clues to the way in which he saw the relationship between labour, socialism and the Liberal party. The story has often been told, but, because historians have underestimated Hardie's commitment to socialism in 1887, the impression left is that Hardie was seeking only to apply pressure on the Liberal party in the name of labourism, rather than following through a principled strategy. [24] What we have to recognise is that Hardie stood, not as a miners' candidate simply, but as a representative of the Labour party, and that his programme included socialist demands. The fact that he appealed to mining interests and that he used a rhetoric as close as possible to that of radicalism should not blind us to these important new harbingers of the future.

Hardie presented himself as a representative of what he called 'the National Labour Party'.[25] This was a name which Champion had given to his breakaway branch of Threlfall's Labour Electoral Association. Hardie insisted that the Liberals must recognise the existence of a Labour party and its right to have its own candidates. He was not against an electoral arrangement between them: indeed, he already foresaw the possibility that serious Labour candidatures would lead to offers of Liberal concessions. Thus he told his followers that the Liberal Association:

may or may not select a candidate. In either case, my advice would be that a Labour candidate should be put forward. Better split the Party now, if there is to be a split, than at a general election, and, if the Labour Party only make their power felt now, terms will not be wanting when the general election comes. [26]

This statement is sometimes interpreted to mean that Hardie envisaged a reunion of the Liberal forces, but it is difficult to believe that Hardie intended it to carry that meaning. In his view, the Liberal party would be better split 'now' precisely in order to give the Labour party time to make its disposition for the general election. In that way, the Liberals would be facing a distinct and separate party, rather than last-minute dissidents; a party which could bargain realistically for the concession of some straight fights against the Conservatives.

As the manoeuvring proceeded, this priority of winning from the Liberals recognition of an organised Labour party with whom they must bargain assumed ever sharper clarity. He would not accept vague promises from national Liberal officials, who had shown often enough in the past that they could not control Liberal caucuses. Francis Schnadhorst, Secretary of the National Liberal Federation, came to Mid-Lanark to arbitrate between Hardie and Philipps. Hardie insisted that any bargain struck with Schnadhorst should be between the two parties. Liberals should recognise openly that the Labour party had a right to a straight fight with the Conservatives in specified Scottish constituencies at the next election. On these terms alone would he agree to withdraw. No such assurances were given, and a conference of Hardie's supporters urged him to go to the poll.[27]

This decision forced a breach with T.R. Threlfall, who had come north to help Hardie at the outset of the contest. Threlfall believed in trusting to the good will of Schnadhorst towards the Labour party, Hardie did not. So Threlfall packed up and left. With him went two radical MPs, C.A.V. Conybeare and A.L. Brown, who had also supp-orted Hardie at first. Later, Sir George Trevelyan came up from London to make one final effort to save the Liberals from the embarrassment of an open rupture with a Labour candidate. He offered Hardie a safe seat at the next election and a salary of three hundred pounds if he would withdraw. This offer put to the test Hardie's seriousness about recog-nition of the Labour party and he spurned it with contempt.[28]

The main emphasis in Hardie's programme was on the miners' collectivist demands: a legal eight-hour day, an insurance and super-annuation scheme, compulsory arbitration in industrial disputes by courts with power to fix a minimum wage and the establishment of a

Ministry of Mines. It is wrong, however, to say that he had no nationalisation to propose other than mineral royalties. The relevant sentence in
his published programme reads, 'nationalisation of royalties *and minerals*'.[29] Now the separation of 'minerals' from 'royalties' should be
read in the light of Hardie's mines' nationalisation proposals laid out in
his first report to the Scottish Miners' National Federation less than six
months previously. In this proposal the state would acquire minerals
and lease them to miners who would work the pits under schemes of
cooperative production. It was a form of nationalisation which
appealed to the independent traditions of the Scots collier.

However, Hardie was careful not to stress the socialist element in his
programme. He spoke at outdoor meetings in his strong, evangelical
style, using rhetoric which Liberal voters knew and understood. His
campaign was for freedom and democracy. The material and moral
elevation of the workers was essential as their foundation. There was
nothing in his programme that sincere Liberals need oppose. And, for
good measure, he added: 'On questions of general politics I would vote
with the Liberal Party to which I have all my life belonged.'[30]

This was no crude calculation of political opportunism, Hardie
sincerely believed that the pristine goals of Liberalism, freedom and
equality for every man under the constitution, were identical with the
goals of socialism. British socialists had long seen their economic
proposals as justified in terms of bringing about a new moral world.
But the Liberal party seemed unable to work towards these goals
because it was thwarted by great property interests, holding it bound
to the principles of freedom of contract and preventing it from enact-
ing those economic measures which would extend cooperation, enlarge
the economic functions of the whole community and foster the
Brotherwood of Man under the Fatherhood of God. As early as January
1888, he had written in the *Miner:*

> Two schools of politicians are now in process of formation or are,
> rather, being forced into existence by our action, the one individual-
> ist, decrying all State interference with freedom of contract in
> the matter of hours and wages, the other Socialistic, recognising
> Parliament as the servant of the people and the protector of the
> weak against the strong and desiring that the principles that have
> done so much for the crofter and the tenant farmer should also be
> applied to the miner.[31]

His election address at Mid-Lanark stated: 'Hitherto, there has been   a reluctance among all parties to interfere with freedom of contract between employer and employed . . . I would support such legislation as would temper the laws of political economy with humanitarian principles.'[32] Thus Hardie's socialism fitted into a pattern of long-term, collectivist amelioration of the conditions of labour, around which would need to be formed a coalition of all men of good will.

So far as programmes were concerned, Hardie's tactics in the contest were to show that he could give firm pledges on labour questions where his Liberal opponent could not. Philipps in reply sought to minimise the distance between them. He proved evasive, however, in face of carefully planted questions from Hardie's supporters in his audiences. He could not give a pledge to support nationalisation of mineral royalties. He could not support the demand for a wages court, because he was against state interference with wages. Only on the legal eight-hour day for miners would he give a straight commitment.[33]

The main Liberal counter-attack was to allege that Hardie was in the pay of Conservative agents who wanted to split the Liberal vote. He was known to be working in association with H.H. Champion, who had got money from the Conservative soap manufacturer, Hudson, for three SDF candidatures in 1885. The Liberal-Labour MP, W.R. Cremer, put it about Westminster that Hardie's funds came from similar sources.[34] This deterred radicals from helping Hardie by speaking for him, and soon the constituency was placarded with jingles in broad Scots denouncing Hardie as a Tory catspaw. One such gem, a parody of Burns, ran:

> There was a lad cam' north frae Kyle,
> In sic a queer, suspicious style,
> I think its fairly worth ma while,
> Tae waste a word on Hardie.

> Hardie is a roarin' boy,
> Ravin' roarin', ravin' roarin',
> Hardie is a roarin' boy,
> Ravin' roarin' Hardie.

> The Liberals keekit in his loof,
> Tae see if he was thorough-proof,
> Quo' they, 'A taltran Tory coof
> Is what we mak o' Hardie.'[35]

In truth, the sources of Hardie's expenses at Mid-Lanark have never been adequately clarified. Champion tried to throw the Liberal press off the scent by getting the socialist novelist, Margaret Harkness, to write to the press stating that she had contributed a hundred pounds. The Liberal papers were not so naive and pointed out that this still left about two hundred pounds of Hardie's published expenses unaccounted for. They would have been even more pressing had they known that Margaret Harkness had confided to her friend, Beatrice Potter, that her statement to the press was untrue and that she had contributed nothing.[36]

The outcome of the election was never in doubt. Hardie finished at the bottom of the poll with six hundred and seventeen votes. Philipps won comfortably, with three thousand eight hundred and forty-seven against two thousand nine hundred and sixteen for his Unionist opponent. One reason for Hardie's low poll was that the large Irish working-class vote in the constituency was thrown against him. Parnell turned deaf ears to the pleas of Michael Davitt and others that the Labour party should be supported by the Irish in Britain. One renegade branch of the Irish National League, the 'Home Government branch' of Glasgow, supported Hardie, but an influential Irish Catholic newspaper looked askance at the 'pack of atheists and socialists' who supported him. Hardie himself made matters worse by lying at a public meeting of Irishmen about his own approaches to the Home Government branch.[37]

But the Irish factor cannot of itself explain Hardie's poor showing. Their own leaders put the strength of the Irish vote at about one thousand three hundred. Hardie estimated that there were about six thousand working-class voters in the constituency, equally divided between coal-mining and iron-smelting. On those figures, there must have been considerable opposition to Hardie among the native Scots miners in Mid-Lanark.[38] No doubt some of this was from Unionists, but Hardie had to acknowledge opposition from Liberal miners in the constituency. The Tattie Strike had not been forgotten. Another noteworthy fact is the low turn-out of working-class voters. Assuming that most of the Unionist voters were middle class and that some of the Liberals were too, then the number of working-class votes must have been very small, especially if the Irish nationalist workers are assumed to have turned out loyally.

Thus Hardie was given a clear sign of the great difficulties of organising the working-class vote in the period of British politics before 1914. Only in a minority of constituencies in Britain was there anything that could be described as an organised working-class electorate. Complex registration provisions kept many working people off the electoral rolls. [39] Labour candidates could hope to do well only where they could build up a powerful electoral machine. In general, this was available only where there was strong trade union organisation and large, enthusiastic bands of voluntary workers. Given these conditions, labour might hope to wrest a few seats from the Liberals and force them to concede straight fights with the Conservatives, but, until a mass trade union movement could be created and electoral law still further democratised, the road to labour rule would be long and frustrating. In Scotland, no such mass trade union support was available and the Scottish Labour party could only have nuisance value.

III

It has been argued that Hardie's vision of a broad labour alliance of trade unions, socialists and other groups working for collectivist and radical measures and slowly evolving a socialist consciousness was a late development in his thinking. [40] The period 1893 to 1895 is then seen as a kind of wild flirtation with socialist extremism to be followed, between 1895 and 1906, by a quiet settling down into cooperation with trade unionists and progressivist radicals.

The establishment and early years of the Scottish Labour party, however, demonstrate that this was not the case. Hardie's actions in this sphere of politics from 1888 to 1894 reveal the same wariness of dogmatic socialist pronouncements such as would scare off collectivist radicals, the same cautious progress towards a completely separate and independent class politics, and the same desire to bargain with the Liberals from a position of strength which characterise the later period. The electoral failure of the Scottish Labour party has obscured this continuity, leading some historians to overlook Hardie's remarkable consistency of purpose and tactical flexibility in pursuing his aim. In addition, the years 1893 to 1895, which saw the peak of the popular socialist revival and of socialist influence in the TUC, aroused the exhilarating hope that a socialist labour alliance would come into existence fully-fledged. Hardie's aggressive socialism of these years was thus a temporary aberration, born of the vitality of the early Independent Labour Party. As that vitality ebbed, he reverted to the cautious approach which he had adopted in Scotland between 1888 and 1894.

Hardie's trimming to the socialist wind in the labour movement will be a major theme in the remainder of this account of his early years.

IV

The Scottish Labour party was formed at a conference in Glasgow in August 1888. Hardie acted as secretary during the preliminary preparations and prepared the draft constitution. Cunninghame Graham took the chair and was elected president of the party. The draft constitution envisaged a federal structure for the party, very similar to that adopted for the Labour Representation Committee in 1900, and the groups represented at the conference were drawn from a broad cross-section of dissidents from Liberalism. In addition to trade unions (among whom the miners were by far the most prominent), there were single taxers, land nationalisers, dissident Irish nationalists represented by John Ferguson, the Glasgow-Irish politician, and Dr G.B. Clarke, the crofters' leader.[41] Few socialists were present, while the official attitude of the SDF and of the Socialist League was intransigently sectarian.

The conference proceeded to draft a programme for the new party. Hardie had kept socialism completely out of the draft, confining himself to labourist reforms and a land tax. The representatives of the Scottish Land Restoration League succeeded in having this changed to land nationalisation. When, however, the socialists tried to commit the party to the nationalisation of all capital used in production Hardie diverted them with a promise that a later manifesto would make it clear that this was the party's ultimate aim. When the manifesto appeared, however, it made no such claim, but called upon the workers of Scotland to imitate the tactics of the Irish nationalists by forming a 'distinct, separate and independent Labour Party' which would 'give the other Parties no rest or peace until their demands are conceded'.[42]

Hardie was concerned to create the broadest possible consensus around the principle of independence from the Liberal party and a programme which served to ameliorate the conditions of the workers. He was just as concerned to attract middle-class radicals to the party as trade unionists: 'If anyone, peasant or peer, is found to adopt the programme and work with the Party, his help will be gladly accepted.'[43] The Labour party must begin and develop as an alliance of men of good will in all classes to promote the interests of labour against the idlers of society:

> Their Movement [he stated] was not in opposition to the middle classes of society. They were a useful class in the existing state of things and could not be dispensed with. Their interests were bound up together and they were to be found fighting side by side against the idlers of society.[44]

We might be tempted to conclude that this 'wily Scot', as Engels was later to call him, had reverted to his pre-1887 views. But these sentiments do not represent a reversion to radicalism. They are really all of a piece with Hardie's Christian socialism. He would always see socialism as coming about through the cooperation of the philanthropic among the middle classes and the respectable among the working class. He would always believe in a Labour party, composed of these elements, as the agitational force which would drive society towards socialism. The ultimate destiny of the Labour party, therefore, was to become a fully-fledged party of socialists and it could never be reabsorbed into the historic Liberal party. 'Liberalism is one thing', he pronounced in 1889, 'Socialism is quite another, and the new Labour Party is Socialistic. It is this which marks the dividing line and the outward and visible sign of it is the eight hour question.'[45]

Given the balance of forces in the Scottish Labour party, however, Hardie had to proceed warily in the matter of socialism. Not all those who supported the new party saw it as a permanent breakaway from the Liberal party. John Ferguson and the Henry Georgeites, such as Richard McGee and David McLardy, saw it as a base from which to permeate the Scottish Liberal Association. Few shared the view of H.H. Champion, who believed that they were engaged in a war to the death with the Liberal party. He argued that even Hardie's Mid-Lanark vote of six hundred and seventeen would be enough to damage the Liberals' chances of winning in several Scottish marginal seats and he urged an intransigent, aggresssive policy.[46] Between these two positions was a third, represented by Cunninghame Graham. Though probably opposed to the idea of reabsorption into the Liberal party, he hoped to win an early agreement from the Liberals to allow the Labour party a straight fight against the Conservatives in certain working-class constituencies. Hardie shared neither Graham's eagerness for an understanding nor Champion's intransigence. He wanted to build the Scottish Labour party into a realistic threat to the Liberals. He was ready to take advantage of any real concessions which that might produce, but he was deeply distrustful of the power of the Liberal party officials at national level to deliver the goods. The only safe policy towards the Liberals was a fighting one.

He therefore lost no time in making the political presence of the Scottish Labour party felt. In the summer of 1889, he was hard at work in a by-election in Ayr Burghs. Pushing aside T.R. Threlfall, who was prepared to offer the Liberal candidate unconditional support, Hardie led a deputation to interview the Liberal. This extracted from him a pledge to support key issues in the SLP programme and enabled the SLP to claim credit for the narrow Liberal majority of sixty-one.[47] A few weeks later, the intervention of the party in Greenock seemed to be equally effective. The local Liberal Association had invited James Hill, a lock manufacturer, to contest the seat at the general election. Hill was an outspoken critic of trade unions, accusing them of under-mining British industry in foreign competition. Hardie published Hill's anti-trade-union remarks in the *Greenock Press,* stirring up the Greenock Radical Association, a working-class body separately organised from the Liberal caucus, to oppose Hill's election. As a result Hill was not invited to contest the division.[48]

The Liberal party managers began to think about concessions to the new Labour party in Scotland. An opportunity arose during the Partick by-election in Glasgow in 1890. The Liberal majority at the general election had been only eight hundred. The SLP had some influence in the division in that one of its affiliates, an assembly of the Knights of Labor, was established there with a membership, it was claimed, of six hundred.[49] Cunninghame Graham, following a decision of the SLP executive, demanded that, in return for support at Partick, the Liberals should accept the Labour programme and give the SLP a free run in three Scottish constituencies at the next general election. This led to a meeting between Graham and the Liberal Whip in Scotland, Sir Edward Marjoribanks. Together, they arrived at an understanding which fore-shadowed the better-known entente between Ramsay MacDonald and Herbert Gladstone in 1903. Marjoribanks agreed that in Greenock and two other unspecified Scottish divisions Liberal headquarters would recommend to the local associations that there should be no Liberal opposition to candidates of the SLP, provided that the Labour cand-idates accepted the Liberal programme in all respects other than labour questions. He stressed, however, that the final decision must lie with the local Liberal associations in question. In return for these somewhat vague promises, the SLP was to instruct its followers in Partick to vote for the Liberal candidate.[50]

Hardie, who took no part in these negotiations, accepted them with great reluctance. The socialist laird was hoping to bluff the Liberals by marching a stage army into every marginal constituency in Scotland. Hardie was never averse to bargaining with the Liberals, but wanted to postpone it until they were strong enough to extract real concessions. He put no faith in Marjoribanks's ability to control the local caucuses:

I confess [he wrote to a member of the SLP] that I do not put much store on them other than they are an official recognition of our existence . . . Mr Marjoriebanks and the wire-pullers generally will require some strict looking after . . . Of course, I will loyally abide by the terms of the agreement entered into by Mr Graham and Mr Marjoriebanks, but I confess I do so with a feeling of reluctance.[51]

Hardie was undoubtedly right to distrust these Liberal promises. The hostility of the local Liberal associations to Labour candidatures had been demonstrated at Mid-Lanark and subsequently in a by-election at West Fife in 1889, when John Weir, the miners' union secretary, had been manoeuvred out of the selection process.[52] Hardie had then insisted that the lesson to be drawn was that Labour must compel the Liberals to fall back by building up its strength. He was right, too, about SLP weakness. The Liberals lost Partick—a clear demonstration to them that SLP strength was not yet worth bargaining about. The constituencies mentioned in connection with the Graham-Marjoriebanks negotiations hastened to repudiate the agreement once the Partick result was known.[53]

The crucial weakness of the SLP lay in its failure to obtain a trade union base in Scotland. In England, 'New Unionism' was carried forward on a wave swelled by the successful London Dock Strike of 1889. In Scotland, 'New Unionism' had no such success. The Scottish miners had gone down to defeat in 1887. A seamen's strike in Scotland, which preceded the London Dock Strike in 1889 and was much larger in size, seemed for a time to offer the SLP leaders agitational possibilities. Hardie and Graham, addressing a strike meeting at Leith, called for sympathetic action in support of the seamen by Glasgow dockers and Scottish miners.[54] Their militancy backfired by provoking a violent outbreak of quarrelling between Scottish labour leaders. Richard McGee, land radical and leader of the Glasgow dockers, and Henry Tait, secretary of the Scottish Railway Servants, both opposed independent labour politics and quickly denounced Graham and Hardie for intervening in the seamen's strike. The opposition of the Railway Servants led Glasgow Trades Council to reject a motion in favour of affiliating to the Scottish Labour party. Other trades councils followed suit.[55] Worse still, a sharp personal rivalry surfaced between Hardie and some of the other miners' leaders. Hardie was jealous of a move by the Lanarkshire miners to have William Small appointed as a member of the Royal Commission on Royalties in 1890 and there was also bad blood between him and the Stirlingshire miners' leader, Chisholm Robertson. Robertson, a self-important political adventurer, could brook no rival in Scottish labour politics. He had taken a leading part in 'New Unionism' among Glasgow dockers and tramwaymen and bitterly resented Hardie's intrusion into the seamen's strike. At a miners' conference in Glasgow, he vehemently denounced Hardie for neglecting the affairs of the Scottish miners by running after the seamen and Hardie was expelled from the conference.[56] Later that year, when Hardie renewed his attack on Henry Broadhurst at the TUC in Dundee, Robertson tried to perform a character-assassination on him by alleging that he had his printing done in non-union shops.[57]

The weakness of the Scottish Labour party's trade union base robbed it of any serious power to threaten the Liberals. As a result, its pro-Liberal elements drifted towards the Liberal party as the general election approached. Ferguson had to be expelled for his public support of the Liberal party. These pro-Liberal tendencies alarmed Champion, who now began to distrust Hardie's credentials as a determined anti-Liberal. They quarrelled in 1889 over the treatment of pro-Liberal trade unionists in Champion's paper, the *Labour Elector,* and Champion now encouraged Chisholm Robertson to set up a breakaway Labour party in Scotland, based on the trades councils of the east coast cities, whose branches of the SLP tended to resent Glasgow domination.[58] By the time the Scottish Labour party went to the polls in the general election of 1892 therefore, it was hopelessly weak and divided and made a very poor showing.[59]

Nevertheless, the foundation of the Scottish Labour party deserves detailed study in any biography of Hardie. It demonstrates the underlying consistency of his view of the relationship between labourism, socialism and Liberalism. He hoped to build up support for a Labour party to a point at which the Liberals would be forced to concede the right to a straight fight with the Conservatives in working-class constituencies. The party would be built up as a broad alliance of trade unions, radicals and socialists and would move only slowly towards accepting socialism as its ultimate objective. This new consciousness would develop out of the experience of struggle with the Liberal party for labour demands and not from the instillation of socialist dogma. Nevertheless there could and would be no reabsorption into Liberalism. This perspective stemmed from his understanding of socialism, which he interpreted to mean the rise of a class-conscious party of organised labour, seeking to mould society after its own image and interests.

Before 1890, there were few socialists in Scotland and these mostly held aloof from the SLP in sectarian isolation. On the international plane, however, Hardie was extending his contact with socialists. He was drawn towards international socialist politics by his experience as a miner. It had made him sharply aware of the international character of capitalist competition. A coal strike or restriction in one country brought orders flooding in from others. Sometimes also it brought foreign blacklegs. In 1887, for example, the Glengarnock Iron Company had brought about twenty Lithuanian Poles into Ayrshire to work as coal-miners. Hardie had seen this as a direct threat to the new Ayrshire Miners' Union and had conducted a virulently xenophobic campaign against the immigrants during the next two years. He accused them of undermining the wages of Scottish miners by being prepared to live on garlic, fried in oil which they filched from street lamps. He alleged that they had brought 'Black Death' and 'immorality' to Scotland and stated downrightly that 'decent men are not going to be turned adrift to make room for beastly, filthy foreigners without knowing the reason why.' He joined Glasgow Trades Council in protesting about Jewish and other immigrant labour and appeared before a Select Committee of the House of Commons to demand control of immigration.[60]

Too much easy sentimentality has been written about Hardie's internationalism stemming from his deep commitment to the brotherhood of man. It fails to see the ideological character of such sentiments and their roots in basic trade union interests. He gradually learnt to moderate his xenophobia and to drop his demand for immigration control as the socialists taught him to look to international labour solidarity to create uniform conditions of labour in all lands, thus making migration by workers unnecessary. Engels and the German social democrats were leading a campaign for international socialist action on the legal eight-hour day, backed by a world-wide stoppage of work on the first of May. Hardie was strongly attracted to the advantages of an international eight-hour day for miners and willingly joined the social democrats in their campaign. In 1888, he strongly attacked British trade union leaders for trying to exclude delegates of Continental socialist organisations from the international conference to be held that year in London. He attended the conference personally and was lavish in his praise of the socialist delegates. He was especially impressed by the French delegates' singing of 'La Carmagnole':

As they stood in a group and made the rafters ring with their sound and the blood tingle with their earnest gestures, I thought of Carlyle's 'Carmagnole Complète' and of Robert Burns drunk, singing 'Ça-Ira' in a theatre in Dumfries, while the rest of the audience cried 'Shame Burns!'

He was beginning to see advantages in not always appearing respectable. He had appreciative words, too, for the London socialists at the conference, Annie Besant, John Burns and Tom Mann: 'Certainly these Socialists know what they are about. They have made up their minds as to what they want and mean to have it.'

Hardie, as so often, managed to appear both practical and futuristic at the same time during this conference. He put forward a resolution calling for the international organisation of all trades and their further linking into a general international confederation. He had very down-to-earth labour goals in mind, but he did not hesitate to connect them with the new gospel of socialism: 'the conference is over . . . Socialism is in the ascendant and everyone knows it. . .Henceforth there can be no more alienation between British and Continental workers. The Broadhurst school has now Hobson's choice facing them—accept the new Gospel or go down before those who will.[61]

Hardie's internationalism always remained rooted in a strong sense of the separate identity and distinctive value of national countries. As his sense of the possibilities of labour cooperation grew, he looked to the different national labour movements to attain power in their own ways and at their own pace, according to different national conditions. In some European countries such as Belgium and Russia, he believed the autocracy of governments would force the socialists to violence by denying popular liberties. In Britain, however, he believed the rise of labour would be peaceful and constitutional, except for isolated incidents when reactionary forces tried to deny basic freedoms such as the right to strike or vote. But the different national labour movements, while each developing at their own pace, would coordinate their demands for common conditions of labour in all civilised countries. He became a strong supporter of the movement for a universal May Day agitation for the legal eight-hour day, and in a miners' international conference in 1890, he called for a miners' strike throughout Europe to win their eight-hour day by legal enactment.[62] Such calls were intended, however, as propaganda rather than as serious policy proposals. They were agitational devices for focusing European public opinion on the issues. Hardie knew that international labour organisation was far from sufficiently well developed to take such a step and he always looked to legislation by national governments as the way to standardise labour laws.

Hardie's internationalism, therefore, stemmed from belief in the value of cooperation between national labour movements and not from either a deep sentiment in favour of the brotherhood of man or from the doctrine that the workers have no country. Far from the workers having no country, he believed strongly that British workers, and their kinsmen in other Anglo-Saxon countries—the United States as well as the colonies—had a unique role to play in extending freedom and civilisation. He did not want to see the British Empire dissolve and the colonial peoples left free to determine their own international roles. Born within a stone's throw of the birthplace of David Livingstone at Blantyre, he shared much of his fellow-Congregationalist's confidence in the civilising mission of the Anglo-Saxons. In 1893, he told a meeting in West Ham that:

> he recognised the fact that the indomitable pluck and energy of the British people had carried the British flag all over the globe and promised to make the British Empire the one great power that would mould the affairs of the world. He thought it was only right that it should be so. If there must be a dominant race in the world's affairs, the safety of weak and struggling peoples could better be entrusted to the British Democracy than to the White Tsar of the North, whose aim was the repression of freedom and the beating back of the current of Democratic feeling.[63]

He was an advocate at this time of imperial federation, which he wrote into the constitution of the Scottish Labour Party in 1888. He wanted Home Rule for every country in the Empire, with representatives of all of them sitting in an imperial Parliament in London.[64]

The root of Hardie's sentiment for the Empire lay in his experience as a miner. All over the colonies of white settlement, in South Africa, in Australia and Canada, he had boyhood friends working in mines and making names for themselves in colonial labour movements. He never went on foreign tours as an international labour leader in later life without making contact with them and his reports to the Labour press back home were always full of detailed facts about the conditions of mining. Like many another lad o' parts in the Scottish mining communities, he had grown up to think of the colonies as fields of endeavour for British labour. In later life, he looked to the British inspiration in the colonial labour movements to bring benign rule to the coloured peoples of the Empire. Labour rule would preserve what he liked to think of as the dignity and simplicity of their pre-industrial way of life, while raising them gradually into democratic practices. In India, he believed, the work had already begun and he was a supporter of the Congress Movement in 1893.[65]

While Hardie was thus widening his international interests, another general election was approaching. The Scottish Labour party seemed to be in disarray and the possibility of developing Alexander McDonald's work seemed to be slipping away. Just as his predecessor had had to look to England for a route of entry into the House of Commons, so Hardie found it necessary to turn his back on Scotland and take advantage of his London contacts. In 1890 he was invited to come forward as a candidate in the East End constituency of West Ham South.

Notes

1. Engels to Sorge, 18 January 1893, reprinted in *Marx-Engels On Britain* (Moscow, 1962), p.579.
2. Lowe, *From Pit to Parliament*, p.76.
3. Morgan, *Keir Hardie*, pp.32ff.
4. McLean, *Keir Hardie*, pp. 25-44.
5. *Ardrossan and Saltcoats Herald*, 24 June 1887.
6. *Miner*, July 1887.
7. P. Smith, *Disraelian Convervatism and Social Reform* (1967), p.150.
8. *Trades Union Congress, 1887, Report of Proceedings*, p.32.
9. Ibid., p.34.
10. *Common Sense*, 15 September 1887; for report of the conference, see *T.U.C., 1887, Proc.*, pp. 34ff.
11. Ibid., p.25.
12. Quoted from *Swansea Herald* in *Ardrossan and Saltcoats Herald*, 23 September 1887.
13. *T.U.C., 1887, Proc.*, p.29.
14. Ibid.
15. Diary Fragment, 6 January 1884.
16. *Ardrossan and Saltcoats Herald*, 18 February 1887.
17. A.F. Tschiffely, *Don Roberto* (1937), *passim.*
18. *Ardrossan and Saltcoats Herald*, 13 May 1887.
19. Ibid.
20. Ibid., 2 September, 11 November 1887; *Miner*, November 1887.
21. Ibid., 15 July 1887; *Commonweal*, 22 October 1887.
22. Ibid.
23. Champion to Hardie, 16 March 1888. Mid-Lanark Corr.
24. Pelling, *Origins of the Labour Party*, pp. 65ff; Morgan, *Keir Hardie*, pp. 23ff; McLean, *Keir Hardie*, p.25.
25. *Scottish Leader*, 18 April 1888.
26. *Miner*, March 1888.
27. For an account of the negotiations see John Ferguson's letter in *Glasgow Observer*, 21 April 1888; for Hardie's terms see *North British Daily Mail*, 29 June 1888; also Conybeare to Graham, 20 April 1888. Mid-Lanark Corr.
28. Our only account of Hardie's part is in his late recollection in *Labour Leader*, 14 March 1913.
29. *Miner*, April 1888; my italics.
30. Ibid.

31. *Miner,* January 1888.
32. Ibid., April 1888.
33. *Scottish Leader,* 5 April 1888.
34. Conybeare to Graham, 20 April 1888. Mid-Lanark Corr.
35. Photocopy in Transport House Library.
36. *North British Daily Mail,* 28 June 1888 for Harkness' letter. See Harford to Hardie, telegram, 13 April 1888, for Champion's contribution. Beatrice Webb, Diary 13 Nov. 1889. (I am indebted to Professor R. Harrison for this reference.)
37. *Glasgow Observer,* 3-14 April 1888; Hardie to Secretary of the Home Government Branch, 24 March and 8 April 1888. Nat. Lib. Scot., acc. 504, mss. 1809/71/2.
38. See *Scottish Leader,* 17 March 1888 for size of Irish vote; see *Miner,* March 1888, for Hardie's estimate of the working-class vote; cf. *Miner,* May 1888.
39. N. Blewett, 'The Franchise in the United Kingdom, 1885-1918', *Past and Present,* 32, 1965, pp.27-56.
40. Morgan, *Keir Hardie,* p.83.
41. *Miner,* September 1888. For draft constitution see ibid., June 1888.
42. Hardie, 'The Pioneer of the I.L.P.', *Socialist Review,* 1914.
43. *Miner,* September 1888.
44. *Scottish Leader,* 18 April 1888.
45. *Labour Leader,* May 1889.
46. Address to the Hamilton Labour Association, n.d.(April 1888?). Mid-Lanark Corr.
47. For accounts of the by-election see *Labour Leader, Labour Elector, Scottish Leader, Ardrossan and Saltcoats Herald,* May-July 1889.
48. *Greenock Telegraph,* 25 July, 1 August, 4 September 1888.
49. *Glasgow Herald,* 21 January 1890; also 27 January 1890.
50. Ibid.
51. Ibid., 3 February 1890.
52. *Scotsman,* 17-20 June 1889; *Labour Leader,* July 1889.
53. *Greenock Telegraph,* 18 February, 14 March 1890.
54. *Scotsman,* 3 June 1889; *Labour Leader,* July 1889.
55. Ibid., June-July 1889; Glasgow Trades Council Minutes, 6-12 June 1889.
56. *North British Daily Mail,* 11, 21 June 1889; *Labour Leader,* May 1889.
57. *T.U.C., 1889, Proc.,* p.23; *Labour Leader,* March, May 1889.
58. *Workman's Times,* 19 March 1892; *Aberdeen Free Press,* 17 March 1892.
59. J.G. Kellas, 'The Mid-Lanark By-Election (1888) and the Scottish Labour Party (1888-95)', *Parliamentary Affairs,* XVIII, 1965, pp.318-29.
60. *Miner,* December 1887; *Ardrossan and Saltcoats Herald,* 18 November 1887; *S.C. on Emigration and Immigration, P.P.,* 1889, X, pp.1409-10, 1419.
61. *Miner,* November 1888.
62. *Ardrossan and Saltcoats Herald,* 13 July 1890; cf. R.P. Arnot, *The Miners,* I, (1949), pp.154ff.
63. *West Ham Herald,* 4 March 1893.
64. *Miner,* September 1888; *Workman's Times,* 3 June 1893, quoting Hardie in *Nottingham Express.*
65. *Labour Leader,* February 1893.

6 FROM WEST HAM TO BRADFORD: THE FOUNDATION OF THE ILP

I

In the years after the Home Rule split in the Liberal party, its managers adopted a policy of showing sympathy towards Labour canditates and Labour aspirations. They encouraged the new progressivism in London County Council politics. The progressives were a broad coalition of radical business and professional men, municipal reformers, Fabian socialists and labour leaders. Their policies were collectivist rather than socialist and they treated organised labour very much as the junior partner in the alliance. They played an important part in the shaping of the famous 'Newcastle Programme', in which, in 1891, the Liberal party wooed labour support by promising state payment of MPs and limitation of the working hours of miners at the end of a long list of traditional radical reforms. It was a far cry from the kind of programme that would have allayed the opposition of labour dissidents like Hardie, yet, until 1892, it must have seemed that the progressive formula would work in constituencies like West Ham South.

The Liberals had lost the constituency in 1886 with a Liberal-Labour candidate, Joseph Leicester of the Glass Bottle Makers' Society, and they then brought forward a new candidate, J. Hume Webster, a wealthy accountant and City financier. He was typical of the kind of progressive businessman then favoured by the party managers for London working-class consituencies. His wealth enabled him to patronise working-men's clubs and to pay canvassers to go round and see that working-class voters were registered. His attitude towards the 'New Unionism', strong among the dockers and gas workers of West Ham, was sympathetic. He contributed to the dockers' strike fund in 1889 and supported the Gas Workers' Union in their demand for an eight-hour day.[1] Those who knew the constituency intimately, however, knew that matters were not entirely plain sailing for Hume Webster. There was much local feeling against him as an alien intruder from his City office. Local businessmen resented his carpetbagging and his 'hanging on the skirts of the strike leaders'.[2] Such suspicion of the combined power of progressivist finance and 'New Unionism' was not confined to the old-style Liberal shopocracy in the constituency. It was shared by the active group of Henry Georgeite land reformers. One of them, Dr John Moir, had written to the press, attacking the militancy of the Dock Strike, condemning socialism and advocating industrial conciliation.[13] Hume Webster was also distrusted by the well-organised temperance lobby, because he would not explicitly support their demands. Temperance was strong in the Nonconformist churches of the district. These, in turn, were being permeated by young activists in the University Settlement at Mansfield House. To this Congregationalist settlement came young men filled with the new 'Social Gospel' of the Nonconformist churches. Like the temperance movement, they wanted to moralise the working class, though they stressed a rather more positive approach by offering wider opportunities for improving leisure rather than a negative condemnation of drinking.

The Irish were normally a power to be reckoned with in the constituency, but in 1890 they were in disarray because of the Parnell divorce case, so that their influence was little felt until after Hardie's election in 1892. Finally, the local trade union leaders, though apparently willing, for the moment, to accept Hume Webster's patronage, aspired to greater representation on the borough council. Under the tactful leadership of Will Thorne, General Secretary of the Gas Workers' Union and a member of the SDF, they achieved their first successes, in November 1890. The way was thus open for a Labour candidate, but there was no obvious choice from among the local men. Thorne, the ablest of them, was unacceptable as a member of the SDF, both to old-style radicals and to the Henry Georgeites. When, therefore, the name of Keir Hardie was mentioned to Dr Moir by Cunninghame Graham,[4] it seemed that he might be just the 'strict' Labour candidate they were looking for. Mid-Lanark had given him a reputation as a fighter against the caucus. His TUC appearances had identified him with the new Labour programme. On the other hand, he was not identified with any socialist sect and, as an outsider, could appeal to all factions in the constituency.

Hardie set out to weld his disparate supporters into a united coalition with considerable tact and not a little opportunism. He appealed first for support to the Mansfield House men, emphasising his former role in the temperance movement. His first public statement called for 'the creation of institutions to relieve the working men from the debasing and demoralising influence of the public house'.[5] He enjoyed from the outset the support of Will Thorne, who rejected the sectarian view of *Justice* that Hardie was a 'tool of the SDF—renegade and Tory intriguer, H.H. Champion'. Thorne understood the importance of building trade union solidarity around an accepted Labour candidate and fell in discreetly behind Moir in support of the newcomer.[6] Throughout 1891, Hardie nursed the constituency assiduously, addressing many meetings and urging his view that a distinct Labour party should be formed in Parliament. Canning Town branch of the SDF gave loyal support, while Ben Tillett, the leader of the Dockers' Union, also spoke for him. Labour solidarity advanced during the year and Thorne, who was returned to the borough council at the top of the poll in 1891, immediately set about organising a Labour bench on the council to get fair wages clauses written into municipal contracts. Some of the trade union councillors who had been supporting Hume Webster now found that Liberal councillors opposed their demands, decried independent labourism and made a dead set at Thorne and Hardie.

Matters thus seemed set for a Labour—Progressive quarrel at West Ham South when, in January 1892, Hardie had the greatest stroke of luck of his life. Hume Webster was found dead in his deer park, having taken his own life. This threw the caucus into disarray. The majority wished to go on opposing Hardie, but Alderman Phillips, secretary of the local railwaymen's union, broke away, urging that Hardie should be supported as the only candidate who could beat the Conservatives.[7] Phillips had been the last important trade unionist in the Liberal-labour camp. Hardie was now in a position to isolate the anti-socialists in the caucus. The key to this move was the temperance lobby and Hardie now strained every nerve to assure them of his temperance convictions. Direct veto of the liquor traffic was placed at the head of his programme for the election. A local Nonconformist minister, Rev. Tom Warren, active in the Mansfield House Settlement, declared Hardie to be a man of religious sympathies with pronounced views on the temperance question. The local temperance newspaper, the *West Ham Herald,* became his warm supporter and remained so as long as he held the seat. Dr. Morison, founder of the Evangelical Union, sent a testimonial on the purity of his moral character. The Council of Nonconformist Churches in the constituency finally passed a flattering resolution of support, referring to Hardie as 'the candidate most admirably suited, both in character and in principles to represent the cause of national righteousness in the Imperial Parliament'.

Confronted by this impressive show of strength, the Websterites made a last desperate attempt to spike Hardie's guns, by bringing forward Joseph Leicester, the Glass Bottle Maker of 1886. But it was too late to stem the tide as the West Ham and District Temperance League swung in behind the Nonconformist Council in support of

Hardie.[8]

Assured of the support of the temperance lobby, Hardie could claim with justice that he was the candidate of the United Liberal, Radical and Labour party of South West Ham. It would clearly be ludicrous for the Liberal party of the Newcastle Programme to oppose such a candidate and the rump of the local caucus could be ignored as typical reactionaries swimming against the progressive tide. As things turned out, even this rump was shepherded into Hardie's fold by Francis Schnadhorst, who seems to have decided to gain what credit he could for Hardie's approaching victory. He met Hardie in the constituency and offered any help he needed. Hardie's blunt reply was, 'Keep out and leave us to fight the battle', but this did not prevent Schnadhorst from working behind the scenes for the withdrawal of Joseph Leicester. This made it possible for the Irish National League to throw its support behind Hardie. On nomination day, his papers carried the signature of the leading member of the Leicester faction.[9]

In the run-up to polling day, Hardie's campaign was vigorous. He opened committee rooms all over the constituency and was indefatigable in outdoor speaking, making three or more appearances each evening and getting up before six to speak again at the dock gates. Colour was given to his campaign by the enthusiasm and insignia of the 'New Unions': 'The platform was a full-sized lifeboat, rigged with mast and ropes and gay with streamers and manned by a crew in uniform. I understand it came from the Tidal Basin Branch of the Seamen's and Firemen's Union'.[10] At midday, there would be more great meetings at the gas works and the whole campaign reached its climax in a series of mass demonstrations on the Saturdays preceding the poll. They were said to be the biggest political meetings ever seen in the constituency, representing every possible interest, 'trade, political, Temperance, friendly, Band of Hope, street urchins, unemployed'. [11]

In truth, working-class people were more involved in politics in West Ham South than ever before. They queued outside Hardie's campaign rooms to work for him as volunteer canvassers.

The poll gave a comfortable victory to Hardie by five thousand two hundred and six votes to four thousand and thirty-six for his Conservative opponent, Major Baines. The heavy poll was due in part to the professional registration work done under Hume Webster, and also in part to the enthusiasm generated by Hardie's campaign. Ordinary people in West Ham felt at last that this was their MP, their spokesman. They carried him shoulder high before a wildly cheering procession, headed by a band, from the Town Hall to the Labour committee rooms.

II

Hardie's conciliatory attitude to the radicals in West Ham South gave rise to misunderstandings. The Liberal party treated him as a supporter of Gladstone and displayed his victory in lights at party headquarters as one of their own. In fact, Hardie had never intended to be anything other than an independent Labour Member. 'My first concern', his election address stated, 'is the moral and material welfare of the working classes, and if returned, I will in every case place the claims of Labour above those of Party.' [12] Indeed, he could congratulate himself on the working out of his basic strategy at West Ham. He had success-fully linked trade unions, radicals and socialists in one coalition and he had forced anti-labour Liberals to accept him as the opponent of the Conservatives with a minimum of concessions. It is sometimes supposed that he did this by leaving socialism out of account and campaigning exclusively on labour and radical issues,[13] but this is inaccurate. As the campaign proceeded, socialism assumed an increasingly prominent place in his pronouncements.

His first manifesto to the constituency in 1890 made no mention of it. He was then making his appeal to small, dissident factions of radicals and Henry Georgeites who were very suspicious of socialism. His programme then demanded shorter hours of labour, Home Rule for Ireland and the Empire, the usual list of political reforms, and the 'resolution of the land question on the lines proposed by Henry George'.[14] His official election manifesto, however, issued shortly before the poll and after he had deve-loped massive trade union support, made quite explicit the link he had always maintained between labourism and socialism. It called for nation-alisation or municipalisation of land, banks, mines, railways, docks, waterways and tramways.[15]

This manifesto suggests that Hardie had been taking socialism even more seriously since coming to London, and it is significant that it was Fabian socialism which provided theoretical clothing for some of his ideas. He joined the Society at this time,[16] and found *Fabian Essays* published in 1889 congenial to his own class-collaborative Christian socialism. It propounded that all monopolies should be nationalised and that unearned income stemmed, in the main, from the monopoly of superior land or site values. It seemed to account for the oligopolistic scale and structure in some industries such as mining and transport. It made political collaboration between labour and middle-class radicals easier by implying that there were many different categories of 'rent' or unearned income, of which the capitalist's profit was but one form, and which could be appropriated to the community gradually. Landlords, rural and urban, might have their rents appropriated first, through heavy taxation, followed by stockbrokers and other rentiers, while the profits of manufacture might be left undisturbed at any rate for a time. Hardie's election address of 1892 displays this Fabian influence. The contest at West Ham was said to be between 'honest industry' and 'useless idlers. . .the absentee landlord, the sweating shareholder, or the gambling and sweating stockbroker'.[17]

Fabian socialism made a strong appeal in the 1890s to working-class dissidents from Liberalism like Hardie. It was more congenial to them than the violent revolutionary bluster of Hyndman and *Justice.* It stressed gradualism, parliamentarism and a consensus across classes. It also implied the need for a moral regeneration through which mankind would overcome selfish instincts and become fit to govern the new economic and technical forces of industrialism.[18]

If, however, the London Fabian Society offered Hardie theoretical confirmation of his most basic political instincts, it deeply disappointed him in its failure to support the growing demand for an independent Labour party. Hardie was present at the 1891 conference of provincial Fabian societies held in London, which heard Bernard Shaw brilliantly expound the London Fabian view that the demand for such a new party, while not to be ruled out in principle, was premature. Shaw's arguments, though intelligible in the context of London, were less applicable in Lancashire and Yorkshire, where Liberals were still bitterly hostile to independent labour candidates. As a result of the negative conclusions of the London Fabians, many of the provincial societies struck out during 1891 on their own course of labour politics. Most notably, the Manchester Fabian Society formed itself into an Independent Labour party and obtained the formidable support of the rising star of socialist journalism, Robert Blatchford. Blatchford had just launched his new paper, the *Clarion,* there. In West Yorkshire, similar moves were afoot in Bradford, where the Labour Union also turned itself into an Independent Labour party. Here also rose another journalistic endeavour, Joseph Burgess's *Workman's Times.* Burgess transferred his editorial office to London in 1891 and in 1892 began to enrol recruits for what he called the National Independent Labour party, though no such organisation then existed.

Meanwhile, in the TUC, the explosion of 'New Unionism' brought a great accretion of strength to the socialist forces. In 1890, the Congress

voted, for the first time, in favour of the legal eight-hour day. Plans
were laid by the socialists and 'New Unionists' to capture the Parliamentary Committee and to commit the Congress to the financing of its
own Labour party. In 1892, the Parliamentary Committee was
instructed to prepare a scheme for financing Labour candidates and in
1893 it laid before Congress a plan for running fifty Labour candidates
at the next election.

It seemed to Hardie that the conditions were ripening for the
creation of the Labour party he had envisaged since 1887, independent,
evolving in a socialist direction, flexible in its relations with other
parties and groups. He determined to use his newly-won position in
Parliament to demonstrate by example the meaning of labour's independence. The hour seemed to have struck for labour's Carlylean hero
to emerge from the shadows of obscurity and usher in the new age by
the compelling force of his mighty deeds. Again and again in those years
he urged the need for a great leader. In 1892 he was preparing the way
for his own coming by pointing to the glaring gap in the forefront of
the labour advance: 'We have no venerable personality around whom
we can rally. Nor have we any kingly man whose presence inspires
respect and commands obedience . . .I have read history in vain if
any great Movement ever reached fruition which had not a person for
its centre.'[19]

The years 1892 to 1895 were to show that Hardie was over-
optimistic about the imminence of a trade union backed Labour party.
The voting strength of independent labourism and socialism was unduly
inflated in the TUC by a number of purely temporary factors. The
miners had worked in alliance with the 'New Unionists' to secure the
vote on the legal eight-hour day, but they were far from committed to
the idea of an independent Labour party. Trades councils, their ranks
swelled by 'New Unionism', were separately represented in the Congress
and, since their delegates were usually of the new party, they
duplicated many of the independent votes. Finally, the 'New Unionism'
itself was to be checked in its growth by employers' counter-attack and
economic depression in the years 1893 to 1895. It was made clear that
no dramatic underlying shift had taken place in the balance of power in
the TUC in 1893, when the new men not only failed to win a majority
on the Parliamentary Committee, but failed to get Hardie elected as its
secretary because the English miners would not have him at any price.

As the hopes of bringing into being a trade-union backed labour
alliance faded in 1893 and 1894, Hardie shifted his emphasis to the
creation of a new vanguard party of committed socialists who favoured

its creation. Previously, he had not felt any need to give formal cohesion to those socialists who believed in a broad, undogmatic Labour party, but as the work of converting the trade unions proved more difficult than anticipated, the ILP gradually altered in his conception from the framework of a labour alliance into the vanguard corps of the labour army.

III

The growing desire for an independent Labour party in 1891 and 1892 enabled Hardie to develop further his idea of a Labour party that would replace the historic Liberal party. No one was more boldly imaginative about the possibilities of labour politics. The election of 1892 had seen the return of John Burns and J.H. Wilson who, like himself, had won their seats in three-cornered contests. Hardie argued that they should work together to form the nucleus of a Labour party in Parliament and to increase pressure on the Liberals to redeem their promises about social legislation. He told a *Daily Chronicle* interviewer on the morrow of his election:

> I hope that we shall soon see the beginning of a new and thoroughly independent Labour Party in the House of Commons. We may be few at first, but we shall attract to us a large number of the new Radicals who have shaken themselves free from *laissez-faire* Liberalism. [20]

This was the Labour alliance strategy of grouping all the collectivist forces around organised labour, but Hardie now drew out the socialist implication that the aim of a Labour party was not just to win this or that measure, but to rule. He invited John Burns publicly to sit with him on the Opposition side of the House and he spelled out the implications of doing so in a speech in his constituency: 'As I understand it, it is a fundamental part of Labour Party policy to remain in opposition (cheers) until the time comes when the Party is able to cross the floor of the House of Commons and form a Labour Government.'[21]

At the same time, he was ready and willing to cooperate with radicals in putting pressure on the Liberal party. He argued that the Labour party should ascertain, in constituencies where it was not strong enough to run its own candidate, which of the two parties would go furthest with its programme and give its support to that candidate. As secretary of the Scottish Labour party, he hailed the rejection, in March 1893, of a Liberal candidate in Banff who was unacceptable to the Labour party there and warmly welcomed the adoption of the radical, Sir William Wedderburn: 'Next to a Labour candidate, Sir William is one of the very best that could be had. So satisfactory was his position to the Labour Party in Ayrshire at last election that everything possible was done by them to secure his return.'[22]

Hardie envisaged from the earliest moment, that the Liberals would offer concessions to a rising Labour party and he was always ready to combine the highest aspirations for labour with a policy of taking advantage of such concessions. It was not a strategy he had to learn after 1895, but one which was implicit in his politics from the beginning of 1887.

This point needs to be emphasised if we are to understand the unpleasant bitterness of the breach between H.H. Champion and Hardie, which took place in 1892 to 1893, and the ferocity of the quarrel with Robert Blatchford over the 'fourth clause' in the constitution of the ILP in 1893 and 1894. With Champion, relations had cooled off shortly after the formation of the Scottish Labour party. Hardie's paper, the *Labour Leader,* which he had brought out in 1889 in succession to the *Miner,* had been merged with Champion's *Labour Elector.* Champion's paper shortly afterwards failed, amidst acrimonious recriminations on the editorial board, which included Hardie. Champion went off to Australia, where he was involved in further labour controversies. Returning to England in 1891, he obtained a post as assistant-editor on the *Nineteenth Century* and threw himself back into independent labour politics. He seems to have become increasingly dependent for his political funds on Conservatives, who saw independent Labour candidates as a way of making trouble for the Liberal party. His old associate, J. Maltman Barry, acted as go-between in raising these funds, and in the run-up to the 1892 election Champion had given donations of one hundred pounds each to Hardie and two other independent Labour candidates. The contributions were paid, apparently anonymously, through the *Workman's Times.*

As an ex-Conservative, Champion nursed an irreconcilable hatred of the Liberal party and he was determined to use his influence to prevent any understanding, tacit or overt, between the emerging independent Labour party and the Liberals. It was inevitable, therefore, that he should come into conflict with Hardie, who believed that such understandings were desirable, and throughout 1893 the two were engaged in a desperate struggle, at first private and finally public, in which the aim of each was to drive the other into a position of political impotence.

Hardie held a master card in this power game as a Member of Parliament, but Champion held a number of strong cards too. It was widely known, for instance, that Hardie had taken money from Champion during the Mid-Lanark contest and after. But Champion's main strength lay in the fact that it was impossible for Hardie to explain openly the grounds of his quarrel with Champion. That would have aroused the antagonism of many leaders of the new independent labour movement who were just as irreconcilable to the Liberals at this time as Champion himself was. The most important of these was Joseph Burgess of the *Workman's Times*. Burgess refused to believe the rumours which flew about that Champion's funds came from the Conservatives and adopted a magisterial tone towards Hardie whenever the latter expressed any sentiments tender to Liberalism. Finally, Champion still had allies in Hardie's own power base, the Scottish Labour party, and hoped to use these to drive Hardie out of its secretaryship.

The first round of the Hardie-Champion struggle was fought over the Newcastle by-election of 1892. The seat had been won for the Liberals at the general election by their prominent leader, John Morley. He had declared himself a committed opponent of interference with the hours of adult male labour and the Independent Labour party of Newcastle had opposed his return at the general election, advising its supporters to vote Conservative. They wanted to repeat the process in the by-election which Morley had to contest as a result of his appointment to office in the new Liberal government. Champion and Barry arrived in Newcastle and encouraged this proposal.[23] Hardie was driven to support this policy only with extreme reluctance. To vote Conservative against a prominent Liberal leader would make it very difficult to win the sympathetic cooperation of radicals. In his own constituency, radicals were putting pressure on him to disavow the deeds of the Newcastle ILP. Hardie therefore sought to out-manoeuvre Champion by calling for a conference of so-called national leaders of the Independent Labour party (which did not yet exist) to be held in the constituency and decide on the best tactics. This only fuelled the resentment of the Newcastle ILP, which did exist and which objected hotly to dictation from outside the constituency. To calm his own constituents, Hardie wrote a letter to Dr John Moir in which he stated his opinion that if Morley had to face Conservative opposition, he should be supported by the Newcastle ILP. These moves aroused the ire of Joseph Burgess, who revealed in the *Workman's Times* that Moir had supported a Liberal against an independent Labour candidate in

Salford at the general election.[24] In a *Workman's Times* leader, Burgess accused Hardie of trying to boss the movement and urged that its leadership should be put formally into commission pending the constitutional establishment of an Independent Labour party at national level.[25'] This sharp reproof pulled Hardie back to the anti-Morley position. It seems clear, therefore, that he would have liked to avoid the open rupture with the Liberals which Newcastle precipitated, but, when forced to choose between keeping the Liberals sweet and setting the independent labour movement into disarray, he regarded the encouragement of the movement as his main priority.

Meanwhile, Hardie's positions *vis-à-vis* Champion had been made more difficult by John Burns. Burns was nettled by Hardie's assumption of a leadership role over the new independent labour movement and deeply concerned that Liberal sensibilities should not be outraged. He wrote to the press revealing that the one hundred pounds apparently paid by the *Workman's Times* to the election funds of himself, Hardie, and J.H. Wilson had really come from Champion and that this raised the strong presumption that they had originated from Conservative sources. Hardie was thus considerably discredited. It appeared that he was willing to accept Champion's money when it suited him, and dictated to others that they should not do so. Burgess increased suspicion that Hardie knew the true donor of the one hundred pounds by declaring in his paper, 'our scruples on this point were removed by Mr Keir Hardie, who stated emphatically to us that he knew Mr Champion's money was not obtained from any political source'. Though Burgess later retracted the obvious implication that Hardie knew his money came from Champion, the denial was widely disbelieved.

The quarrel with Champion became still more public when the publication of Hardie's election accounts showed that he had received another contribution of one hundred pounds from no less a figure than Andrew Carnegie, the Scottish-born steel magnate of the United States. This revelation coincided with a bitter and bloody strike at Carnegie's Homestead steel mills which outraged labour opinion in Britain. Hardie was subjected to a shower of protests from trades councils and other labour organisations up and down the country. Trade union opinion in the Scottish Labour party was shocked, and Champion stoked it up by writing to a Scottish newspaper denouncing the actions of foreign plutocrats who tried to hire working-class representatives in Britain to betray their class to latter-day Liberalism.[26]

Carnegie's real reason for supporting Hardie remains obscure. He was informed by Scottish Home Rule supporters that Hardie would support their cause in Parliament, but Hardie vigorously denied that he had given any pledges in return for Carnegie's money.[27] He decided to restore his slipping position in the movement by a dramatic gesture. In 1890 he had resigned his secretaryship of the Ayrshire Miners' Union and he had been presented with an honorarium of about one hundred pounds, which he had made over to his wife as security for the family while he should be a Member of Parliament. He now used this money to send a donation of one hundred pounds to the Homestead strikers and challenged the labour movement to make good the sum to his wife, in order 'to test to the full how much of a reality and how much of a desire to injure me there is in the public declarations made by trades councils and similar organisations'.[28] Joseph Burgess warmed to the gesture and opened an appeal for subscriptions to make good Mrs Hardie's loss, but the damage to Hardie's standing is seen by the fact that money trickled in only slowly and the full amount was never recovered.

A decisive struggle with Champion could not now be long delayed and the underlying strength of Hardie's position began slowly to reveal itself. His position in the Scottish Labour party was far from being so vulnerable as Champion assumed. In the Glasgow district, his position had been strengthening rather than weakening. Hardie had compensated for his quarrels with Scottish trade union leaders by attracting a new Christian socialist type of activist to the party. By the end of 1893, they held leading positions and were loyal in the main to Hardie, with whose politics they sympathised. The president, J.W. Warrington, and the secretary, Archie McArthur, of the Glasgow district of the SLP, were both members of a body called the Glasgow Christian Socialist League. McArthur founded the Labour Army in 1891 to conduct propagandist lectures in association with the SLP. Christian and ethical socialists preached from its platforms and attendances at its lectures grew from under fifty at the beginning to over a thousand in 1895. McArthur, who took a leading part in developing socialist Sunday schools in the 1890s,[29] felt a strong bond of sympathy with Hardie.

So also did the strange personality, C.W. Bream Pearce. The son of a Chartist, he was also active in the Glasgow Christian Socialist League. His main allegiance, however, belonged to the Brotherhood of the New Life, an American society dedicated to the preaching of what it called social betterment. The Brotherhood owned a prosperous vineyard at Fountain Grove in California and employed its members as agents for the distribution of its products in the wine trade throughout the world. Bream Pearce, as one of these agents, had sworn on oath to use all the profits from the trade, apart from his business and living expenses. 'for theo-social purposes'. [30] About 1892, he formed a close and lasting friendship with Hardie, whom he regarded as a man endowed with the same inspiration as the Brotherhood.

Hardie's ability to attract the support of relatively well-off Christian and ethical socialists was to have a great deal to do with his ability to create and maintain a charismatic position in the ILP. It also led him into many quarrels over the use of political funds, since Hardie treated contributions from such sources as gifts, given by disciples and symp- athisers to further his heroic work, rather than as contributions to a political organisation to be disbursed under strict principles of demo- cratic control. The effect of these dealings was often to give Hardie an independent position within the ILP by which he could claim to speak for the rank-and-file of the party and to be more truly representative of its wishes than those who disagreed with him. In 1893, Hardie took advantage of these techniques in launching the new *Labour Leader,* in succession to the paper which had died in 1889. It was launched as a monthly in 1893 as the organ of the Scottish Labour party. During that year, Hardie attracted large donations from Bream Pearce and others. Pearce contributed two hundred pounds alone. [31] Although these donations were made nominally to the Scottish Labour party, Hardie used the fact that they had been contributed by his personal symp- athisers to persuade the party to plough them into an expansion of the *Labour Leader,* which was converted into a weekly and considerably enlarged in 1894.

Hardie's conception of labour journalism was modelled closely on the methods of W.T. Stead. He believed in sensationalist exposures which would shock the conscience of society. For such work, the in- dependence of the owner-editor of the paper was deemed to be crucial. His conscience and his heroic deeds were to be reflected in its camp- aigns. The contradiction in this, which involved Hardie in so much trouble with the ILP, was that while insisting on his own absolute editorial control, he also insisted that the *Labour Leader* was the voice of the ILP and did not hesitate to demand sacrifices of effort from party branches to keep it afloat. Moreover, in struggles with his critics, he took care to ensure that his point of view was over- whelmingly represented and he frequently suppressed or misrep- resented the views of his critics. When the paper blossomed into an expanded weekly in 1894, for instance, he brought his Christian socialist allies into it as paid members of the editorial staff. Archie

McArthur ran the children's column; 'Lily Bell' (Mrs Bream Pearce) ran the women's column. David Lowe, another Christian socialist from Dundee, became assistant-editor. Hardie kept his own name and doings prominently before the readers of the paper, and he was always referred to in its columns by his editorial colleagues as 'The Chief'.

As events were to show, the venture of 1894 had been planned on an absurdly grandiose scale which far outran available financial support. Members of the Glasgow Labour Literature Society, a cooperative print-ing press formed to produce socialist propagandist liberature over a wide spectrum of political views, found that their printing expertise was being used to produce the *Labour Leader* in expensive format while SLP funds were withheld from any other publishing ventures. This was the root of the fierce quarrel between Hardie and the society which broke into the press and even the law-courts in 1895. [32] For the moment, however, these problems were concealed and Hardie was strengthened in the emerging independent labour movement by the possession of his own paper.

He was helped also by the image which Fleet Street fastened upon him as a labour representative. From the outset, he was intent on flouting the conventions of the House of Commons. He was determined that its procedures, rules and style should not turn him into yet another nondescript labour representative. His task was to speak independently for labour and independent he would be. On the day of the opening of Parliament, he flouted the usual stylishness of the occasion by driving up from West Ham in a brake crammed full of enthusiastic supporters. Mounted behind was a cornet player, who played the *Marseillaise* as they approached Westminster. As Hardie jumped from the brake and strolled across Palace Yard, lobby correspondents, avid for unusual details to enliven the boredom of lengthy word-pictures of the scene, turned to see that the new Member had been aggressively uncomp-romising in his style of dress. Next morning, there appeared in the press nearly as many versions of Hardie's attire as there were newspapers. It is therefore very difficult to be sure what Hardie really did wear, but we may quote the *Clarion's* description as one most sympathetic to him: 'his usual brown tweed suit, bedecked for the occasion by a bright red flower and an aggressive looking blue and white rosette, whilst his head covering, a tweed travelling cap, looked very con-spicuous amongst the shining grey of tall silk hats.'[33]

There is room for doubt as to whether Hardie intended his dress on this occasion to have any class significance, but we should not rush to the opposite conclusion from that of Hardie's ILP biographers who thought that it had. A tweed suit was, at that time, quite customary as Sunday best for a Scottish artisan. Hardie wore one habitually, though in later life he often assumed bizarre clothing for public appearances.[34] This theatrical trait in his personality was already evident in the strange deerstalker hat, a flaunting gesture at the conventional dress of the Liberal-Labour MP of the day, but Hardie's main intention seems to have been to make the point that he felt no exaggerated awe of Parliament and intended to go there in his ordinary, everyday clothes. The press, however, exaggerated the class significance of his action. Typical was the reaction of the correspondent of the *Daily Telegraph,* who gave his readers the following eye-glass view of the incident:

> The House is neither a coal store, a smithy nor a carpenter's shop; and, therefore, the entrance of Mr Keir Hardie in a blue serge coat and vest, yellow checked trousers, and a flannel shirt which carried no collar upon it, left a painful impression which the workman's tweed cap was powerless to subdue.[35]

The supercilious tone and the obvious exaggeration of such comments was deeply offensive to Hardie, but he well knew how to turn adverse publicity to his own advantage. Many correspondents confused his deerstalker cap (which he had worn as a convenient all-weather cap during his open-air campaign in West Ham) with the peaked flat cap of the industrial workers, then coming into general use. He hastened immediately to acquire such a cap and to have himself photographed in it.[36] In this he showed a truly Carlylean feeling for the symbolic importance of dress. The myth of the cloth cap gesture lived on in the British labour movement, symbolic of its pride of class, and nothing did more at the time to identify Hardie with the emerging force of independent labourism in British politics.

Moves towards the establishment of a national independent Labour party were gathering momentum in 1892 and, in January 1893 the ILP was born at a conference held in Bradford. It is often held that the new party was Hardie's creation, but the evidence suggests that it did not develop as he had intended and that he remained very ambivalent towards it during the first year of its existence. He did not conceive of the ILP at the outset as a propagandist agency for socialist labourism, which it soon became, but as the framework for an alliance of trade unions, radical and socialist bodies such as he had endeavoured to create in Scotland in 1888. He had high hopes in 1892 of a victory for independent labour in the Trades Union Congress and he approached the business of framing a constitution for the new party with circum-spect awareness of the susceptibilities of the trade unions. He proposed that the new party should have a federalistic constitution like that of the SLP. It should stand clearly for the independence of Labour from all other parties and have a collectivist programme, socialistic in tend-ency. He did not propose that it should declare a specific commitment to socialism. While leaving a great deal of freedom to its local con-stituency organisations, it should have an executive responsible for giving advice to these organisations on electoral tactics. It should not tie itself down to a rigid opposition to all other political parties, but should decide on its policy in the light of circumstances.[37] At the TUC in September 1892, the Parliamentary Committee was instructed to prepare a scheme for the financing of labour representation and Hardie took the chair at a special conference of delegates sympathetic to the formation of an independent Labour party. The conference set up an arrangements committee under the care of George Carson, of the Scottish Labour party, and within three months a conference was planned for setting up an independent Labour party at Bradford.

The conference met on 13 and 14 January 1893. Hardie was elected as its chairman and warmly received by the delegates. It proceeded to adopt a federalist constitution with an executive called the National Administrative Council to implement the policy laid down by annual conferences. Owing to a widespread provincial distrust of being bossed from London, the Council was given no right to initiate policy and no right to impose Parliamentary candidates on constituency branches. It was to accept contributions to party funds only if they were offered without strings, a provision designed by Joseph Burgess to counteract Champion's influence. The Council was thus a weak and circumscribed body, with no permanent chairman and with representation determined on a geographical basis.

In his opening address from the chair, Hardie stressed the democratic spirit of the new movement which, he claimed, had been maturing among the working classes. Labour now desired, he said, its own polit-ical expression. He stressed that freedom must have an economic as well as a political dimension, but he said little specifically about socialism.

The desire among the delegates to give the party a socialist commit-ment was strong, however. Although a proposal from the Scottish Labour party to include the term 'socialist' in the party's name was rejected, the conference nevertheless went on to declare that the aim of the party was the common ownership of the means of production, distribution and exchange.

In the discussion of election tactics, Blatchford and the Manchester delegates vigorously advocated that the fourth clause of their local constitution should be written into the national constitution. Their fourth clause laid down that no member of the ILP should vote for any other candidate in an election if no ILP candidate was in the field. Such a policy would have made impossible the flexible relationship with the Liberals at which Hardie aimed. On the other hand, there was undoubtedly widespread suspicion of the danger of intrigue, and the delegates, while utterly rejecting the fourth clause, provided that the party's election tactics should be settled by special conferences.

Hardie stood for no office in the new party and kept his own Scottish power base intact during the first year of its existence. The reason for this ambivalent behaviour seems to lie in his doubts as to the value of the instrument created at Bradford for serving his purpose. He had got the federalist constitution he wanted and he could have had no objection to the broad statement of socialist principle written into the constitution. But Champion's supporters were influential on the new Administrative Council, which included his old enemy, Chisholm Robertson. If the ILP were to develop along Championite lines, all hope of attracting the trade unions into affiliation with it and of pursuing a flexible policy towards the Liberals would be ruined. It seemed right, therefore, to stand back, give his Parliamentary activities time to enhance his standing in the party and guard the Scottish Labour party from falling under Champion's control.

But a showdown with Champion could not long be delayed. In February 1893, Hardie's close associate, John Lister, treasurer of the ILP, stood as the party's candidate in a by-election at Halifax. Lister set out to woo radical voters as Hardie had done at West Ham and declared publicly that there was no difference between advanced radicalism and socialism and Hardie came to Halifax to speak for him in the same vein. Champion got his lieutenant, J.L. Mahon, to publish a manifesto denouncing these tactics.[38] In the following month, Champion again intervened, this time in the Grimsby by-election where the ILP had refrained from putting up a candidate against Henry Broadhurst. This provoked a strong attack on the ILP from Liberal-Labour spokesmen, who denounced it as a clique financed by Tory gold. In addition, Joseph Burgess discovered that Champion had gone behind the back of the National Administrative Council to offer some ILP branches funds for running candidates in their constituencies. Burgess was now convinced that Champion was working in the pay of Maltman Barry and the Conservative party and he launched a blistering series of articles against him in the *Workman's Times.*

Hardie had no desire to see Champion's past career raked over and his own associations with him too closely scrutinised. He tried at first to dissuade Burgess from publishing his attacks on Champion and Barry, but when this proved impossible, he took the precaution of publishing a long article in the *Labour Leader,* giving his own highly coloured account of his relationships with Champion. He minimised Champion's contribution to his own career, making it seem that he, and not Champion, had initiated the attack on Broadhurst at the TUC in 1887. He repeated the old falsehood that all his Mid-Lanark expenses had come from Margaret Harkness and minimised his own willingness to make use of Champion's funds to get the Scottish Labour party started. Taken as a whole, the article amounted to a clear demand to Champion to submit himself to the discipline of the National Administrative Council of the ILP or clear out of the party altogether.[39]

Champion counter-attacked in Hardie's power base. Some of the miners' leaders in the Scottish Labour party, such as Chisholm Robertson and William Small, had not forgotten or forgiven their old quarrels with Hardie. At the Trades Union Congress in Belfast in 1893, Champion tried to spread disaffection among them. But the Christian socialist group around Hardie stood firm. A letter from Champion, apparently delivered by mistake to the *Labour Leader* office, was opened and revealed that one of the SLP organisers was in Champion's pay.

When Champion came north to speak at a meeting in Glasgow, he was given a hot reception by a packed and noisy meeting. The audience stamped, shouted and sang, refusing to let him deliver his prepared address and demanding to be told the truth about his intrigues in the party. A man sat in a conspicuous position in the gallery, blowing bubbles from a large jar labelled 'Hudson's Soap', a reference, of course, to the Tory gold scandal of 1885.[40]

Now almost completely discredited in Glasgow, Champion's last card was to play upon the old jealousies between Clydeside and the east coast cities, Aberdeen, Dundee and Edinburgh. He attempted to revive the Scottish Trades Council's Labour party under Chisholm Robertson, but the attempt failed, partly because Hardie had secured the support of the Dundee leader, David Lowe, as assistant-editor of the new *Labour Leader,* and partly because the financial contributions which Hardie was drawing to the Scottish Labour party by this time rendered Champion's money less attractive. By the end of 1893, it was clear that Champion was isolated and impotent within both the ILP and the SLP and he packed his bags, shut down his paper, the *Labour Elector,* and left for Australia.[41]

Hardie's activities in Parliament were by now enhancing his reputation and wiping out for the time being old memories of Carnegie, Tory gold and the like. There was widespread belief in the ILP that the Administrative Council had been weak and ineffective in its first year of existence and that a strong man was needed to give it direction. It was proposed to create a new office of president of the party and Hardie was pressed to stand for election. The ILP appeared to be growing rapidly. It was claimed that there were over four hundred branches in existence. Tom Mann had agreed to replace the old Scottish land nationaliser, J. Shaw Maxwell, as secretary. Hardie decided to accept the invitation to become president of the party and to merge the SLP branches into it as Scottish branches of the ILP.

This decision represents a new emphasis in Hardie's underlying strategy. There were by now clear signs that the anti-socialist view was still in the majority in the Trades Union Congress, blocking all progress towards the kind of labour alliance Hardie had wanted to build up. The socialists had been unable to wrest the secretaryship of the Parliamentary Committee from the Liberal-Labour Charles Fenwick. John Burns, now working closely with the Fabians and antipathetic to hostile attacks on the Liberals, had gained election to the Parliamentary Committee. Above all, the Congress, notwithstanding its acceptance of a new scheme to finance fifty Labour candidates for Parliament (a scheme which was quietly put into cold storage), rejected a motion proposed by Hardie in 1893 that the Labour party should sit in opposition until the time came for it to form a Labour Cabinet.[42]

It seemed that the process of converting the unions to his view of socialist labourism would be a longer process than he had thought. He now began to see the wisdom of calling on the ILP to conceive of itself as the vanguard of the labour army, jealously guarding its independence and blazing the trail which the organised labour movement must eventually follow. A party of dedicated socialists who abjured the sectarian isolation of the SDF and identified itself with the interests of labour seemed to be the necessity of the hour.

This did not mean that Hardie abandoned the attempt to promote a labour alliance, merely that he felt now a greater importance in having a propagandist organisation to campaign for it. The Scottish Labour party had already developed along this path. Originally conceived by Hardie as a federal labour alliance, it had quickly lost its formal trade union support. By the beginning of 1893, it had become a party of labour activists with Christian socialist leanings, the vanguard itself of a broader labour alliance. At the end of 1893, it held a conference in Glasgow of trade unions, cooperatives, radicals and socialist organisations. It drew up a programme of broad collectivist demands, rebuffed an SDF attempt to commit it to the class struggle and adopted a broad, undogmatic statement of socialism as its ultimate goal.[43] Hardie took the chair at this conference and there can be no doubt that it represented the kind of coming together of labour, radical and socialist organisations he had always wanted to see. It was to be seven years, however, before British trade unions could be brought to such a conference in England and even in Scotland matters still failed to develop beyond the stage of talking at conferences. No machinery was set up by this conference to carry its decisions into effect and a Scottish Workers' Representation Committee was not formed until 1900.

For the immediate future, therefore, the ILP was the only instrument to hand for making propaganda for socialist labourism and the mood and tone of the ILP generally was far more militant and menacing towards the Liberal party than Hardie had so far been prepared to be. Hardie's militant attacks on the Liberals in 1894 and 1895, essentially an aberration from the strategy he had followed hitherto, can only be understood with reference to the temper and the balance of forces within the Independent Labour Party, which he had now committed himself to lead.

IV

It was Hardie's role as the best-known propagandist of the ILP in the 1890s, to create an alternative socialism to that of the SDF in Britain. Many writers have found great difficulty in summing it up coherently and relating it to any socialist tradition. It has already been suggested that it is best seen as a new form of Christian socialism and it was in this form that it made its strongest appeal in the ILP. It was Christian socialism brought up to date by some of the precepts of social democracy and placed at the service of organised labour. It was an outlook which, for Hardie, had its origins in the year 1886-7, but the years of the early nineties saw some further notable developments under the stimulation of Hardie's experience in London and of competition with the SDF.

The most striking development was the adoption of the SDF assertion of and explanation for the increasing immiseration of the British working class in the 1880s and 1890s. In a series of articles contributed to the *Weekly Times and Echo,* a London radical paper, in 1892, he wrote of 'the increasingly keen competition at home and abroad', which, he said, was sharpening remorselessly the competition of workers in the labour market. Employers, driven by the need to keep down costs, were driving their workmen harder and dismissing them as soon as age began to slow them down. Men were being paid off by large industrial concerns to join the ranks of the unemployed at forty-five years of age. Simultaneously, the introduction of machinery and the collapse of English agriculture were swelling the ranks of the surplus population for which no regular employment could be found. In the search for cheap labour, other industries were exploiting weak and defenceless workers. Into the sweaters' dens of the East End of London were being sucked the pauper Jewish aliens from Eastern Europe. Within a radius of one mile around St Paul's Cathedral, twenty thousand women and girls worked for three and six a week, supplementing these starvation wages by going on the streets.[44] Thus was created that reserve army of labour which hung about the skirts of trade union organisation, making it impossible for it to exercise effective bargaining power against capital.

Besides providing a persuasive explanation of the poverty which had baffled him since youth, socialism had also furnished the policy proposal of nationalisation, and it is interesting to see how Hardie developed in these years his demand that the mines should be nationalised as a means of abolishing the poverty of the miners. It is sometimes argued that socialism was a kind of afterthought for Hardie, added late to his land radicalism as a means of broadening the electoral base of the Labour party he hoped to build.[45] This is, however, far too crude a view of Hardie's life as well as his political situation. It ignores the fact that his labourism had always entailed a view of the emancipation of his class and it misunderstands the ways in which Hardie's socialism could appeal to the kind of people who supported him in the ILP.

Hardie had believed since 1887 that nationalisation of industries where large-scale capitalism had reached monopolistic proportions was the only way to ensure that the poverty of their workers was eliminated. He did not propose to wait until some remote future before raising the question of nationalisation. From his first entry into Parliament he raised the demand for mines nationalisation, and the draft Bill which he presented in 1893 provides an interesting insight into the way in which he related socialism to the interests of organised labour. The mines were to be run by a Ministry of Mines. Democratic control by Parliament was to ensure fair trade union conditions for miners, a legal eight-hour day, a minimum wage and a legal apprenticeship. It would be a cost on the industry to ensure these conditions, as well as pensions for retired and disabled miners. The state would ensure that the industry met this cost by regulating the supply of coal to guarantee a standard price, in return for which the consumer would be assured of a regular supply of coal from an industry freed from industrial disputes occasioned by the class struggle between miners and great coal companies.[46]

The occasion of Hardie's Bill was the first national coal strike organised by the Miners' Federation of Great Britain in 1893. What his proposal amounts to, however, is simply to use the power of the state to create the harmony between consumer and producer which he had hoped at one time would be created by class collaboration between miners and coalmasters. If we substitute enlightened coalmasters for the state, the Bill of 1893 reads exactly like his mining notes between 1882 and 1886. Now, the miners' emancipation from poverty is to be the work of an enlightened parliamentary democracy in which the consumers offer fair wages in return for an essential commodity and in which the producers agree to accept wages that are fair in the light of the circumstances of the industry. It was now to be the work of the Labour party to agitate the question with the electorate until it so stirred the social conscience that it won its demand.

Here, however, we arrive at the point where ILP and SDF socialism parted company. Nationalisation depended, in Hardie's view, on building a labour alliance, but the building of a labour alliance in turn depended on the amelioration of that excessive competition in the labour market which rendered trade unions powerless. Before the real agitation for socialism could begin, the unemployed and underemployed must be materially elevated so that they would become morally fit for the responsibilities of the labour movement. Before its agitation for socialism could become effective, the Labour party must first agitate effectively for the improvement of the poor.

Now what is usually left unsaid is that Hardie applied nothing of socialist principle to this preliminary problem of putting an end to the competition of the unemployed and the underemployed with those who were in work. Whereas the SDF insisted on regarding the unemployed as citizens of one commonweal with the workers, having the same right to work and to sustenance from the processes of social production, Hardie saw them, or at least some of them, as the unfit, incapable of surviving in the conditions of competitive capitalism and he was prepared to collaborate with those anti-socialist collectivists who wanted to take them out of the labour market altogether. By this means he hoped to free organised labour from the incubus of wage-cutting blacklegs so that it could develop its industrial and political power and begin its true work of transforming society into the Godly Commonwealth.

Thus Hardie's Christian socialism was still, as it had been in 1886, directed towards the moral elevation of the lumpen-proletariat. In a sermon delivered in 1893 from the pulpit of the West Ham Congregational Church, he stated: 'If the common people be righteous and lovers of justice, the laws passed in their name will be righteous and just. Otherwise, they may be very much the reverse.'[47] He believed that desire for the moral recovery of the working class was spreading among the upper classes but the movement was checked by its being embroiled with the reactionary property interests of Mammon. The Christian churches were too often pharisaical, and collectivist radicals in the Liberal party truckled to the interests of party and government. Yet, insistently, the lines of Tennyson's 'Jubilee Ode' were penetrating into the conscience of society:

> Is it well that while we range in science,
>   glorying in the time,
> City children soak and sadden sense and soul
>   in city slime?[48]

The ILP, as Hardie conceived it, was to be a band of dedicated, self-sacrificing, heroic men and women from all classes, fighting uncompromisingly for the application of the principles of the Sermon on the Mount to the laws of distribution of economic wealth. Each week, the front page of the *Labour Leader* blazoned forth this signal from its masthead:

> God give us men! A time like this demands
> Strong minds, great hearts, true faith and ready hand;
> Men whom the lust for office does not kill;
> Men whom the spoils of office cannot buy;
> Men who possess opinions and a will;
> Men who have honour; men who will not lie.

And in 1893, he told the ILP, 'The nation from which heroism hath departed is in a fair way to drop out of the race of Progress.'[49]

In one important respect, however, Hardie's Christian socialism had been modified since 1887 and it is the respect in which he remains historically significant. His alliance with the representatives of social democracy had liberated him to express an enhanced pride in labour as the one social force which strove relentlessly for progress. The Christian socialists of the 1850s had seen the organised labour movement as a kind of lump to be leavened by the inspiration of enlightened, philanthropic superiors. The impact of socialist agitation in the 1880s had released Hardie's feelings of self-respect and class pride and he now looked to organised labour as the movement which was instinct with the cooperative principle of brotherhood. The striving of ordinary working people for righteousness and justice was the force which would stir the consciences of the rich whose material and intellectual assistance would, in turn, help labour to give legislative form to its moral aspirations. But 'labour' in this context did not mean the working class as a whole, not even the organised labour movement as a whole. The great mass of the workers were sunk in poverty and ignorance. The organised workers were too absorbed in the day-to-day struggle for material survival to have anything more than an unconscious, instinctive striving for socialism. Only the flower of the working class could envisage the full glory of what life might be like under socialism and these had to form a vanguard to go before and teach the way by example.

But a vanguard party must be financed and must find its material resources from outside the mass of the working class. Hardie was well aware that the ILP must depend for its existence as a propagandist party in a parliamentary system on the resources of sympathetic middle-class supporters. Appealing for election funds for the party in 1894, he said, 'there are hundreds of men . . . in sympathy with the Movement to whom five pounds, ten pounds or twenty pounds is a bagatelle'.[50] And on another occasion he stressed, 'These rich sympathisers have a duty to themselves and to humanity in connection with this election fund'.[51] Such rich sympathisers were mostly Christian and ethical socialists, who contributed to a party which they believed to be working for the long-term moral and material elevation of the poor. They would not have contributed to a party which agitated on principles of treating the poor and the unemployed as people with the same right to work and to the same living conditions as all members of society.[52]

This was the source of the difference between the SDF and the ILP and the source of so much of the bitterness which the SDF felt towards

Hardie. They believed that he was trying to build a party which compromised socialism with patronising middle-class people who drew distinctions between the deserving and the undeserving poor. They often found Hardie an enigmatic and puzzling figure, uttering apparently revolutionary rhetoric, but leading the party on lines of class compromise and class collaboration. In fact, the ambivalences of Hardie's socialism can be readily understood when we see that he had not abandoned that borderline position between social classes which the *Ardrossan and Saltcoats Herald* had provided for him in the 1880s. Whereas in those days he had looked to collaboration with the evangelical middle classes of Ayrshire to give him a secure role as spokesman and champion of his class, he now looked to the Christian and ethical socialists of the middle class to provide the finance that would enable him to speak for his class in journalism and labour politics. Insofar as this enabled him to move from a Liberal-labour to a socialist labour position it had a radicalising effect on his politics. It enabled him to speak as the prophet of labour, free from the inhibiting influences of a party or trade union official. But it also meant that he remained encapsulated in a middle-class life-style, more Bohemian perhaps, and more challenging to the security of the Liberal party, but still remote from the hardships and sacrifices of the poor, towards whom he now expressed compassion and condescension instead of the condemnation and censure of the evangelical past.

Hardie liked to view himself as an outcast, living with the down-and-outs of society. Yet all the evidence suggests that the life of the ILP took him further and further away from the personal experience of insecurity and victimisation which was the common lot of the poor. Adam Birkmyre, a rich, Scottish manufacturer who owned what had once been Robert Owen's New Lanark mills, provided an interest-free loan which enabled him to build a large stone house on the outskirts of Old Cumnock.[53] To its quiet rural seclusion he would retreat when the round of Parliamentary life became too depressing. Most of his political life, however, was spent on the platform, in committee rooms, living overnight in hotels and travelling by day on railway trains. These were not the places to make intimate contacts with the unemployed, the casual dockers and the sweated women. They were encountered only as audiences, as objects of pity. Between the political activist in the ILP and the casual East End worker was set a gulf of life-style that was almost unbridgeable.

A sense of Hardie's remoteness from and lack of real understanding of the life of the poor comes over in his reporting in the *Labour Leader* of his observations of East End life. Hardie was no Mayhew, and he lacked even the respect which Charles Booth felt towards a way of life of which he could not approve but which he appreciated as having its own dignity and its own values. Hardie's compassion is always forced into sensational descriptions which are intended to shock in the manner of the exposure pamphlets of Andrew Mearns and other commentators of the 1880s. We get from Hardie, as we get from these earlier writers, the sense of an alien observer, penetrating into darkest England:

> About midnight on Saturday, I was with a friend, prowling round the slums in the neighbourhood of Drury Lane. It was a depressing sight. In some of the side courts, each doorway contained two or three women, who, in the cool of the night, were enjoying a rest and a bit of gossip. There they sat or stood, most of them nursing children, while scores of unkempt and almost naked little savages darted hither and thither, engaged in childish games.[54]

We feel in this passage the watchful eyes of the outsider, scanning the scene for the well known symptoms of social disease. As before, it is the women who are tested, for the prevalence of vice or virtue among the women will be the bane or hope for the next generation.

It is to the gin shops that Hardie seems drawn for his evidence:

> Women, each with a struggling child under her arm, clawed and tore at each other, whilst the night was made hideous by their yells and curses and the screams of the terror-stricken children. One of these fights, we learned from the victor as she gathered her hair together and bound it into a knot behind, was undertaken to prevent another of the sex going home to live with a man whose wife lay sick in the same room. The woman was scratched and torn, but . . . glorying in the fact that she had effected her purpose. What a mixture of bestiality and chivalry.[55]

We sense in passages such as these the abiding horror of the city which Hardie had acquired in boyhood and the ambivalent feelings which the energy and unconventionality of life among the working-class poor set up in him. He still wanted to escape from this life, to end its night-marish confusions and to restore the world to the imagined simplicity, health and moral order of the rural past. In Hardie's rhetoric, the British Mayday became less an international propagandist strike for common labour conditions, and more a symbolic celebration of the rural revival that socialism would bring: 'Imagine the village common, thronged with a group of happy lads and lassies dancing round the Maypole, with the elders quaffing their nut brown ale, and telling their mighty deeds of other days, while children roamed and played as only children can.'[56]

Hardie attracted to the ILP many men and women who occupied this border position between social classes. They sincerely hated the poverty, the squalor and the ugliness of late-nineteenth century industrial life, but they too often assumed that the poor would want the life-style which they wanted for themselves. All too often, they created in the party's branches an atmosphere that was precious and highly moral, emphasising temperance and culture and refinement. Theirs was not a party that would develop intimate contact with poor people themselves, and their lack of understanding became reflected in their inability to apply their socialist principles to the question of the relief of poverty which they rightly saw to be the practical question of the hour in working-class politics.

It was this willingness to leave socialism out of the question of relief for the unemployed which helped to embitter relations with the SDF in the 1890s and to make it so difficult to create socialist unity thereafter. The history of the relations between the two British socialist parties is too often written as if the issues were simple: the sectarianism of the SDF is singled out for condemnation; the ILP is praised for its consistent efforts to relate to the trade union movement. Yet the issues cannot be thus limited. Time and again it was the SDF which generated the socialist policies which proved to have longest relevance to the problems of working-class poverty. Time and again it was the ILP which compromised with non-socialist collectivists to lead the labour movement into blind alleys. The sectarianism of the SDF should be seen as a reflex to the willingness of socialist labourism to compromise the interests of the poor. The result was a tragic confusion of effort at a time when socialists most needed to be united in a common fight to carry their principles in the trade union movement. For this confusion, Hardie and the Christian socialist tradition are just as responsible as the worst anti-trade-unionism to be found among the social democrats. Nowhere is this more clearly to be seen than in Hardie's handling of the question of the unemployed in Parliament between 1892 and 1895.

Notes

1. The best account of West Ham politics in this period is an unpublished paper by Mr P. Whatmough of the Centre for Social History, University of Warwick.

I have greatly benefited from reading Mr Watmough's essay..

2. *Stratford Express,* 4 January 1890.
3. Ibid., 14 September 1889.
4. Ibid., 4 January 1890.
5. Ibid., 24 May 1890.
6. *Justice,* 17 May 1890.
7. *West Ham Herald,* 20 February 1892.
8. Ibid., 7, 9, 18 July 1892; *Daily Chronicle,* 17 July 1892.
9. *West Ham Herald,* 18, 25 June, 1 July, 1892.
10. *Workman's Times,* 25 June 1892.
11. Ibid., 2 July 1892.
12. Stewart, *Keir Hardie,* p.67.
13. McLean, *Keir Hardie,* pp.43ff. Morgan, *Keir Hardie,* p.51.
14. *Stratford Express,* 24 May 1890.
15. E. Hughes (ed.), *Keir Hardie's Speeches and Writings from 1888-1915,* p.20.
16. A.N. McBriar, *Fabian Socialism and English Politics* (Cambridge, 1962), p.295.
17. Hughes, *loc.cit.*
18. D.M. Ricci, 'Fabian Socialism, a Theory of Rent as Exploitation', *J. of Brit. Studies,* ix, 1969, pp.105-21.
19. *Labour Prophet,* March 1892.
20. *Daily Chronicle,* 5 July 1892.
21. *West Ham and Stratford Express,* 13 August 1892.
22. *Labour Leader,* March 1893.
23. See *Daily Chronicle,* 16-27 August 1892, for an account of the by-election.
24. *Workman's Times,* 23, 30 July 1892. Moir was disposed to an understanding with the Liberals. In 1892 he tried to arrange for a straight fight by himself against the Conservatives in South Monmouthshire. See *Labour Leader,* 5 December 1891.
25. *Workman's Times,* 20 August 1892.
26. *National Observer,* 8 October 1892.
27. *Workman's Times,* 16 August 1892.
28. Ibid., 20 August 1892.
29. F. Reid, 'Socialist Sunday Schools in Britain, 1892-1939', *Int. Rev. Soc. Hist.,* xi, 1966, pp.18ff.
30. *Labour Leader,* 27 April 1895.
31. Ibid., 23 November 1895.
32. *Mr James Keir Hardie v. the Labour Liberature Society* (Glasgow, 1895).
33. *Clarion,* 6 August 1892.
34. J. Bruce Glasier, *James Keir Hardie, a Memorial* (Glasgow, 1919), p.63.
35. *Daily Telegraph,* 7 August 1892.
36. See portrait in *Labour Prophet,* May 1893, and *Labour Annual* (1897). For the deerstalker see portrait in *Labour Prophet,* September 1892.
37. *Workman's Times,* 18 October 1892.
38. See E.P. Thompson, 'Homage to Tom Maguire', in A. Briggs and J. Saville (eds.), *Essays in Labour History* (1960), p.287.
39. *Labour Leader,* April 1893; *Labour Elector,* May-June 1891; J. Burgess, *Will Lloyd George Supplant Ramsay MacDonald?* (Ilford, 1929?), p.83.
40. *Workman's Times,* 30 September 1893.
41. *Aberdeen Free Press,* 7 March 1892.
42. *T.U.C.,* 1893, *Proc.,* p.48.
43. *Labour Leader,* January 1894; Lowe, *Souvenirs,* p.170, describes this as a conference of the Scottish Labour party, but the Leader report makes it quite clear that the SLP was only one of the organisations represented.
44. *Weekly Times and Echo,* 18 December 1892.
45. McLean, *Keir Hardie,* pp.52ff.

46. *Labour Leader*, December 1893.
47. *West Ham Herald*, 22 April 1893.
48. Ibid., 22 October 1892.
49. *Workman's Times*, 20 February 1893.
50. *Labour Leader*, 14 July 1894.
51. Ibid., 7 April 1894.
52. See ibid., October 1893, for contributions to SLP election fund.
53. Stewart, *Keir Hardie*, p.13.
54. *Labour Leader*, 28 July 1894.
55. Ibid.
56. *Labour Prophet*, May 1893.

7 MEMBER FOR THE UNEMPLOYED

I

The problem of the unemployed had been the subject of vigorous discussion since the SDF had led the famous riots in London in 1886 and 1887.[1] Discussion had turned around two broad issues: first, how to relieve men who were genuinely looking for work without sending them to the Poor Law which involved a test of actual destitution and the stigmatisation of disfranchisement. Many radicals agreed that men who were genuinely out of work ought to be more humanely treated. There was, however, anxiety about demoralisation, of paying 'loafers' who were unwilling to do a fair day's work. Various schemes of relief were tried and had come under severe criticism. The Mansion House Fund had been condemned by the Charity Organisation Society as indiscriminate alms-giving to the clever pauper as well as the genuinely destitute. Relief works, encouraged by Joseph Chamberlain in his period of office at the Local Government Board in 1886, were criticised as leading to work being inefficiently done, because the unemployed who were recruited were not up to the standard of the best labour. There was also the difficulty that relief works required local authority expenditure and the authorities were reluctant to set them up as it brought unemployed men flocking in from other areas which did not take the trouble to do so. Finally, farm colonies had been the subject of experiment. They were vigorously advocated by the Unitarian minister, H.V. Mills, whose book *Poverty and the State* had attracted much attention. He proposed to set up farm colonies where the urban unemployed could be sent to live and work to provide their own means of subsistence. Finance would be provided from voluntary and/or local authority sources. Although criticised as likely to attract the wrong kind of unemployed, the farm colony idea received considerable support in the 1890s from such bodies as the Salvation Army, as an appropriate way of helping the genuinely unemployed and reforming the 'loafer'.

It was characteristic of all these proposals that they treated the unemployed as a separate class for whom special provision had to be made. Even temporary relief works involved the provision of a special category of work for unemployed men who must be registered and directed to them.

A second category of proposals, by contrast, concentrated on the problem of expanding the aggregate demand for labour by extending the sector of public enterprise in the economy. The Social Democratic Federation demanded the 'organisation of labour', by which it meant that all productive activity should be undertaken by public authorities concentrating on production for use rather than profit, producing food, building houses and extending the area of public service generally. This demand for the complete socialisation of the economy attracted little support outside the SDF. The Fabian Society advocated a more gradualist policy, involving extension of local authority Works Departments into such areas of urban improvement as housing, road building, parks and the like. By and large, the socialist emphasis was on providing more employment through public enterprise. The radicals feared the socialist implications of municipal enterprise and tended to concentrate on schemes for helping the unemployed rather than providing public employment.

Concentration on the question of providing work for the unemployed long obscured the important question of out-of-work maintenance. The Charity Organisation Society heavily emphasised the danger of demoralising men by paying them money to live in idleness. Socialists also disliked charity and tended to demand work rather than payment for the unemployed. Nevertheless, the issue of a state unemployment benefit was in the air and, in 1895, an article in *Justice* proposed out-of-work pay as the most rational way of relieving the unemployed during periods of bad trade and criticised farm colonies, municipal relief works and other such palliatives.

In 1892, the attitude of the Liberal leaders to all such proposals was entirely negative. The unemployed, they held, were not a problem for central government but for local authorities. Hardie had long seen that this issue would be a particularly embarrassing one for the Liberals and that it could be used to fuel the demand for independent labour action in politics. Immediately after his election for West Ham South, therefore, he began to operate as the Parliamentary mouthpiece of a campaign already under way in London. The SDF were organising demonstrations which often involved them in clashes with the police over rights of assembly. Hardie put down a motion for the opening of Parliament, calling for an autumn session to discuss the problem, but, owing to a procedural muddle, the motion was not taken.

As soon as Parliament reassembled in February 1893, Hardie raised the question of the unemployed again. He put down an amendment to the Queen's Speech, regretting its failure to notice the industrial depression and its effect on the unemployed. None of the radical or labour members would second his amendment. John Burns, pursuing his policy of not embarrassing the Liberals, argued that it was too early to challenge them on this question. The government had their hands full with Irish Home Rule, he said, and needed time to think out a careful and coherent policy. By focusing on this one issue, Hardie was leaving out of account other good things that the government could do for labour, such as helping forward the miners' eight-hours Bill. An open display of disaffection would only encourage the Conservatives.[2]

Given this attitude on the part of Burns and the radicals, Hardie would have missed his opportunity to voice his concern over unemployment but for an offer from Colonel Howard Vincent, a Conservative Protectionist, to second him. Vincent was one of a group of 'Tory Democrats' in the House who linked fair trade, imperial consolidation and alien immigration with the question of unemployment. They had their own reasons for approving of Hardie's conduct, but there is no reason to think that Hardie deliberately preferred their help to that of Burns or of radicals. The choice for him was a simple one. He must accept help where he could get it, or join the ranks of private Members on the government benches who jostled and competed to force on the Ministers their personally favoured policy proposals.

The House was crowded when Hardie rose from the seat once occupied by Parnell to move his amendment. Dressed in his notorious tweed suit, cloth cap and wearing a muffler round his neck, he spoke confidently and clearly. In a discursive speech, he went out of his way to disparage both the socialist demand for increased municipal enterprise and the demand of his Conservative supporters for fair trade. The latter, he claimed, would aggravate social and industrial evils, while the former could only be a spasmodic response to bad trade. He demanded a minimum wage of sixpence an hour and a forty-eight-hour week in government workshops, with anti-sweating clauses in government contracts. He did not explain how these measures might help the unemployed. Experiments with shorter hours had recently shown that the working day could, in circumstances of technical innovation, be shortened without any new labour being employed. Hardie simply ignored this evidence. For those who remained unemployed, the remedy lay, he argued, 'in enabling men to provide themselves with the means of subsistence', and he urged the establishment of home colonies on idle lands. In conclusion, he warned the Liberal Members of the fate that might await them at the polls if they voted against his amendment.[3]

The president of the Board of Trade, A.J. Mundella, replied with the government's completely negative view that the issue was one for local authorities. Only one radical Member, Murray MacDonald, spoke in support of Hardie, and only one other, L.E. Atherley Jones, son of the Chartist, Ernest Jones, went into the lobby with him when he forced a division at the end of the debate. The remainder of his one hundred and nine supporters were Conservatives, giving colour to the charge made during the debate by the Liberal-Labour Member, W.R. Cremer, that Hardie was a catspaw of the Conservatives.

Considering the embarrassment he had caused the government, the Liberal press treated Hardie's speech kindly. There was widespread Liberal sympathy for the unemployed, but a feeling that Hardie had offered no new suggestions. The radical *Daily Chronicle* spoke of 'the simplicity of the speech, the plain roughness of the orator's dress, the homeliness and yet directness of his language, and the rough, but interesting face [which] combined to give Mr Hardie a real success'.[4] In an editorial, the paper advised the government to waste no time in bringing forward a sound scheme for dealing with the problem. Even the Conservative-inclined *Daily News* commented that 'The social condition which leaves so many able and willing workers in enforced idleness cannot be logically or politically defended'.[5] In short, the message to Hardie was that he had made a dignified protest, which honoured his election pledges. He should now keep quiet and let the government get on with devising a policy.

Hardie, however, had no intention of letting matters rest. Out-of-doors, the ILP and the SDF expected him to use Parliament as a forum for the agitation of social questions and he would have to embarrass the government and annoy the radicals still further. The radical and labour Members responded quite naturally by keeping him somewhat at arm's length. They were wary of being drawn into ploys for causing the government difficulty. Hardie was, however, able to turn this weakness into a source of strength. The more the radicals held aloof from his campaign, the more colour they gave to his charges of aloofness from the sufferings of the unemployed. In June 1893, he seized on a case which lent support to his claim that ageing workmen were prematurely thrown onto the industrial scrapheap. A workman named Pluck had committed suicide after being dismissed from his employ in a government dockyard. At the inquest, the contractor who had employed Pluck stated that he had dismissed him on instructions from a government official that no workman over the age of forty-five should be employed on contract labour. When Hardie had gone to Pluck's home to investigate the case, he found that the man had earned seventeen shillings a week, had been dismissed shortly after presenting a petition against conditions in the dockyards and that his body still lay in his home unburied because his widow was too poor to pay the funeral expenses.[6]

The Pluck case was exceedingly embarrassing for the Liberals and for their labour supporters. Conditions in government workshops and dock-yards had been the subject of a TUC campaign since the early 1880s and the new government had been expected to do something quickly about them. In a series of probing Parliamentary questions, Hardie forced the Civil Lord of the Admiralty to confess that pressure had in fact been put upon the contractor to dismiss Pluck and other workmen who looked as though they were getting a bit old for the job. But when Hardie tried to get an adjournment debate on the matter, only twelve radical members supported him.[7]

The Liberal press accused Hardie of bringing his case before the House without properly notifying the other radical members and branded him as ineffective, but Hardie soon found another way of making his point. The occasion was the motion of An Humble Address of Congratulation to the Queen on the marriage of her grandson, the Duke of York. It was a ceremonious Parliamentary occasion, with a packed House of Commons gathered round an eminent and ageing Prime Minister. In the full glare of publicity, Hardie rose to move an amendment which stated that 'there is nothing in the recent Royal marriage which calls for special mention in this House'.

> His sympathies [he said] were as keen as those of any man and, just because they were so, he was impelled to call attention to the fact that, while that House today had time and to spare to offer congratulations to those who stood in no need of them, it had no time to consider the case of those who mourned, the poor and the needy and those who had no helpers. Twice during the present session he had asked — once the Prime Minister and once the President of the Local Government Board — if time would be given to consider the case of the thousands of men who were unemployed in this great city and on both occasions the answer had been that it would be impossible to interrupt the ordinary course of public business.[8]

Hardie kept worrying at the question of unemployment during the rest of 1893. Twice he moved the adjournment and, on the second occasion, was successful in getting the support of enough Members to hold a debate. This time he made a new suggestion – a Select Committee to consider all proposals for helping the unemployed. He made several proposals for expanding employment. The government should place orders for eight to ten fast cruisers, giving one of the contracts to his own constituency. It should draw up schemes for afforestation and foreshore reclamation. However, it was not on measures for expanding employment that he put his main emphasis, but on the question of relief for the unemployed. He was cooperating behind the scenes with some of the London radicals who were bent on getting the government to revive the Elizabethan Statutes giving power to local authorities to purchase land on which to set the unemployed to work. In the *Labour Leader* he reprinted an article by the London progressive, J. Theodore Dodd, setting forth the view that the relevant sections of the Elizabethan Statutes had not been repealed by the New Poor Law of 1834.[9] He followed this with a series of Parliamentary questions, which elicited from the Law Officers an acknowledgement that Dodd's view was technically correct. The Law Officers added, however, that the government did not believe the Elizabethan Statutes could be implemented without fresh legislation.[10] Hardie responded by issuing a manifesto asking all pressure groups concerned to demand greater powers for local authorities to acquire land for relief works, farm colonies and similar schemes. In July 1893, Hardie and Archibald Grove, Member for West Ham North, led a demonstration of the local unemployed committee, including Will Thorne, to interview the Mayor of West Ham who told them that the council was sympathetic but needed more powers to acquire land.[11]

This growing emphasis on palliatives began to place strain on Hardie's relationship with the SDF. They wanted him to conduct a campaign for the extension of public enterprise. They looked, quite correctly, with suspicion on the motives of philanthropists like A.F. Hills, director of the Thames Iron Works, whose shipyard lay in Hardie's constituency and for whom he had demanded one of the battle-cruisers. Hills was prepared to put up money for relief works in the borough of West Ham, but was not prepared to pay trade union rates for the work done. He exemplified the danger of submitting the relief of the unemployed to philanthropy in farm colonies and special relief projects. Throughout the winter of 1893, the SDF conducted their own campaign in the East End of London to persuade the local authorities to undertake municipal enterprise at ordinary trade union rates of wages. Their demonstrations often led to violent clashes with the police.

Hardie was not unwilling to exploit the provocative tactics of the SDF for his own purposes. He hoped that the threat of disorder would help to frighten the authorities into introducing relief schemes. He took part in at least one unemployed demonstration, which was broken up by the police, and was himself somewhat roughly handled by them.[12] On several occasions during 1894, he advised the unemployed to steal food and to engage in 'harmless' attacks on property, such as the smashing of street lamps.

Hardie's campaign has been criticised as a mistaken approach to the problem of getting the Liberals to do something about the unemployed.[13] It is argued that many Liberals were already sympathetic to the kind of experiments he wished to promote and that a more discreet form of pressure would have been more effective. This, however, is a doubtful argument. As H.V. Emy has shown,[14] radicals disposed to collectivist measures were numerically weak in the Liberal party and were divided into many factions. The government had little to fear from them in the way of pressure so long as they did not face agitation in their constituencies. Their attitude throughout 1893 had been entirely negative. Hardie's persistent pressure, however, proved embarrassing to them. In the *Labour Leader,* he published division lists showing how they had voted on his motions. He taunted Gladstone for his negative responses: ' "We have never done anything", says Mr Gladstone, "and therefore it would not be wise to do anything." . . . Mr Gladstone might as well say, "We have never passed a Home Rule Bill and therefore we won't pass one." '[15]

As the government's majority was reduced by by-election defeats in 1894 and as the preoccupation of Lord Rosebery (who succeeded Gladstone when he retired in that year) encouraged an increasingly negative approach to domestic questions, Hardie's publicity on the unemployed question began to have a telling effect.

He stepped up his campaign with another outspoken attack on the sycophancy shown to the Royal Family. In June, the President of France was murdered by an assassin and on the same day nearly four hundred miners were killed by an explosion in a colliery in South Wales. In the House of Commons, Sir William Harcourt moved a vote of condolence with the French people. Hardie rose and asked if the vote of condolence could embody an expression of sympathy with the families of the Welsh colliers, but Harcourt impatiently brushed the intervention aside. Hardie felt keenly this slight to the mining community. It seemed to him to epitomise the callousness of polite and comfortable society towards those who toiled to provide their creature comforts. It awakened his own boyhood memories of underground terror and social stigmatisation.

When, therefore, the House interrupted its proceedings to pass an Address of Congratulation to the Queen on the birth of a son to the Duke and Duchess of York, Hardie put down an amendment protesting at the time of the House being wasted on a matter which did not concern it. This move once again brought him into the press headlines. He rose to speak in a House where the silence was cold and contemptuous. 'I owe no allegiance to a hereditary ruler', he began, and went on, as an angry murmur of interruptions disturbed the silence, 'and I expect those who do to allow me the ordinary courtesies of debate.' From this point onwards the speech became a gladiatorial combat between the lone figure at the cross benches and protesting Members on all sides. His intention was to tell them plainly the common man's view of the monarchy and of the practices and ceremonies which surrounded it. He said he felt it necessary to protest against a law which required a Minister of the Crown to be present at the birth of a successor to the Throne. 'It is a matter of small concern to me', he stated bitingly, 'whether the future ruler of the nation be the genuine article or a spurious imitation.' He referred to the reputation of the Prince of Wales as a gambler and slum landlord. Through a crescendo of interruptions, he said of the newborn infant, the future King Edward VIII:

> From his childhood onward, this boy will be surrounded by syco-phants and flatterers by the score. . . A line will be drawn between him and the people whom he is to be called upon some day to reign over. In due course, following the precedent which has already been set, he will be sent on a tour round the world, and probably rumours of a morganatic alliance will follow . . . and the end of it all will be that the Country will be called upon to pay the bill . . . The Government will not find an opportunity for a vote of condolence with the relatives of those who are lying stiff and stark in a Welsh valley, and if that cannot be done, the motion before the House ought never to have been persisted in either. If it be for rank and title only that time and occasion can be found in this House, then the sooner that truth is known outside, the better for the House itself.

He sat down amid the same stony silence that had greeted him. The Speaker put the question and a general shout of 'aye' was greeted by a solitary voice, ringing out in broad Scottish vowels, 'no'.[16]

This outspoken protest aroused great enthusiasm in the Independent Labour party for its new president. It seemed to them that a common man had risen up to tell their betters, in plain language and without mincing matters, what the common people thought of them. 'Nothing that I have done or left undone [wrote Hardie] seems to have touched such a responsive chord as this.'[17] It took two men two hours to read all the letters that came pouring in. A London newspaper editor found his compositors dancing wildly round the type-setting room, waving a copy of Hardie's speech, and singing 'La Carmagnole'.

Outside the socialist movement, however, it seemed that Hardie had committed a most dreadful *faux pas*. He had outraged the Conservative party. He had driven yet another wedge between himself and radical back-benchers and had appeared to justify the view that this ILP was a disaffected clique of irreconcilables whose extremism would alienate many potential Liberal dissidents. This view seemed to be confirmed on the day after Hardie's speech when an ILP candidate in a by-election at Sheffield polled only twelve hundred and forty-nine votes.

As the autumn and winter drew in, however, it became clear that the existence of the ILP could not be entirely ignored. The party was much more successful in another three-cornered contest at Leicester, where Joseph Burgess polled four thousand one hundred and two. In London, the weather became so cold that the Thames froze over and the unemployed agitation reached new heights. Unemployed Committees of ILP, SDF and trades councils were set up in a number of centres. Hardie addressed a large demonstration in Trafalgar Square in December 1894, and when Rosebery visited Stratford at the end of the year, he was confronted by an unemployed deputation headed by Hardie and Archibald Grove. Hardie asserted that the number of unemployed in the country under prevailing conditions must be in excess of one million. The figure was hailed with general incredulity in the press, but a house-to-house census in West Ham lent support to Hardie's 'guesti-mate'.[18] By the opening of Parliament in 1895, it was clear that the Liberal government was tottering to the end of a very unsuccessful period of office. Its majority was much depleted by by-election defeats. It was increasingly difficult to fend off Conservative censure motions. The confident expectation at the time of the 'Royal Baby' episode that all further cooperation between Hardie and the Conservatives would henceforth be at an end was proved dramatically wrong. Hardie once again put down an amendment to the Queen's Speech referring to exceptional unemployment in industry. Radicals, sensing danger to working-class constituencies, began to make threatening noises to the government. The influential London progressive, J.W. Benn, let it be known that he would vote against the government and the radical leader, Labouchere, also made representations behind the scenes.[19] The Conservatives prepared to fall in behind Hardie's motion. In a last minute move to avoid defeat, the government agreed to Hardie's demand of November 1894, and set up a Select Committee to inquire into distress from want of employment.

II

Hardie had been successful in forcing the question of the unemployed into the government's thinking. He was given credit for this on all sides of the socialist movement. But there had been growing signs of division between him and the SDF about the kinds of solutions he proposed. The demand for ten new battleships had caused particular offence and was branded as chauvinism. Now, in 1895, Hardie's conduct of the campaign before the Select Committee widened these divisions much further. Appearing as a witness before the Committee, he proposed that the government should set aside one hundred thousand pounds to be spent by joint committees of local authorities and voluntary agencies in providing relief during the bad weather. Relief should take the form either of food distribution or of relief works. No out-of-work pay was to be given, because to pay men money for doing nothing would demoralise them.[20] The SDF were appalled. They argued that Hardie should have carried socialist proposals before the Committee. He had made no mention of the organisation of labour, had derogated out-of-work pay and had ignored even Fabian proposals that local authorities should reserve spending on public works for periods of slack trade. Hardie, they concluded, had completely failed to understand the economics of the question and had shot off at a tangent.[21] To his critics Hardie replied that his concern had been distress and he had wanted immediate emergency action for the suffering unemployed. After that he could, and would, have talked about providing employment.

Yet there is not much evidence that Hardie was very greatly concerned with the expansion of employment. Writing in the *Weekly Times and Echo* in 1892, he stated:

I am unable to endorse the cheery optimism which sees, in the immediate future, the absorption of the out-of-works in the regular army of labour, either by a process of the shortening of the hours of labour, joined to an increase of municipal activity and better enforcement of the laws of sanitation, or by an extension of our foreign trade.[22]

This was a side-swipe at proposals which had then been put forward by John Burns on behalf of the Fabians and by Joseph Chamberlain. However, as radicals like J.A. Hobson began to come forward with proposals for government to create jobs and so stimulate consumption, Hardie picked up their ideas with more optimism, but, apart from the battle-cruisers, he had no suggestions to make for stimulating urban employment. His positive suggestions were those of afforestation and foreshore reclamation, which went back to his father's republican days and beyond.[23]

Hardie's major concern was to see farm colonies established. 'The most feasible proposal yet made', he wrote in 1892, 'is that of the communal home colonies, where the inmates would produce everything necessary for their own maintenance, but no manufactured goods for sale on the open market.'[24]   And again, in 1895, he argued that the government should establish municipal farms and workshops, 'that, we might, in a very few years, have a flexible system of enabling the out of works to work and so feed themselves'.[25] The demand for revival of the Elizabethan Statutes was conceived as a means of enabling local authorities to buy lands and establish farm colonies upon them.

Hardie spoke and wrote of land colonisation as if it could be a stepping stone to a Communist Utopia:

It was said that if work was found for those who are unemployed, it will mean the break-up of our industrial system. He believed this was so and that was one reason why he advocated this solution so strongly . . . If it could be shown that land and labour, freed from the incubus of the landlord and the usurer, could produce all the necessities and a good many of the luxuries of civilised life from four or five hours labour out of twenty four, then it appeared to him that a good many would want to leave the gas works and docks, the Thames Iron Works and factories and go into the unemployed colonies, where life would be sweeter, purer and easier.[26]

The social republicanism of the Land and Labour League of his father's day had expressed similar aspirations for a return to Arcadia, and Hardie's enthusiasm for farm colonies stemmed, in part, from his own deep-seated longing for a rural way of life far from the hell of industry and the city, in which so much of his childhood and youth had been spent. He had recently acquired rural peace in his private life with the building of his new home, Lochnorris House, on the banks of the Lugar. 'Living as I do', he told the House of Commons, 'in a quiet country village, which nestles among the hills of Scotland, where Nature's charms are lavishly bestowed and where there are no unemployed, the miseries of a great industrial centre strike me with all the more force because of the contrast.'[27] On to the casual workers of West Ham, some of whom were recent migrants from the depressed agriculture of Essex, Hardie projected his own fantasies of rural innocence:

> Let them picture to themselves a tract of land which men of agricultural tastes were engaged in cultivating. The women would look after the dairies, poultry yards, flower gardens and all the rest of it. The food supplies would be raised on their own estate and there would be fresh eggs for breakfast and chicken soup occasionally. Beef and mutton would be raised and nearly all things would be to hand, which, compared with life today, would be as heaven to the hell of the old theologians.[28]

Here, as so often, it is impossible to take Hardie's apparently naive and innocent rehetoric at face value. There was a good deal of the self-interest of the organised trade unionist beneath the altruistic longing for the new moral world. He was still thinking, like the skilled Scots colliers of old, that the land was the place where the surplus industrial population ought to go, instead of flooding into their jobs and undercutting their rates. He did not seriously think that Britain could be restored to an agricultural way of life. His farm colonies were to be refuges, asylums for the unemployed, the ageing workmen, the disabled, to take them out of competition in the labour market. They were to produce only for their own subsistence and nothing for sale in the market. They were to be institutions which would humanise the Poor Law by enabling the worker to provide for his own subsistence without the stigmatisation of disfranchisement entailed by the provision of outdoor relief. Even here, Hardie wavered between the sentimental philanthropy of the Unitarian minister, H.V. Mills, whose book, *Poverty and the State,* had done so much to arouse enthusiasm for land colonies when it appeared in 1886, and the harsher attitudes of Social Darwinist reformers who looked to German experiments with labour colonies as a means of disciplining the hordes of work-shy who were alleged to hang about the ranks of the genuinely unemployed. The farm colony, Hardie suggested, would be a tougher place for the loafer than the Poor Law stoneyards or oakum-picking sheds. 'Treat them as you will and, above all, see that it is made impossible for them to propagate their species.'[29]

Stripped of its nostalgic, 'back to the land' rhetoric, Hardie's enthusiasm for farm colonies would have subjected the unemployed to a regime which was at best puritanical and at worst cruel. It was a vision of a regimented society that would have gladdened the hearts of his Covenanting forebears. He quoted with approval the chairman of Mile End Board of Guardians who said: 'He would have a system of registration of worthless casuals, so as to prevent them migrating from one district to another, and he would strengthen the law so that those who would not work could have the alternative of prison.' Hardie added, 'I call these words of wisdom and trust they will receive serious consideration from the Government.'[30]

Far from criticising Hardie maliciously, the socialists treated him too leniently, for they assumed that his emphasis on these old-fashioned remedies arose from lack of education and incapacity. They stemmed quite logically, however, from his Christian socialism. He looked forward to a regulation of the poor out of which alone the higher life could grow for those who were fit for freedom. He quoted Carlyle on the point with enthusiasm:

> I foresee that the regimentation of pauper bandits into soldiers of industry is but the beginning. It would make us once more a governed community and *civitas dei* if it please God. The nomads of the labour market, seeing such example and its blessedness, will say, 'Masters, you must regiment us a little. We will enlist with the State otherwise'.[31]

Social democrats were appalled by Hardie's vision. Was this to be the outcome of ILP socialism, for all its lofty sentiments? Were they to be read lectures about the bureaucratic implications of their state socialism, only to see Hardie sell the poor and exploited to the tender mercies of middle-class philanthropy? Hardie's rhetoric exalted industrial freedom. His policies opened the way to industrial servitude.

In fact, Hardie was at odds with many in his own party over the farm colonies policy. The inaugural conference of the ILP, acting under the guidance of Edward Aveling, had specifically rejected it in 1893 and demanded 'remunerative work for the unemployed' instead. Although the policy was reinstated by the 1895 conference,[32] not all

ILP socialists thus turned their backs on modern industrial conditions. Manchester ILP advocated urban rehousing to absorb the unemployed into work. The Scottish Labour party was deeply divided over the farm colony policy. Leeds ILP also advocated municipal housing.[33] In 1895, H. Russell Smart began a sustained campaign to get the ILP to commit itself to the demand that the local authorities should provide work for anyone who applied for it. Smart emphasised the possibilities of agricultural revival, but he scornfully rejected labour colonies — 'they might be called colonies, but they would really be prisons'.[34]

Such criticisms were obscured by the wave of support for Hardie in the ILP in 1894. Hardie seemed to give a clear lead in independence from the Liberal party, and there were many articulate members who shared his Christian socialist outlook. They surrounded Hardie with an aura of hero-worship, comparing him to Cromwell, who, it was thought, had also denounced a corrupt, out-dated and useless Parliament. Hardie's friend, J.C. Kenworthy, the Tolstoyan advocate of community life, published the following fulsome tribute: 'His head is of the high moral type, with a finely developed forehead, denoting perception and reason of the kind called common sense. His brown hair is worn long and curling, something like the glory round the head of a saint in a painted window, and he goes unshaven.'[35] Hardie took good care that such opinions were given prominence in the *Labour Leader.* Its advertisement columns advised readers of the merits of the 'Keir Hardie Boot' and told them where they could buy a cabinet-photograph of him from a photographer who also supplied portraits of Gladstone and Salisbury.

It must be borne in mind that Hardie was very lonely during these first years in Parliament. He felt ostracised and friendless in the House of Commons, and the hard travelling and speaking at meetings, often in the open air where he had to shout to be heard, wore him down and brought on bouts of depression. The work also placed heavy strain on his marriage. He had done his best to provide Lily Hardie with some of the fruits of success, making over money to her and building a large, comfortable house in a fashionable quarter. But she resented the movement for the long absences which left her with the burden of his children and she could never quite believe that it was all respectable. Her health collapsed under the strain and she was seriously ill at the end of 1894. Hardie had to cancel a projected visit to the United States and Lily was far from completely recovered when he left her for a long tour there in the autumn of 1895.

The adulation of ILP members was thus some consolation for the loss of political friendships and the backbiting of socialist quarrels, but the sympathy of a like-minded woman proved harder to replace. In 1893, he fell in love with the bright eyes and playful ways of Annie Hines, daughter of Alfred Hines, an Oxford veteran of the Socialist League. Annie, with her four sisters, was prominent on the platforms of local meetings to spread socialist propaganda in the agricultural region around their home. They sang socialist songs and conveyed an atmosphere of exuberant high spirits and attracted the attentions of other wandering propagandists besides Hardie.[36] He made Annie's acquaintance during a stay at the village of Claydon in the summer of 1893: 'They walked by shady grove and murmuring brook, hand clasped in hand and heart throbbing against heart. His cheek to hers he oft did lay and love was ever the tale he told.'[37]

Hardie went on to pour out his loneliness to her in a brief, but intense correspondence:

> I have been in the dumps myself and know what it means to be there. For one thing it doesn't pay. But like the wind of which we know not whither it cometh or goeth, so too is it with fits of depression. . .There is no balm for weariness of heart like being able to place your head on a sympathetic breast and there hear sweet true strong words of encouragement. . .Sympathy, of the helpful kind, is very largely sentiment or communion of spirit and if the marriage tie or rather the wedded life degenerates into a business partnership, the direct product of this finer, higher feeling may be checked and no hypothetical freedom gained will compensate for its [word illegible − loss?].

It is very doubtful, however, whether passages such as these point to loneliness and frustration as the source of Hardie's political drive. If anything, they rather suggest the reverse, that the loneliness and isolation resulted from his burning ambition to right the class injustices he had experienced and saw in life around him. He reveals to Annie his sense of the price he must pay in loneliness for the role of knight-errant he has taken upon himself:

> The knight, as was the custom in those days, was engaged in slaying the monsters with which the land abounded and which flourished on the bodies and souls of men, women and children. Silent and gloomy was the knight as he went about his task and few there were with whom his heart could hold communion. While others feasted and

made merry he retired to his own cave and communed with the spirits of the mighty dead, or made moan over the evil the monsters were working in the land.

The relationship withered quickly, however, like the yellow flower which Annie gave him on one of their Claydon walks. Hardie could not afford the scandal which open relations with her would arouse. He wanted her to spend a week with him in London, perhaps even to get a job there. She visited him there only once, for a day. Hardie paid several further visits to her in Oxford, but Annie's father began to raise difficulties about him seeing so much of her. In the last letter of their extant correspondence, Hardie cancels an arrangement to see her in Oxford lest 'It might lead to further complications and unfounded suspicions'.

It was thus as a lonely and isolated man that Hardie pursued his strategy of independent labourism. With the exception of Frank Smith, his close friend and host in these first Parliamentary years, there were few in the movement in whom he felt able to confide. He even tried going to a spiritualist seance to converse with Parnell and Robert Burns — 'the spirit of the mighty dead'? — but it turned out to be a political hoax and he laughed it off in the *Labour Leader*.[38] But the loneliness was real enough and derived essentially from the fact that Hardie had no broad area of support for his political strategy. Social reformers in Parliament shunned him for his commitment to class politics. Fellow socialists distrusted him for his ambiguous independence and political opportunism. He could not, therefore, explain his policy in explicit terms and he relied on his deeds to win him loyal and unquestioning support. Even to a close collaborator like David Lowe, assistant-editor on the *Labour Leader,* he often seemed roughly impatient and reserved.[39]

III

Hardie's campaign on behalf of the unemployed in Parliament made him seem more intransigent towards the Liberals than he really was. His rhetoric in 1894-5 reflected the mood of the ILP. It conveyed the impression that the days of the Liberal party were numbered and that within a very short time — two or three elections at most — British politics would be completely transformed into a struggle between the Conservative-Whig alliance and a Labour party. Behind him, the party was spoiling for its first electoral battle. Large polls in three-cornered contests at Halifax and Leicester in 1894 and again at East Bristol in 1895 encouraged over-optimism. A plethora of ILP, candidates appeared, many of them in constituencies in which the ILP could not hope to do well. The spirit of Champion and Blatchford was far from extinct.

The contradictory stance of Hardie's politics in these years stems from this fact. He needed the ILP for the work of converting the trade unions and he had to be wary of alienating its more enthusiastic anti-Liberals. Personally, he would have liked to repeat the West Ham strategy of drawing radicals into *de facto* alliance with the ILP, but the activities of Championites and enthusiasts for the fourth clause made such a strategy impossible to expound or practise very openly. Nevertheless, there is some evidence that he did what little he could to signal his desire for a working arrangement with the Liberals. In June 1894, writing in the *Labour Leader,* he qualified the statement that ILP batteries must be trained on the Liberals with the words 'for the present'.[40] A little later, the strength of the ILP is stated to lie in isolation, but again 'for the present'.[41]

He used his paper to argue strenuously though oracularly against Blatchford's championship of the fourth clause during 1893 and warned the ILP conference against adopting it in his presidential address in 1894. The fourth clause would have made any West Ham type of understanding impossible. The party showed that it was unwilling to tie its hands as Blatchford suggested and that, at the same time, it distrusted intrigues by its leadership when it followed the line proposed by Edward Aveling requiring that the party's electoral strategy be settled by a special pre-election conference.[42]

Hardie had to acknowledge, in an article in the *Nineteenth Century,* that feeling in the ILP was strongly anti-Liberal 'for the present', and gave it as his opinion that the pre-election conference would recommend abstention by ILP voters in constituencies where no socialist candidate was in the field.[43] He seemed to rule out any electoral arrangements or understanding with the Liberal party: 'I would rather fight the next election on independent lines and lose in every case, my own included, than win ten or twelve seats as the result of a compact or compromise.'[44]

Yet as the collapse of Rosebery's government approached in the spring of 1895, Hardie began to argue publicly that the policy of abstention might be unwisely rigid. He criticised the strict independence with which the London ILP fought the LCC elections in March 1895.[45] He followed this by opening a correspondence column for discussion of the issue in the *Labour Leader.* Summing it up, he hinted at the possibility of local agreements with the Liberals: 'It seems. . .as if the two wisest courses open are abstention and voting in certain districts according to the special circumstances of the district', and he instanced Glasgow as one district where 'the ILP is entitled to expect the benevolent neutrality, if not the actual support, of the Liberal Party'.[46]

When the pre-election conference met, a motion from Bradford ILP sought to qualify the abstention policy by empowering the Administrative Council to give over-riding instructions to party branches according to its own discretion.[47] The proposal was strongly attacked by the delegate from Manchester and lost by forty-five votes to sixty-two, branches voting in proportion to their membership. There is no evidence that Hardie directly inspired the Bradford motion, but its sponsors must have known that he had expressed at least an open mind on the issue. It seems highly likely that Hardie wanted to keep open until the very eve of the election the room to manoeuvre some kind of arrangement with the Liberals, since he proposed from the chair that the decision of the election conference should not be announced to the press or otherwise made public 'until a later period'.[48] The high temper of the party caused this suggestion to be rejected also.

The 1895 election, therefore, saw a pitched battle between the ILP and the Liberal party. No seats were left free for straight contests between the ILP and Conservatives, and the South West Ham Liberals were encouraged to run a candidate against the ILP president. They needed no encouragement. They had not forgotten Hardie's opposition to the re-election of John Morley, nor his collaboration with Conservatives in Parliament. Some of the trade unionists broke away from Hardie's camp and there was discontent also in the temperance lobby, who were outraged by Hardie's public rejection of local veto in favour of municipalisation of the drink traffic. This curious abandonment of the teetotal principles of his youth was almost certainly occasioned by the opposition of the SDF and of the Gas Workers' Union to the principle of local option.[49]

Finally, Hardie was unpopular with Irish nationalists (reorganised after the disarray occasioned by the Parnell divorce) for his attacks on the Liberal party, while the Catholic clergy were alienated by his opposition to voluntary schools. Hardie had tried to conciliate official Liberal and Irish nationalist opinion by fulsome praise of Gladstone's speech introducing the second Home Rule Bill. He had even appeared on the same platform as Gladstone when the Liberal leader opened a working-men's college in London. But all this went for nothing, though the Liberals were unable to agree on a candidate to oppose him. He was defeated by 775 votes by his Conservative opponent, a result which was posted up at Liberal headquarters as a Liberal victory. Hardie replied by denouncing the efforts of the Liberal managers against ILP candidates and declaring that the party would vote Conservative in retaliation at the next election.

Nationally, the results were equally disappointing for the twenty-eight ILP candidates who went to the poll. None was elected and many polled derisory votes, especially in Glasgow.[50] There was some consolation to be found in the defeat of the Liberals as foretold by the ILP. Radical opinion had been disgusted by Rosebery's performance and the failure of the party to press forward such elements of the Newcastle Programme as Welsh disestablishment or the reform of electoral registration. Property interests, on the other hand, continued their drift to Unionism in defence of Constitution, Church and Empire. There was consolation too for the ILP in the defeat of John Morley at Newcastle and in high polls for their candidates at Leicester, Halifax and West Bradford. With an average of fifteen hundred votes for each of its candidates, the ILP had shown that it was a serious disruptive force with which the Liberals would have to reckon if they wished to return to power.

Hardie, however, became the object of criticism from pro-radical elements in the ILP (such as the recent recruit, James Ramsay MacDonald) who blamed him for the bellicose attitude of the party towards the Liberals. They claimed that it had cost the party votes and influence in Parliament. They forgot that Hardie had been applying, with some reluctance, the policy of the ILP, decided by a considerable majority at its special election conference. Moreover, with hindsight, there is no reason to think that the ILP rank-and-file acted mistakenly in maintaining pressure on the Liberal party through 1895. The Liberal governments of 1893 to 1895 could hardly have been more behind-hand in responding to the interests of organised labour. They had failed to carry the miners' eight-hour day, despite strong support from many of their own back-benchers. They had aroused the criticism even of John Burns and J.H. Wilson by their readiness to send troops to intervene in industrial disputes in the Hull docks and the mining industry in 1893. The Select Committee on the unemployed had reported that there was no need to alter the position taken up by the government that relief was a matter for local authorities rather than Whitehall. Liberal associations at constituency level were often, of course, more radical than their governments, but they had shown no enthusiasm for adopting Labour candidates in increased numbers. It seemed, therefore, that there would remain a need for a tough, intransigent class party which could attract radical support away from the Liberals and force them into making concessions.

Hardie, therefore, saw no reason to moderate the policy he had been pursuing since 1887. He went on pouring scorn and contempt on the Liberals as a party dominated by capitalists and landlords. At the same time he stepped up his efforts to arouse trade unionists to an acceptance of the need for independent class politics. He was able to predict the hardening of trade union opinion in favour of independent labour representation because the first reports were already coming into the *Leader* office of anti-picketing decisions in the lower courts. His confidence that the trade unionists would soon come over to the position he had advocated since 1887 was therefore unabated. What he was now concerned to ensure was that, when trade union opinion did swing their way, it did not find the ILP either sunk in 'the flabby imbecility known as Liberal-Labourism',[51] or dug into a position so intransigent as to make cooperation impossible. As events were to show, 1895 was not to be a major turning-point for Hardie, but for the new party which he was determined to continue to lead.

Notes

1. G. Stedman Jones, *Outcast London* (Oxford, 1971), pp.281ff; J. Harris, *Unemployment and Politics: A Study in English Social Policy, 1886-1914* (Oxford, 1972), pp.51ff.
2. *Daily Chronicle*, 7-8 February 1893.
3. Ibid; *H.C. Debs., 4th Ser.*, 7 February 1893, viii, col.726.
4. *Daily Chronicle*, 8 February 1893.
5. *Daily News*, 8 February 1893.
6. *West Ham Herald*, 17 June 1893.
7. Ibid., 3 July 1893.
8. *H.C. Debs., 4th Ser.*, 14 July, 1893, XIV, col.1580-1.
9. *Labour Leader*, August 1893.
10. Ibid., September 1893.
11. *West Ham Herald*, 12 July 1893.
12. *Labour Leader*, 1894.
13. Morgan, *Keir Hardie*, p.72; Poirier, *The Advent of the Labour Party* (1958), p.62.
14. H.V. Emy, *Liberals, Radicals and Social Politics 1892-1914* (Cambridge, 1973), pp.47-51.
15. *Labour Leader*, January 1894.
16. *H.C. Debs., 4th Ser.*, 28 June 1894, XXVI, col.463-4; *Daily Chronicle*, 29 June 1894.
17. *Labour Leader*, 14 July 1894.
18. *West Ham Herald*, 22 December 1894, 9 February 1895.
19. *Labour Leader*, 23 February 1895; Emy, *Liberals, Radicals and Social Politics*, p.59.
20. *S.C. on Distress from Want of Employment, 1895, P.P.*, VIII, 1895, evidence of James Keir Hardie, qq.700ff.

21. See *Labour Leader,* 13 April 1895, for Hardie's reply to Hyndman's criticisms; ibid., 6 July 1895, for Aveling's criticisms.
22. *Weekly Times and Echo,* 25 December 1892.
23. Ibid., 18 January 1895.
24. *Weekly Times and Echo,* 25 December 1892.
25. *Labour Leader,* 19 January 1895.
26. Reported in *West Ham Herald,* 19 August 1893.
27. *Weekly Times and Echo,* 25 December 1892.
28. *West Ham Herald,* 19 August 1893.
29. *Labour Leader,* 26 January 1895.
30. Ibid., 4 August 1894.
31. Ibid., 9 January 1895.
32. The Independent Labour Party, *Report of the First General Conference (1893),* p.12; *Report,* 1895, p.26.
33. *Labour Leader,* January 1894 and 8 May 1895; *Clarion,* 14 October 1893.
34. *Labour Leader,* 29 June 1885.
35. *Weekly Times and Echo,* 24 June 1894; *Justice,* 30 July 1894, for complaints about hero-worship of Hardie.
36. D. Laurence (ed.), *Bernard Shaw's Collected Letters, 1874-97* (1965), p.359.
37. Hardie to Annie Hines, n.d. (June 1893?) Nat. Lib. Scot. Hardie's letters to Annie Hines cannot be dated with precision. The postmarks of surviving envelopes, together with internal evidence, suggest that most were written in June 1893. More precise dates for the quotations which follow are impossible to give, but the whole correspondence is not large and the quotations will be easily located.
38. Stewart, *Keir Hardie,* p.70.
39. Lowe, *From Pit to Parliament,* p.76.
40. *Labour Leader,* 23 June 1894.
41. Ibid., 1 November 1894.
42. *ILP Conference, 1894, Report,* pp.11f. Cf. *Clarion,* 4, 11 February 1893.
43. Hardie, 'The Independent Labour Party', *Nineteenth Century,* CCXV, January 1895, p.1.
44. *Labour Leader,* April 1893.
45. Ibid., 9 March 1895.
46. *Labour Leader,* 17 May 1895.
47. *Minutes of the Special Election Conference of the ILP., 4 July, 1895.* N.A.C. Minutes.
48. Ibid.
49. See *West Ham Herald,* 5 May 1894 for Hardie's change of policy; see *Workman's Times,* 2 July 1892, for complaint by Assistant Secretary of the Gas Workers' Union that Joseph Leicester's temperance views had been unpopular with working men in 1886.
50. Pelling, *Origins of the Labour Party* (2nd edn., 1965), p.166.
51. *Labour Leader,* 3 August 1895.

8 CONCLUSION

Keir Hardie has long been an enigma to biographers and historians. Early hagiography founded the myth of the saintly, crusading man of the people, whose instinctive class feeling enabled him to become an outstanding class leader. Recent scholarship has raised many problems concerning this myth, without, however, resolving the most fundamental of them. In spite of work done on Hardie's early life,[1] and two complete biographies,[2] controversy continues over many basic questions concerning Hardie's politics and personality.

The source of his indomitable inner drive has remained obscure. Biographers have seemed unsure about the balance of social and psychological factors. In the work of Kenneth O. Morgan, sexual frustration seems to be more important in explaining Hardie than class consciousness.[3] Yet Hardie's sense of commitment to his class is obvious on almost every page of his writings and speeches. Here also, biographers have been right to insist on ambiguities. Militancy sits uneasily alongside class-collaborationist sentiment; sympathy with the poor and exploited is shadowed by fear of the slum-dweller and the loafer.

On the question of Hardie's political development, there has been most disagreement, perhaps, as to the date at which he become a socialist. The year 1887 was suggested,[4] but Morgan believed that no definite date could be assigned, while McLean, though accepting 1886-7 as a turning point, sees it as recording commitment to an old-fashioned agrarian socialism which had no relevance to late nineteenth-century industrial society. Morgan holds Hardie to have achieved a unique fusion of radicalism and socialism, without any very precise definition of what was one and what the other. Can Hardie's socialism be located within any tradition at all, or is he merely a protagonist of labourism, as McLean would have it, who used socialist rhetoric instrumentally to broaden the basis of support for a Labour party? Were Hardie's apparent political gyrations related to any strategy at all, and if so, did he aim at anything more than increasing the influence of labour within a capitalist society?

This book has tried to throw light on some of these questions by presenting a fully-documented account of Hardie's early life and formative years. It has sought to penetrate into the obscurities of

Hardie's childhood behind the veil of myth which still surrounds it. It has tried to present his early manhood in the context of the Scottish mining community, with its subtle complexities of occupation, status and tradition. It has tried to understand the problems of being an independent working-class leader in a society where such independence was very difficult, perhaps impossible, to achieve. It has tried to maintain a balance between Hardie's views of organised labour, the working class and the many strands of tradition which fed into the popular socialist revival of the late 1880s and the early 1890s. It has looked for an explanation of Hardie's personality or consciousness in terms of that cult of heroic leadership which was so powerful in nineteenth-century politics and art.

The inner driving force which impelled Hardie in Labour politics was the personal experience of class oppression. It affected him at a tender age, when he was dismissed without a hearing by the Glasgow baker who employed him. It was built into the fibre of his family life while he worked for the iron companies in Lanarkshire in the 1860s and 1870s. The power of great capital to frustrate the independence of the working man was made clear to him by his mother's conflict over the monopoly claimed by the company store, by the use of Cornish, Irish and other immigrant workers to undermine trade unionism and by the arbitrary and violent reductions of wages after 1873. Moreover, to be a collier in that community was to be stigmatised by respectable opinion as a black, heathen outcast, to which, in Hardie's case, was added the anxiety of knowing that he was illegitimate, and a sense of insecurity which probably made him nurse fantasies of high-born parentage. We need scarcely look further for the psychological roots of a personality which could be stiffly unbending or touchingly deferential, according to the sincerity it found in others.

Hardie' sensitive nature was fostered by the intense pride of the traditional Scots colliers. Fascinated by powerful myths of their emancipation from serfdom and of their lost peasant status in small-scale mining of the early nineteenth century, they dreamed of a future in which labour would reign as an equal partner with capital in the coal-mining trade. Small masters would become managers and workers would become owners. The rentier class of directors, landlords and idle shareholders would be eliminated. The pits would be worked for the benefit of consumer and producer alike. The consumer would get a steady supply of a vital commodity in return for which the producers would expect a fair wage, good housing, land on which to grow their basic food requirements and a share in the running of their industry through trade unions and cooperation. This was the dream, the fantasy world, of a frustrated labour aristocracy.

Hardie imbibed these fantasies and believed they could be brought about by the collaboration of working men and enlightened, sympathetic masters. For him it seemed an escape route from the hell of industry, into which he had been born, to a rural Arcadia, which had always seemed near but unattainable. Once let the cooperation of capital and labour be established and there would be no competition for jobs, no separation of the worker from the land, no violent fluctuations of trade, no poverty and no luxury. Instead, there would be initiated a kind of stationary state in which all would share alike the simple comforts of a self-sufficient society. Then would be restored to the working man that simplicity and independence which Robert Burns had celebrated. It was a vision of the new moral world which had haunted many kinds of skilled workers since the Industrial Revolution, as their control over the means of production was obliterated by the relentless growth of large-scale capitalism.

Hardie imbibed the myth through a trade unionism which it had helped to sustain, the trade unionism of which Alexander McDonald was the head and symbol. It was the trade unionism of men who saw themselves as a skilled elite and it required insistence on the separateness of their interests from those of the mass of migrant workers who poured into the mining industry during the rise of the great iron companies from 1832 to 1873. The mass of deprived humanity, badly housed, low-paid and disorganised were less than captivated by the outlook of the skilled collier. They worked in thick coal-seams, where the hewer's skill counted for little. Apprenticeship restrictions would have prevented them from bringing in relatives or mates to work alongside them at the pillars and stalls. Restriction of output offered them only smaller earnings, already diminished by short-time working and company fines and deductions. They wanted a union which would mobilise their class power to strike against wage reductions imposed arbitrarily by the companies. Leaders who could not maintain a posture of trade union aggression were sooner or later repudiated by mass meetings of miners, at which the great majority of non-unionists out-voted the elite of organised men.

Throughout his trade union and political life, Hardie displayed an ambiguous irresolution between the outlook of the traditional Scots colliers and the class-consciousness of the rank-and-file. He could never see the contradiction between fighting in the interests of an organised elite of the workers, and fighting for generalised class interests which embraced the poorest sections. His was always the mentality of the self-improving Scots collier in contention with the despised and illegitimate outcast. He could feel for the pains and grievances of the poor, but he could never identify with them. He despised them for their lack of moral discipline. They lacked the qualities needed to build the trade unionism of skilled men, patiently and peacefully. They seemed abandoned to selfishness, hedonism and Mammon-worship. One moment they were clamouring for a strike; the next, they were quarrelling among themselves as to who was getting the most out of it. Any miners' agent who got involved in leading them soon found himself dragged into such quarrels, of district against district, unionist against non-unionist. Strike movements fell apart, leaving the agent high and dry, exposed to the tender mercies of employers. Hardie was determined thtat this would not happen to him. He had seen too much of poverty in childhood to court any risk of being plunged back into it. He would not be driven into social ostracism and the life of a wandering agitator. Carlyle, he concluded, was right. The majority of men were fools and only an élite was capable of the sobriety, self-discipline and thrift which would sustain trade unionism.

Hardie, therefore, could never see the miners' emancipation arising from their own class solidarity. Those who had the discipline and capacity for organisation must work in alliance with sympathetic and enlightened members of the middle class to raise the mass materially and morally. Only then could the power of labour begin to be felt in society. But it was organised, respectable working men who had the most compelling interest in bringing this about, since they lived closest to the abyss of poverty and exploitation. It was from them that heroes would arise to expose the dreadul conditions of industrial life. They would shock the rich out of their luxurious languor and win them to collaboration with labour for the uplifting of the poor.

Hardie's belief in the disinterested concern of middle-class, and especially intellectual middle-class people towards the poor, was lifelong. He never tried to formulate to himself the conflict which might exist between the material interests of the poor and their moral coercion in the interests of organised labour. He never resolved the tension in his outlook between the poor as enemies and as brothers of organised workers. He welcomed mass agitation as an opportunity to publicise the grievances of the poor and he sustained such agitations by appealing to the common class interest of all workers. But, in the last analysis, he was content that something, anything, should be done if only it would remove the drug of their competition in the labour market. It is not possible to see Hardie's political development in terms of progression from labour aristocrat to mass working-class leader.

This ambiguous social outlook meant that Hardie often acted as a drag on the development of class-consciousness in the labour movement. Between 1882 and 1886, he abandoned his proto-socialist approach to the miners' problem and retreated into confusing concessions to the middle-class radicalism of small coalmasters and petit-bourgeois radicals on whose social support he was heavily reliant. His insistence on class collaboration with them acted as a drag on the Hamilton and Blantyre miners as they thrashed out the issues of class politics between 1884 and 1886. Only when the strike of 1886-7 revealed the combination of powerful coalmasters and iron companies and the unreliability of radicals to defend basic trade union freedoms of skilled miners did he revive and reinvigorate his former enthusiasm for socialist ideas. His faith in the goodwill of Liberal coalmasters and newspaper-owners was severely shaken. The arguments which Small, James Neill and others had been putting to the miners were now unanswerable. They must seek the solution of their problems in the nationalisation of their industry and the direction of its profits towards the maintenance of their standard of living. The road ran straight on to independent class politics.

It is in this sense that we may speak of Hardie as being converted to socialism by the crisis of 1886-7 in the Scottish coal industry. From that moment onwards, socialism meant to Hardie the independent, class organisation of labour in politics, struggling for its own class interest and not stopping short until it had attained the nationalisation of mines and other great monopolies which frustrated the power of workmen to control their own destinies. In that year, he joined Mann, Champion and the Engels-Marx-Aveling group in pioneering a new Labour party, which would be a class party, not a pressure group in a broad, populist coalition, since it would insist on the interest of labour coming first on the political agenda. Since the Liberal party lay in the grip of its 'Whig' landlords and capitalists, such a Labour party would be the inevitable resting-place of all radicals who wanted to see harmony restored between the classes in society. There could be no stopping point short of Labour government and a society in which participation in productive labour, by hand or by brain, was the badge of entitlement to citizenship and a share in the fruits of social industry. To see Hardie as interested only in social reform or instrumental trade union demands is to ignore the importance he attached to socialism as marking the dividing line of class interest between the party of labour and the parties of property. Socialism, at the outset of a new Labour party, might be but the aspiration of a few far-seeing pioneers, but class interest must steadily force the workers to adopt socialism as the only complete solution to economic subjection.

Socialism, therefore, must be kept before the Labour party by political agitation until adopted fully into its demands. Thus, in 1887, nationalisation of mines and other industries was included in the programme which Hardie proposed for a new Labour party. A few months later, he told the Scottish Miners' National Federation that nationalisation of the mines must be their ultimate objective. The demand was again included in his election address at Mid-Lanark in 1888. At West Ham South in 1892, public ownership figured more prominently and more sweepingly in his election address. In his first session as a Member of Parliament he brought forward a Mines Nationalisation Bill in the name of the Scottish Labour party. There is no doubt, when all the evidence is fully reviewed, that Hardie took the nationalisation of modern industry seriously.

To draw attention to the timing and content of socialist ideas in Hardie's political development is not, of course, to argue that he became a Marxist, openly or covertly. He retained the attitudes of the skilled Scots collier all his life. He never abandoned the view that the poor constituted as great a check on the development of a powerful Labour party as did the monopolists of land and capital. Class politics, and hence socialism, could never be effective until the material and moral elevation of the poor was complete. The organised labour movement might have to act in very militant style in order to shock the rich into sympathy with the plight of the poor, but the poor could not be elevated without the collaboration of the rich. The programme for the elevation of the poor could not, therefore, be evolved along class lines, like the programme for achieving the economic freedom of organised labour. Hardie's poverty programme was a confused muddle of collectivist labourism, Social Democratic palliatives and Christian philanthropy, dressed up to look like stepping-stones to the cooperative commonwealth. It included state regulation of hours and wages in the sweated trades, payment of old age pensions out of funds raised by progressive taxation rather than workers' contributions, and the gathering of the unemployed into farm colonies isolated from the labour market by the proviso that they were to produce only for their own subsistence. It was, as before, a programme which hovered uncertainly between socialism and the state regulation of the skilled

Scots colliers.

Nevertheless it would be wrong to insist on a sharp disjunction between Hardie's views on social reform and his socialism. They were easily accommodated in his respectable miner's outlook as different but connected agencies of labour's rise to class power. In Hardie's mind, they became fused into a new form of Christian socialism, which undoubtedly had a strong appeal in the ILP, dominated as it was by idealists bent on rescuing the poor. It was not a form of Christian socialism defined by theological dogma. Hardie's Christianity eventually broadened into an acceptance of all transcendental creeds and his other-worldliness was rooted in the pesant values of the rural poor among whom he passed his childhood. What defines his socialism as 'Christian' is the evangelical belief that the poor were sunk in sin from which they could be elevated by the Grace of Jesus Christ. It was the class-consciousness of the rank-and-file miners which forced into his outlook the view that their elevation might have as much to do with higher wages as with discipline to higher moral standards. But in either case, Hardie saw the disciplining and the bettering as an act of sympathy on the part of the rich. It followed that the rule of labour could only come into being by the heroic work of an alliance between organised working men and rich sympathisers who placed their material and mental resources at the men's disposal in the fight against Mammonism in all classes.

Between about 1888 and 1893, Hardie hoped that the political formation of this heroic alliance would be a Labour party, formed as an alliance between trade unions and sympathetic middle-class groups of all collectivist and democratic shades. In order to hold open the door of the new Labour party to such middle-class sympathisers, he stressed their common interest with labour in the struggle against the rentiers. Federal constitutions were prepared, first for the Scottish Labour party, and then for the ILP, and any socialist formula which over-stressed class struggle, or which implied expropriation of capitalists and landlords was resisted. In terms of fundamental strategy, therefore, Hardie had nothing to learn after 1895. He had been struggling to bring it to fruition in Scotland from 1888 to 1894.

As the movement for the creation of an independent Labour party gathered strength in England from 1891, Hardie welcomed it and prepared to give it leadership by opposition to the Liberals in Parliament. But he held aloof from the ILP as established in 1893, suspicious of its intransigence. He was strengthening his own power base in Scotland and no doubt looked to the overwhelming of the ILP's anti-radical elements by the early adhesion of the Trades Union Congress to independence. His decision to accept the leadership of the ILP in 1894 is to be related in part to the defeat of the Championites, in part to the overthrow of the Manchester Fourth Clause, and in part to the failure of socialists and 'New Unionists' to capture the TUC in 1893. Faced with this impasse, Hardie needed a broader platform from which to campaign for his strategy of a trade union party which was at once independent, socialistic and prepared to work with radicals for social reform. After the events of 1893, he could be fairly sure that the ILP could fulfil the role of a vanguard party for this strategy.

Hardie's vision of a class party of organised labour working in collaboration with middle-class radicals did not go unchallenged. The SDF, quite understandably, denied the socialist credentials of a party whose programme for the reduction of poverty bore so little relationship to its declared socialist objective and which was so ready to subject the unemployed to the mercies of middle-class philanthropy. Their criticisms of Hardie cannot be dismissed as merely malicious or carping. He had failed entirely to demonstrate how socialism was relevant to the problem of creating more jobs or to providing adequate relief for men out of work. More government contracts for battleships might certainly have done something, but that was scarcely a policy to which socialists had yet reconciled themselves. Foreshore reclamation and reafforestation might have some small effect, but were of little relevance to the problems of an archaic industrial economy, hard-pressed by foreign competition. Hardie never campaigned for the socialist proposals of urban rehousing and improvement. His basic concern was not really with jobs for the unemployed, far less for the right to work, but with removing the unemployed from competition with organised labour in the market. Some of the seeds of socialist disunity were thus sown in the consciousness of the frustrated labour aristocracy of the Scots coalfields. The Lanarkshire collier who set more store by the support of sympathetic middle-class opinion than by the solidarity of working-class agitation had emerged as the leader of a new socialist party which emphasised the importance of the moral conversion of the rich and the uplifting of the degraded poor.

Notes

1. Reid, 'Keir Hardie's Conversion to Socialism', in Briggs and Saville (eds.), *Essays in Labour History*, pp.17-46.
2. Morgan, *Keir Hardie;* McLean, *Keir Hardie.*
3. Morgan, p.58f.
4. Reid, pp.40ff.

Little evidence has so far come to light on Hardie's attitude to his own illegitimacy. Early hagiographers respected the secret knowledge which Hardie carefully guarded throughout his life. Nevertheless, there were other signs and hints that Hardie felt the position keenly. Emrys Hughes, Hardie's son-in-law, hinted that rows between Hardie's mother and stepfather over 'the bastard' affected the boy and left him with a desire to obtain equality before the law for illegitimate children.[1] More recently, the present writer drew attention to the manuscript account by Allan A. Durward of his own investigations into Hardie's antecedents.[2] Durward's inquiries were made around Hamilton in 1923, and he wrote his manuscript, 'The Truth about James Kerr alias James Keir Hardie and the ILP', in 1949, when he was nearly eighty years of age. A copy of the manuscript was made by Mr Henry Pelling from the original, when it was in the possession of Mr Dennis Bell of Glasgow University. Mr Pelling's copy is still in his possession at St John's College, Cambridge, and the extract below is reprinted with his permission.

Durward may be regarded as a hostile witness. In 1888 he joined the Aberdeen Socialist Society, which supported H.H. Champion in his struggles with Hardie. Later, Durward was a member of the Social Democratic Federation. Was he, therefore, over-credulous about the gossip he picked up concerning Hardie's beliefs about his parentage? His glaring error about the age of Hardie's mother at his birth does nothing to increase one's confidence in his report.[3]

Some corroboration, however, seems to come from Hardie's own pen. In the *Miner,* December 1887, there appeared a short story under the head, 'Wee Jamie Keekie'. It was unsigned, but the style in general and the use of Scots in particular are very characteristic of Hardie's writing at this time. The story has been analysed in chapter 1, and is reprinted here in full because the *Miner* is a rare journal.

(A) Extract from 'The Truth about James Kerr alias James Keir Hardie and the ILP', by Allan A. Durward

James Kerr was born at Langbrannock (or Leybrannock?) near Holytown, Lanarkshire. His mother, Mary Kerr, at work in a *turnip- or hay-field* near the village on 15th August, 1856, and there *in the open air,* gave birth to her child before being carried to her home in the village. Her mother, Agnes Kerr, registered the birth, making an X on the register as she could not write her name, at the parish registrar's office in the neighbouring village of Holytown, where the register can still be examined for verification. A marginal note, dated March, 1857, intimates that *William Aitken,* collier, *was declared the father of James Kerr* in his absence, after being summoned to appear at the Sheriff's Court in Hamilton. According to local report, he denied paternity, but was said to have disappeared on receipt of the summons, having been *bribed* by the real father, with the concurrence of Agnes Kerr, the grandmother, and a doctor practising in the neighbourhood and residing in Airdrie. The mother, at this time, was a young girl of sixteen. Just afterwards, she went into domestic service and the grandmother gave the custody of the child, now chargeable to the Parish, into the keeping of an old woman who had several other parish children in her keeping. Here the child remained for some years, being generally known as *Keir,* the local pronunciation of Kerr. He is said to have attended the local school and got there probably all the schooling he ever had up to six or seven years of age. His mother, while in service in Glasgow, met and married a ship's carpenter named *Hardie* and the parish authorities handed the child over, as the young couple's responsibility, and he was ever afterwards known as Keir Hardie and signed his name as *J.* or *James Keir Hardie,* and in his entry in *Who's Who* and all his biographies, no mention is made of his years prior to his mother's marriage, although mention is made of a rather pitiful story about his being sacked without wages as a message boy for turning up late for work. Ship-building has always had its *slump* periods and Hardie, the step-father, after a long period of unemployment, and his step-son were in the pits during the hey-days of coal mining in the early seventies during the Franco-Prussian War. A close chum of these days said that Hardie confided in him the facts of his birth and concluded his story in these words, 'Aye, he was a damm sight prouder to think himself the son o' a doctor who disowned him than the dacent man wha gae him and his mither a name and brocht him up.'

(B) Wee Jamie Keekie, reprinted from the Miner, December 1887, p.187

Wee Jamie Keekie was everybody's wean. There were few houses Righa' that Jamie had not made his way into, and not into the houses only, but somehow he managed to get into the hearts of the people as well. Whenever a 'tap, tapping' was heard at the door of a house, the following colloloquy was almost sure to follow:—

'Wha's that?'

'Wee Jamie Keekie wantin' in, for his feet's caul' an' his shin's din.'

And then the door would be opened and the little fellow admitted. Though the door stood wide open, and the day was the hottest in summer, the formula had to be gone through. Little wonder he was a favourite. When he turned up his round laughing face, and looked with his clear blue eyes that seemed, young as he was, to be wells of liquid light, and said in his own simple, childish way — 'Wee Jamie Keekie, let me in, my feet's caul' an' my shin's din,' an instinctive feeling rose within the bosoms of even ordinary people to take him in their arms. Who he was, and where he had come from, no one knew. At the time of which I am now writing he was about four years of age. On a New-year's morning one of the inhabitants of Brownstone had been out first-footing, and returning home for breakfast not exactly 'fou,' but with 'a drappie in his e'e,' he stumbled and fell over a basket which was lying on the road at one end of the village. His companions laughed immoderately at his fall, and on getting up, Adam — Adam Goodheart was his name — turned round and gave the basket a tremendous kick, and at the same time gave vent to a volley of swearing directed against the woman, whoever she might be, who had left the basket for him to fall over. But now a strange thing happened. Proceeding from the basket came a strange cry, evidently that of a child awakened out of its sleep, and Adam at once, bemuddled as he was, ran forward and picked up basket and everything in his arms and made for his own door, which fortunately was not far distant. He was followed by his tipsy companions, who made fun of his burden. The continued cries of the child, however, kept Adam from minding his companions, and so on reaching home he called out — 'Kate! here's yer newerday for ye.'

Kate, honest woman, had been 'nursing her wrath' most of the night, and was prepared to give Adam a bit of her mind anent his conduct in having been out of his own house all night. Her curiosity, however, completely overcame her anger when she saw her husband's burden and heard the cries proceeding from the basket, and so she at once flew to the relief of the child. On removing some of the blankets in which it was enveloped, she revealed the face of a chubby-cheeked, golden haired, blue-eyed 'greetin' wean' apparently between two and three years old. Under Mrs Goodheart (sic) care it was soon sound asleep, and on opening its eyes again it began repeating the words — 'Wee Jamie Keekie, let me in, mine feet's caul' an' mine shin's din;' and from that day forth he was Wee Jamie Keekie.

Where he came from no one knew, but as the Goodhearts had no children of their own they adopted him, and he was soon a favourite in every miner's house in Brigha'.

Five years have passed away and Wee Jamie Keekie has grown to be a lad of seven years. Times were hard, and money scarce, and as Goodheart liked a dram, it so happened that his circumstances were no better than they should have been. The New Year was approaching and the prospects of a good spree at the holiday season were not bright. Under these circumstances it was proposed that Jamie Keekie should be taken into the mine. Ah! you lads may read this, your lines have been cast in pleasant places. There were no School Boards then to compel attendance at school nor mine Regulations Acts to prevent children from being taken into the pit, and so Wee Jamie was well happed up and marched off to work. It makes one laugh to think of a child of seven years working. He was not expected to do any work. But then he was entitled to a 'quarter-ben,' and that was a consideration. For the first few weeks he lay wrapt up in Goodheart's plaiding jacket. He was not allowed a lamp, and the time passed wearily enough. And now happened a strange thing. Jamie had been in the mine for a number of weeks, and Hogmanay was come. He had learned the way to where a spring of pure water bubbled up out from the pavement of the mine, and on the night before Hogmanay, Jamie was sent to fill a flask with water. The two were alone in the mine, Adam being at the time working a double shifted place. He was allowed a lamp to go for the water, his foster father agreeing to have a smoke till he returned. After waiting for full fifteen minutes and there being no sign of the boy's return. Adam began to get uneasy, and he concluded that Wee Jamie Keekie had either lost his way, or that his lamp had gone out. With this idea he began to shout at the pitch of his voice. The sound echoed and re-echoed along the passage of the mine, but brought forth no other sound. Then he thought of making his way to the place where the water hole was, in the hope that he might find the boy there. With this idea he began to grope his way along, shouting as he went.

New Year's Day, Brigha' and the whole country side is in a ferment. Wee Jamie Keekie and Adam Goodheart are both amissing. Since the night when they were seen going to their work in the mine nothing has either been seen or heard of them. Search parties have been sent into the mine, and every neuk and crannie had been carefully examined, but still no trace of the missing ones could be found. Men believed in those days that the devil sometimes came and took men away, body and soul, and the older people were quite convinced that the man and the boy had been spirited away. The more practical believed that either the two were still in the mine, or else they had been murdered during the night and their bodies been buried or carried out and thrown into the water. I should here explain that the mine was driven in from the side of a glen, and some 30 feet below the entrance, Calder water flowed on its way to the sea. During the summer months the stream was not of much consequence, but after a spate of rain it roared along with great volume and force. The authorities were communicated with, and they agreed to have the river dragged. After this had been done, parties were still as far from a solution of the mystery as ever, as nothing was found. The bloodhounds were suggested. These were brought in and put on the track. Goodheart's jacket was lying at the spot where Wee Jamie had laid it down when he set off for the water, and this gave the animal the scent, which he at once took up and followed first to the water hole, and then to the edge of a fall, where he seemed to lose it. No matter from what point he started, he always finished at the same spot, and yet he never seemed satisfied. He kept sniffing the air, and at times gave utterance to a low whine, and when (sic) looking up at his keeper as if pleading for help to unravel the mystery. But all was in vain. Some of the younger and more fiery spirits were of opinion that the fall should be cleared away; but the manager and several others were positive in their assertion that the fall had lain there for months, and that they could not by any possibility be under it. And so the matter had to drop, and the mystery remained; but the miners, as they went along the passages of the mine, frequently declared that they were startled by hearing strange wailing sounds, and sometimes even a well-known voice repeat, 'Wee Jamie Keekie, let me in, ma feet's caul an' ma shin's din.' It might only be imagination, or it might be the air whistling through the building, but it at least showed that the memory of the sunny-hearted, blythe-faced laddie was green in their hearts. And what about Kate, Goodheart's wife? She, poor body, never recovered from the shock. At first she refused to believe that husband and boy were both gone. Reason reeled under the shock, and she went about from house to house asking for her ain Jamie Keekie. Strange that the name of her husband was never once mentioned by her in the hearing of any one. One morning some miners going into the mine at an early hour saw an apparition in front of them — that of a figure robed in white — and the next instant the air was filled with the most unearthly wailing sound that they had ever listened to. They were just on the point of turning to run away when some one remarked — 'Oh, it's only poor Kate,' and on further examination this turned out to be the case. She had evidently been in the mine all night searching for her lost ones. Alas! poor Kate. How strong is even a foster mother's love!

In the year of grace 1854 some men were working in a pit near to the scene of the mysterious disappearance of twenty years before. One day a strange rumour ran through the pit. Some old workings had been pricked, and the black damp was coming out in great volume. The men were thrown idle for several days until the damp was cleared out. Then men were set to work to try to find out the extent of the old workings. It was known that the ell coal had been worked from the old mines; but this was a splint seam, and no knowledge remained of it ever having been worked. On examination it was found that what had been gone through on was an old shaft which had evidently been sunk blind from the ell to the splint coal, but nothing else had been done. But they found more. In clearing out the bottom of the shaft some broken delf was discovered, an old tea flask, and a *human skeleton*. Aye, and there was a record left. A stone and a large pin were found together, and on the stone 17 strokes were marked. What did it tell? That for 17 days Adam Goodheart — for his skeleton it was — had been alive at the bottom of that shaft. He had cried while his strength remained, and then, when utterly exhausted, he had lain down and died the slow, lingering death of cold and hunger. His, then, were the cries heard by his fellows for days after his disappearance, though at the time they put it down to imagination. Poor Adam! Let us hope that even down in the darkness of the mine he gave his heart to the loving Saviour, and died trusting in His salvation.

Last scene of all! On the New Year Day of 1855 a few kind-hearted neighbours were gathered round the dying bed of Jamie Keekie's Kate, as she had come to be called by the children. It was evident that the poor wasted creature on the bed had not long to live. They had tried to tell her about the finding of her husband's bones, but the intelligence had no interest for her. But now as the body kept getting weaker the mind grew stronger. For some time she had evidently been sleeping, but now she opened her eyes, and, looking round in a strange dazed kind of way, said, 'Surely I maun hae been dreamin', for I thocht I heard wee Jamie speakin' an' Adam tae.' The kindly women saw that reason was returning, and one of them said soothingly —

'Vera likely ye did hear them speak tae ye, at least ye'll sune see them baith.'

Ere the words were spoken a knock was heard at the door, and on it being opened a well-dressed gentlemen asked if Mrs Kate Goodheart lived there. On being answered in the affirmative, he walked in with the remark that he wanted to see her. As he advanced to the bedside the eyes of the dying woman turned towards him, a new light broke her countenance, as, raising herself up on her elbow, she exclaimed –

'Ye're no Wee Jamie Keekie, but yet Jamie Keekie a' the same.'

The strong man's eyes were full of tears as he bent over and kissed the thin lips of his foster mother, and said –

'Yes, mother, I am Jamie Keekie; and I want you to live that I may in some measure repay your kindness to me.'

'Ah, laddie!' said Kate, 'its no tae be. But, oh, am gled, gled tae ken that ye werena foul'y murdered; an' Jamsie,' – and here her voice sank to a whisper – 'I'm gaun hame tae the better laun, an' jist as ye hinna disappointed me here, will ye noo promise tae meet me there?'

There was a longing look in her eyes, the words had been spoken with a great effort, and Jamie, taking the dying woman by the hand uttered a solemn 'I will.'

A smile passed over Kate's countenance, she quietly lay back on her pillow, and gave up her spirit to her God.

And now a word of explanation. Jamie Keekie was the son of Sir John Broadacre. His father, however, was thrown from his horse and killed a few months after his son's birth. An uncle who had a longing eye to the estate, and who knew that only the child stood between him and it, bribed the nurse to put the child out of the way. She, either through ignorance or to save her conscience, took this to mean that she was to take the child away from his mother. This she managed easily enough, and the result was the finding of it by Adam Goodheart, as already told. It so happened, however, that the uncle was part proprietor of the Brownstone mines, and one day, during a visit, he saw wee Jamie Keekie. There was no mistaking the boy, and so another abduction had to take place. This time it was bargained that the man should take the boy across the sea. He accordingly watched his chance, followed Jamie to his work in the mine, and when the boy came out for the flask of water, he pounced upon him and bore him off. For years they lived in California, and, to his credit be it said, Mosson, the abductor was kind to the little fellow, and did his best to educate him. One day, however, Mosson took ill, and when he found himself, as he supposed, dying made a clean breast of everything he knew, and so it happened

192 Appendix I: Hardie's Illegitimacy

that he knew all about the first abduction. He did not die, however, but young Broadacre, as he was now called, had learned too much not to desire to learn more, and so he set sail for Scotland, Mosson bearing him company. The rest is soon told. He had no difficulty in identifying himself, and his mother welcomed to her arms her long-lost son. The uncle, when he learned that he was fairly baulked, determined to make the best of a bad bargain and go and see the young heir. To get his courage up to the point, he went and filled himself drunk, and, while riding to fulfil his mission, his horse stumbled, and he was thrown and killed on the spot.

Sir John Broadacre never married. He spent his whole life in doing good, and whenever anybody wanted to specially touch his feelings, they had only to get some little child to sing in his presence —

> Wee Jamie Keekie, let me in;
> Ma feet's cauld, an' ma shin's din.

Notes

1. Hughes, *Hardie*, pp.15f.
2. Reid, 'Keir Hardie's Conversion to Socialism', in Briggs and Saville (eds.), *Essays in Labour History*, p.21.
3. However, this error may not be so wildly inaccurate as it seems. Mary Hardie was close to her twenty-sixth birthday in August 1856. Durward, at the age of eighty, may simply have made an arithmetical error in calculating her age as sixteen instead of twenty-six. It is also possible that sixteen resulted from a typographical error.

APPENDIX 2: THE SONS OF LABOUR

The influence which the events of January to May 1887 had on Hardie's political development has been discussed in chapter 4 of this work. Hardie's first programme for a new Labour party is here reproduced from the *Miner* of July, 1887, together with an extract from the leading article which introduced it.

Item 12 of the programme shows that Hardie intended the socialist element to cover at least as much of 'modern' industry as railways and mines. His statement that, 'I am . . . with my present lights prepared to champion every bit of it and show the reason for its being there and the means to its accomplishment', indicates that the socialist element was integral to the programme and not merely tacked on to attract support. The passage from 'The Liberal Party has done good service in the past', to the end of the leader, shows that Hardie could already envisage the replacement of the historic Liberal party by an entirely new party.

The curious title, 'Sons of Labour', is an echo of the American movement, 'Knights of Labor', whose rapid growth in the United States Hardie had watched with interest. The Knights of Labor had a few branches in Britain[1] and the Lothian miners' leader, William Bullock, sought to extend their principles among Scottish miners from 1887 under the title 'Sons of Labour'.

(A) From leading article, 'Labour Representation', signed J. Keir Hardie, Miner, July 1887

There is something even more desirable than the return of working men to Parliament, and that is to give working men a definite programme to fight for when they get there, and to warn them that if they haven't the courage to stand up in the House of Commons and say what they would say in a miners' meeting, they must make room for someone else who will. . .

I append to this a programme for discussion. I don't say it is either perfect or complete. It does not give details. It deals with general principles, leaving the details to be worked out as occasion may require. I am at the same time, with my present lights, prepared to champion every bit of it and show the reason for its being there and the means to its accomplishment. It is framed to be read by miners, but has an

193

interest for every working man, inasmuch as that which hurts or helps one class of the community will also hurt or help every other ...

We require, however, a new Party to carry it out. The Liberal Party has done noble work in the past in securing civil and religious freedom. It is, I believe, prepared to carry this part of the work forward to completion. There, it seems to me, its work ends, as in all matters affecting the rights of property or capital or interfering with 'Freedom of Contract', there is not, nor has there ever been, much to choose between Whig and Tory.

It would be for the Sons of Labour, then, to take up the work where the Liberals of today leave it off and carry it forward to completion by removing every obstacle which hinders the worker from enjoying the full fruits of his labour.

(B) The Sons of Labour: Programme of the New Labour Party, devised by J. Keir Hardie, Miner, July 1887, p.98

Object
To improve the material, mental and moral condition of the people.

Method
Organisation of political power in every constituency in order to secure the return of candidates pledged to our programme.

Programme
1. Power to control or prohibit the liquor traffic to be vested in the inhabitants.
2. Payment of Members of Parliament, including official election expenses, by the State or from the rates.
3. Adult suffrage.
4. Triennial Parliaments.
5. Abolition of all non-elected authority.
6. A graduated income tax on all incomes over three hundred pounds a year.
7. Re-assertion of national rights in the soil and the re-enaction of a State rent.
8. Promotion of home colonies and cultivation and reclamation of waste land.
9. Free education.
10. To establish an eight-hour labour day in mines and wherever else it may, on inquiry, be found judicious.

11. To establish a national insurance fund.
12. Railways, minerals and mines to be owned by the State, the purchase price to be paid in annuities only.
13. Improved homes for working people by the compulsory erection of healthy dwellings.
14. Protection of household effects to the extent of twenty pounds from seizure for debt.
15. The establishment of tribunals for the assessment and settlement of all labour disputes.
16. Direct taxation and abolition of customs duties on all articles of food.

Note

1. H.M. Pelling, 'The Knights of Labor in Britain, 1880-1901', *Ec.H.R.*, 2nd Ser., IX (1956).

BIBLIOGRAPHY

Primary Sources

1. Manuscript

Auchinleck, Parish of, Minutes of the School Board, ii, 1883-1899. County Buildings, Ayrshire

Ayrshire Miners' Union, Account Book, 1887-9. Emrys Hughes, Esq., MP, Cumnock

John Burns Papers. British Museum, Add. Mss. 46281-46118

H.H. Champion, Correspondence relating to the Mid-Lanark By-Election, 1888. Copies in the possession of Mr H.M. Pelling, St John's College, Cambridge

Cumnock Congregational Church, Minute Books, 1882-4. Clerk of the Church, Cumnock

Engels Papers. International Institute of Social History, Amsterdam

Glasgow and District United Trades Council, Minute Book, 1889. Mitchell Library, Glasgow

James Keir Hardie Correspondence. National Library of Scotland, Acc. 504, Ms. 1809/71-6

Hardie-Hines Correspondence. National Library of Scotland, Acc. 4494

James Keir Hardie, Book of Press Cuttings relating to the Scottish Labour Party. Emrys Hughes, Esq., MP, Cumnock

James Keir Hardie, Diary Fragment, 1884. Copy in the possession of Mr H.M. Pelling, St John's College, Cambridge

Independent Labour Party. Minutes of the National Administrative Council. London School of Economics Library

Murray Col. Int. Inst. Soc. Hist., Amsterdam

Scottish Labour Party, First Annual Report of the Executive, n.d., 1889. Incomplete photocopy in Library of Transport House, London

Scottish Liberal Association, Minute Books, 1886-92 (press cuttings). University of Edinburgh

Scots Ancestry Society, Report on Ancestry of James Keir Hardie, 1965

B. Small, Papers relating to Her Father, William Small. Scottish National Library, Ms. Acc. 3359

2. *Printed*

A. Trade Union Sources

Ayrshire Miners' Association, *Rules,* 1881. Scottish Record Office, Fs 7/3

Ayrshire Miners' Union, *Rules,* 1886. Scottish Record Office, Fs 7/18

Minutes of Miners' National Conference, Nov. 1886. Webb Trade Union Collection, London School of Economics

Minutes of Miners' National Assembly, Jan. 1887. Webb Trade Union Collection

Minutes of Miners' National Conference, Apr. 1887. Webb Trade Union Collection

Minutes of a Conference of the Miners of England, Scotland and Wales, Oct. 1887. Webb Trade Union Collection

Scottish Miners' National Federation, *Rules and Secretary's Report,* 1887. Webb Trade Union Collection

Scottish Miners' National Federation, *Rules of the Larkhall Branch,* 1887. Webb Trade Union Collection

Trades Union Congress, *Reports,* 1887-92. Congress House.

B. Parliamentary Papers, etc.

Decennial Census of the Population of Scotland, 1881

House of Commons, *Debates*

Report on the Blantyre Colliery Explosion and Report of the Commission of Inquiry on the Blantyre Explosion. *P.P.,* 1878, XX

Reports of H.M. Inspector of Mines for the Western Division of Scotland. P.P., 1878-88

Royal Commission on Labour, 1892, Minutes of Evidence. *P.P.,* 1892, XVIII, XXXVI

Royal Commission on Mineral Royalties, 1890, Minutes of Evidence, *P.P.,* 1890, XXXVI

Royal Commission on the Truck System, Report. *P.P.,* 1871, XXXVI

Select Committee on Distress from Want of Employment, Evidence, *P.P.,* 1895, VIII

Select Committee on Emigration and Immigration, Minutes of Evidence. *P.P.,* 1889, X.

C. Newspapers, etc.

Aberdeen Free Press (Aberdeen)
Ardrossan and Saltcoats Herald (Ardrossan)
Chicago Chronicle (Chicago, Illinois)

Christian News (Glasgow)
Commonweal (London)
Daily Chronicle (London)
Daily News (London)
Daily Telegraph (London)
East and West Ham Gazette (London)
Glasgow Herald (Glasgow)
Glasgow Weekly Mail (Glasgow)
Greenock Telegraph (Greenock)
Hamilton Advertiser (Hamilton)
Justice (London)
Labour Elector (London)
Labour Leader (Cumnock, 1889; London, 1893-1915)
Labour Prophet
Labour Tribune (West Bromwich)
Miner (Cumnock)
National Observer (Glasgow)
North British Daily Mail (Glasgow)
Paisley Daily Express (Paisley)
Review of Reviews (London)
Scotsman (Edinburgh)
Scottish Leader (Edinburgh)
South Essex Gazette (London)
Weekly Times and Echo (London)
West Ham and Stratford Express (London)
West Ham Herald (London)
Workman's Times (Huddersfield)

D. Works of Reference

Bartholomew's Gazetteer of the British Isles (Edinburgh, 1887)
Catholic Directory (1870 and 1880)
Dictionary of National Biography
Dod's Parliamentary Companion (annual)
R. Hunt, *Mineral Statistics of the United Kingdom* (annual)
Labour Annual
May's British and Irish Press Guide (1880)
Naismith's Hamilton Directory, 1878-9 (Hamilton, 1879)
D. Pollock, *Dictionary of the Clyde* (Edinburgh, 1891)
J. Saville and J. Bellamy, eds., *Dictionary of Labour Biography*,
    I (1972)

E. Published Collections

D. Laurence, ed., *Bernard Shaw's Collected Letters, 1874-97* (1965)
Marx-Engels on Britain (Moscow, 1962)

F. ILP Publications

ILP Conference Reports 1893-1900

Secondary Sources

3. Works Published before and during Hardie's Life-time

A. Books

A.J. Beaton, *The Social and Economic Condition of the Highlands of Scotland since 1800* (Stirling, 1906)
D. Bremner, *The Industries of Scotland* (Edinburgh, 1869)
Robert Burns, *Selected Works,* (Oxford, 1904)
Thomas Carlyle, *Chartism* (1830)
—— *Heroes and Hero-Worship* (1888 edn)
—— *Latter-Day Pamphlets* (1850)
—— *Past and Present* (1843 edn)
—— *Sartor Resartus* (1831)
—— *The French Revolution* (1903 edn)
J. Denvir, *The Irish in Britain*(1892)
H. Fawcett, *Pauperism, Its Causes and Remedies* (1871)
—— *Manual of Political Economy* (4th edn 1876)
R.L. Galloway, *Annals of Coal Mining and the Coal Trade, Second Series* (1904)
Henry George, *Progress and Poverty* (1881)
R. Giffen, *Essays in Finance, Second Series* (1886)
F.H. Groome, *Ordnance Gazeteer of Scotland* (1885)
T. Honeyman, *Good Templary in Scotland* (Glasgow, 1894)
E.G. Howarth and M. Wilson, *West Ham, A Study of Social and Industrial Life* (1907)
R. Howie, *Churches and the Churchless in Scotland* (Glasgow, 1892)
S. Jevons, *The British Coal Trade* (1915)
K. MacDonald, *Social and Religious Life in the Highlands* (1902)
A. Miller, *The Rise and Progress of Coatbridge* (Glasgow, 1874)
H.V. Mills, *Poverty and the State* (1886)
B. Potter, *The Co-operative Movement* (1893)
Second Statistical Account of Scotland (1845)
L. Stephen, *Life of Henry Fawcett* (1885)
H.J. Steven, *The Cumnocks, Old and New* (Kilmarnock, 1899)

T. Stewart, *Among the Miners of Larkhall* (1893)

S. Taylor, *Profit-Sharing between Capital and Labour* (1884)

J. Warwick, *History of Old Cumnock* (Paisley, 1890)

P.T. Winskill, *The Temperance Movement and its Workers,* III (1892)

B. Pamphlets

Distribution and Statistics of the Scottish Churches (Edinburgh, 1886)

Scottish Home Rule Association, *Statement of Scotland's Claim for Home Rule* (Edinburgh, 1886)

4. Biographies of Hardie

D. Carswell, *Brother Scots* (1927)

J. Cockburn, *The Hungry Heart, a Romantic Biography of Keir Hardie* (1956)

G.D.H. Cole, *Keir Hardie* (1941)

M. Cole, *Makers of the Labour Movement* (1948)

H. Fyfe, *Keir Hardie* (1935)

J. Bruce Glasier, *Keir Hardie, the Man and his Message* (n.d., 1919)

E. Hughes, *Keir Hardie* (1956)

—— *Keir Hardie, Some Memories* (n.d.).

—— *Keir Hardie's Writings and Speeches* (Glasgow, n.d., 1928)

F. Johnson, *Keir Hardie's Socialism* (1922)

Garth Lean, *Brave Men Choose* (1961)

D. Lowe, *From Pit to Parliament* (1923)

I. McLean, *Keir Hardie* (1974)

J. Maxton, *Keir Hardie, Prophet and Pioneer* (1939)

K.O. Morgan, *Keir Hardie* (Oxford, 1967)

—— *Keir Hardie, Radical and Socialist* (1975)

W. Stewart, *Keir Hardie* (1921)

W. Straker, 'In Memoriam James Keir Hardie, M.P.', in *Monthly Circular,* October 1915, Northumberland Miners' Mutual Confident Association

5. Autobiographies, Biographies and Memoirs

W.H.G. Armytage, *A.J. Mundella, 1825-97, the Liberal Background to the Labour Movement* (1951)

R. Page Arnot, *William Morris, the Man and the Myth* (1964)

C.A. Barker, *Henry George* (New York, 1955)

R. Blake, *The Unknown Prime Minister* (1955)

A. Briggs, *Victorian People* (1954)

J.L. Garvin, *Life of Joseph Chamberlain,* I (1932)

J. Bruce Glasier, *William Morris and the Early Days of the Socialist*

Movement (1921)

W. Martin Haddow, *My Seventy Years* (Glasgow, n.d)

L.S. Hunter, *John Hunter, D.D., a Life* (1921)

R.R. James, *Rosebery* (1963)

D. Lowe, *Souvenirs of Scottish Labour* (Glasgow, 1919)

W.R. Moody, *Life of Dwight L. Moody* (2nd edn, n.d.)

J. Morley, *Life of Gladstone* (1908)

J.W. Robertson Scott, *The Day Before Yesterday* (1951)

R. Smillie, *My Life for Labour* (1924)

J. Symons, *Thomas Carlyle* (1952)

E.P. Thompson, *William Morris* (1955)

A.F. Tschiffely, *Don Roberto* (1937)

C. Tsuzuki, *H.M. Hyndman and British Socialism* (Oxford, 1961)

H. West, *R.B. Cunninghame Graham* (1932)

6. Histories, Monographs, etc.

R. Page Arnot, *History of the Scottish Miners* (1955)

—— *The Miners, I, 1889-1910* (1949)

W. Ashworth, *Economic History of England, 1870-1939* (1960)

F. Bealey and H. Pelling, *Labour and Politics 1900-1906* (1958)

E. Eldon Barry, *Nationalisation in British Politics* (1965)

S.H. Beer, *Modern British Politics* (1965)

A.L. Bowley, *Wages and Income in the United Kingdom since 1860* (Cambridge, 1937)

W. Boyd, *Education in Ayrshire through Seven Centuries* (1961)

E.H. Phelps Brown, *The Growth of British Industrial Relations* (1959)

P. Hume Brown, *History of Scotland* (Cambridge, 1911)

K.D. Buckley, *Trade Unionism in Aberdeen* (Edinburgh, 1955)

J. Burgess, *Will Lloyd George Supplant Ramsay MacDonald?* (Ilford, n.d., 1929?)

J.H.S. Burleigh, *Church History of Scotland* (1960)

D.L. Burn, *Economic History of Steel-Making* (1940)

T.H. Burnham and G.O. Hoskins, *Iron and Steel in Britain, 1870-1930* (1930)

J.L. Carvell, *The New Cumnock Coalfield* (Edinburgh, 1946)

J.H. Clapham, *Economic History of Modern Britain*, II and III (Cambridge, 1932 and 1938)

J.Clayton, *The Rise and Decline of Socialism in England* (1926)

H.A. Clegg, A. Fox and A.F. Thompson, *History of British Trade Unionism since 1889*, I (Oxford, 1964)

G.D.H. Cole and R. Postgate, *The Common People* (5th edn, 1949)

R. Coupland, *Welsh and Scottish Nationalism* (1954)

J. Cunningham, *Church History of Scotland* (Edinburgh, 1882)

P. Deane and W.A. Cole, *British Economic Growth, 1688-1959* (Cambridge, 1962)

H.V. Emy, *Liberals, Radicals and Social Politics, 1882-1914* (Cambridge, 1973)

H. Escott, *History of Scottish Congregationalism* (Glasgow, 1960)

J.R. Fleming, *Church History of Scotland* (Edinburgh, 1927-33)

H.H. Geith and C. Wright Mills, *From Max Weber* (1948)

P. Geyl, *Debates with Historians* (1955)

Glasgow and District United Trades Council, *Centenary Brochure* (Glasgow, n.d., 1958?)

I.F. Grant, *Economic History of Scotland* (1964)

D.A. Hamer, *Liberal Politics in the Age of Gladstone and Rosebery* (Oxford, 1972)

H. Hamilton, *The Industrial Revolution in Scotland* (Oxford, 1932)

J.E. Handley, *The Irish in Modern Scotland* (Cork, 1947)

H.J. Hanham, *Elections and Party Management* (1949)

J. Harris, *Unemployment and Politics. A Study in English Social Policy 1886-1914* (Oxford, 1972)

R. Harrison, *Before the Socialists* (1965)

E.J. Hobsbawm, *Labouring Men* (1964)

K.S. Inglis, *Churches and the Working Class in Victorian England* (1963)

J.B. Jefferys, *Story of the Engineers, 1800-1945* (1945)

T. Johnston, *History of the Working Classes in Scotland* (Glasgow, 1946)

J. Joll, *The Second International* (1955)

G. Stedman Jones, *Outcast London* (Oxford, 1971)

P. d'A. Jones, *The Christian Socialist Revival, 1877-1914* (Princeton, 1968)

E.P. Lawrence, *Henry George in the British Isles* (East Lansing, Michigan, 1951)

M. Lindsay, *The Lowlands of Scotland* (1956)

H.M. Lynd, *England in the 1880's* (New York, 1945)

A.M. McBriar, *Fabian Socialism and English Politics, 1884-1918* (Cambridge, 1962)

J. McBryde, *Park Road E.U. Congregational Church, Hamilton: Centenary Brochure* (1954)

S. Maccoby, *English Radicalism, 1853-86* (1938)

A.M. MacKenzie, *Scotland in Modern Times* (Edinburgh, 1943)

J.D. Mackie, *History of Scotland* (1964)

J. MacKinnon, *Social and Industrial History of Scotland since the Union* (1929)

W.G. McLaughlin, Jnr. *Modern Revivalism* (New York, 1959)

I.M.M. MacPhail, *History of Scotland*, II (1956)

S. Mechie, *The Church and Scottish Social Development, 1780-1870* (Oxford, 1960)

F. Mort, *Lanarkshire* (1910)

C.A. Oakley, *The Second City* (1946)

J.E. Orr, *The Second Evangelical Awakening in Britain* (1949)

J. Paterson, *History of Ayrshire* (1863)

H.M. Pelling, *History of British Trade Unionism* (1963)

—— *Modern Britain* (1960)

—— *Origins of the Labour Party* (2nd edn Oxford, 1965)

—— *Popular Politics and Society in Late Victorian Britain* (1968)

P.P. Poinnier, *The Advent of the Labour Party* (1958)

J.B. Pringle, *British Regional Geography, the South of Scotland* (2nd edn, 1948)

G.S. Pryde, *Scotland since 1603 to the Present day* (1961)

—— *Social Life in Scotland since 1707 (1934)*

R. Rait and G.S. Pryde, *Scotland* (2nd edn, 1954)

B.C. Roberts, *The Trades Union Congress* (1958)

E. Roll, *History of Economic Thought* (1945)

J. Ross, *History of Congregational Independency in Scotland* (Glasgow, 1900)

W.W. Rostow, *British Economy of the Nineteenth Century (Oxford, 1949)*

J.W.F. Rowe, *Wages in the Coal Industry* (1923)

J.E. Shaw, *Ayrshire, 1745-1950* (Edinburgh, 1953)

P. Smith, *Disraelian Conservatism and Social Reform* (1967)

T.C. Smout, *History of the Scottish People, 1560-1830* (1969)

E.R. Strauss, *Irish Nationalism and British Democracy* (1951)

J. Strawhorn, *The New History of Cumnock* (1966)

J. Strawhorn and W. Boyd, *Third Statistical Account of Scotland, Ayrshire* (Edinburgh, 1951)

D. Torr, *Tom Mann and his Times* (1956)

S. and B. Webb, *History of Trade Unionism* (2nd edn, 1920)

S. Webb and H. Cox, *The Eight Hour Day* (1891)

E. Welbourne, *The Miners' Unions of Northumberland and Durham* (Cambridge, 1932)

B. Willey, *Nineteenth Century Studies* (1949)

J.E. Williams, *The Derbyshire Miners* (1962)

R. Williams, *Culture and Society* (1961)

J.A. Wilson, *Contribution to the History of Lanarkshire* (1936-7)

K. Wittig, *The Scottish Tradition in Literature* (Edinburgh, 1958)

L.C. Wright, *Scottish Chartism* (Edinburgh, 1953)

7. Articles, Pamphlets, etc.

H.L. Beales, 'The Great Depression in Industry and Trade', *Ec.H.R.*, 1st ser., V 1934

N. Blewett, 'The Franchise in the United Kingdom, 1885-1918', *Past and Present*, 32, 1965, pp.27-56

A. Briggs, 'The Welfare State in Historical Perspective', *Archives Européennes de Sociologie*, II, 1961, pp.221-58

A.J. Youngson Brown, 'Trade Union Policy in the Scots Coalfields', *Ec.H.R.*, 2nd ser., VI 1953

J.R. Campbell, *Burns the Democrat* (Glasgow, 1945)

R.V. Clements, 'British Trade Unions and Popular Political Economy', *Ec.H.R.*, 2nd ser., XIV 1961-2

G.D.H. Cole, 'Some Notes on British Trade Unionism in the Third Quarter of the Nineteenth Century', *International Review for Social History*, II 1937

D.W. Crowley, 'The Crofters' Party, 1885-92', *Scottish Historical Review*, XXXV 1956

A.E.P. Duffy, 'New Unionism in Britain, 1889-90, a Re-Appraisal', Ec.H.R., 2nd ser. XIV 1961-2

R. Haddow, 'The Miners of Scotland', *Nineteenth Century*, September 1888, p.362

J. Keir Hardie, *The ILP: A Historical Sketch of the Movement* (1894)
—— 'The Pioneer of the I.L.P.', *Socialist Review*, XII, 69, 1914, pp.113-17

J.G. Kellas, 'Highland Migration to Glasgow', *Bulletin of the Society for the Study of Labour History*, XII 1966
—— 'The Liberal Party and the Scottish Church Disestablishment Crisis', *English Historical Review*, LXXIX 1964
—— 'The Liberal Party in Scotland 1876-95', *Scottish Historical Review*, XLIV 1965

J. Leatham, *Glasgow in the Limelight* (Turriff, 1924)

H. MacDiarmid, *Burns Today and Tomorrow* (Edinburgh, 1959)
—— Cunninghame Graham, a Centenary Sketch (Glasgow, n.d., 1952)

B. McGill, 'Francis Schnadhorst and Liberal Party Organisation', *J.M.H.*, XXXIV 1962

T.W. Moody, 'Michael Davitt and the British Labour Movement, 1882-1906', *T.R.H.S.*, 5th ser., III 1953

A.E. Musson, 'The Great Depression in Britain, 1873-96, a Re-Appraisal', *Journal of Economic History*, XIX 1959

H.M. Pelling, 'The Knights of Labor in Britain, 1880-1901', *Ec.H.R.*, 2nd ser., IX 1956

F. Reid, 'Keir Hardie's Conversion to Socialism', in A. Briggs and J. Saville, eds., *Essays in Labour History*, (1970)

F. Reid, 'Socialist Sunday Schools in Britain, 1892-1939', *Int. Rev. Soc. Hist.*, XI, 1966, pp.18ff

—— 'The Independent Collier', *New Edinburgh Review*, 1975, pp.30-3

D.C. Savage, 'Scottish Politics, 1885-6', *Scottish Historical Review*, XI 1961

J. Saville, 'Henry George and the British Labour Movement', *Bulletin of the Society for the Study of Labour History*, No.5 1962

J. Strawhorn, 'New Milns, the Story of an Ayrshire Burgh', *Coll. of the Ayrshire Arch. and Nat. Hist. Soc.* 1948

Unattrib., *Mr James Keir Hardie v. the Labour Literature Society* (Glasgow, 1895)

D.W. Urwin, 'Development of the Conservative Party Organisation in Scotland until 1912', *Scottish Historical Review*, XLIV 1965

W. Whitely, *J. Bruce Glasier, a Memorial* (n.d., 1920)

J.E. Williams, 'Labour in the Coalfields', *Bulletin of the Society for he Study of Labour History*, no.4 1962

8. Unpublished Theses

T.J. Byres, 'The Scottish Economy during the Great Depression, 1873-96, B Litt., Glasgow University, 1963

D.W. Crowley, 'Origins of the Revolt of the British Labour Movement from Liberalism', Ph.D., London University, 1952

J.G. Kellas, 'The Liberal Party in Scotland, 1885-94', Ph.D., London University, 1962

F. Reid, 'The Early Life and Political Development of James Keir Hardie', D. Phil., Oxford, 1968

INDEX